The T-Shirt Quilt:

Design and Create Your Own Memory Quilt In One Weekend

By Marie Anderson

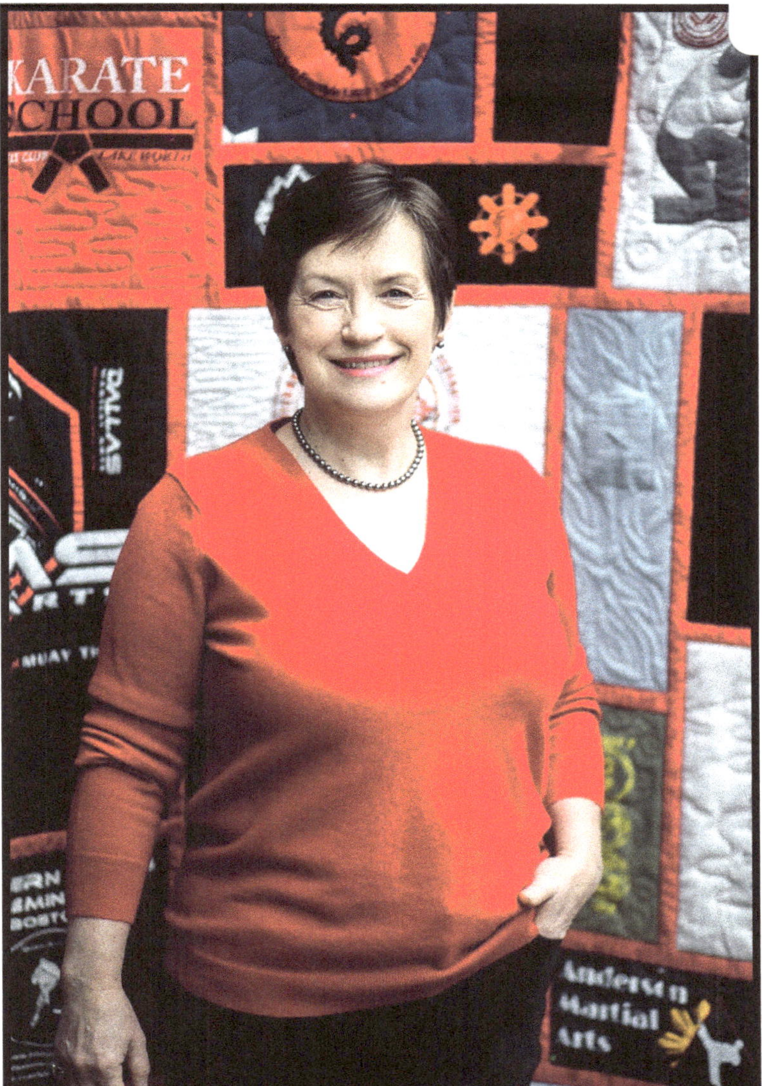

Dear Reader,

Thank you for purchasing this book. I am happy that you share my interest in quilting. This book covers just one of the many types of quilting I do.

If you are interested in contacting me regarding:

- T-shirt quilting

- Leather quilting

- Art quilts

- Private consultations/private lessons on your specific project

- Workshops

- Speaking engagements

- Classes

or if you have a question for me, you can contact me through my website, *www.mariescustomquilting.com*. I look forward to hearing from you.

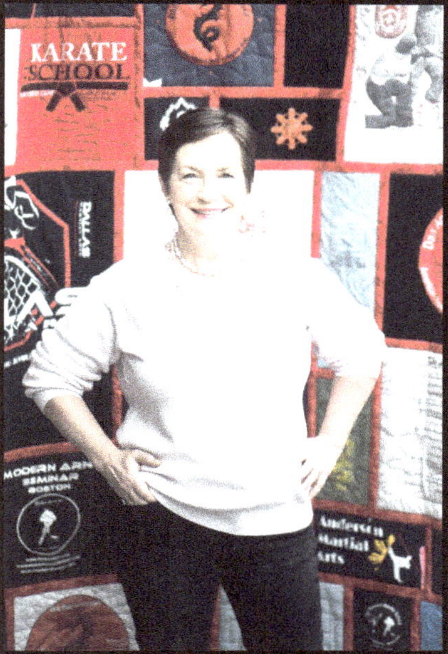

Marie Anderson

Yours,

Marie Anderson
Marie's Custom Quilting

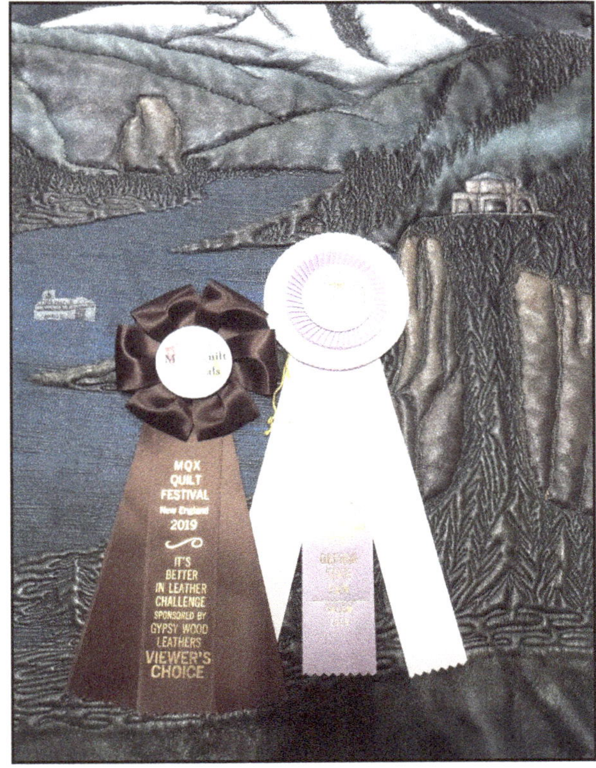

"Home" - An award winning leather quilt by Marie Anderson

Published by
Angels Rest Productions
PO Box 12
Bridal Veil, Oregon 97010

Manufactured in the United States of America, or in the United Kingdom when distributed elsewhere.

Cover design and photo by: Marie Anderson
Interior design: Dan Anderson
Photos of Marie Anderson by: Kate Holt Photography

Author's URL: mariescustomquilting.com
ISBN 978-0-578-59858-1

ENDORSEMENTS

"This book was an absolute delight! The instructions were clear and there were many useful tips I had   not considered before. This book can take any beginner and make then feel like a pro. Not only was there   information on t-shirts but how to use hoodies as well. All the math was laid out for me in the examples which immediately had me visualizing my old t-shirt pile and the potential it has. Marie suggest several different ways of going about the quilt but also stresses the importance of creativity and what works for you. The whole book is infectious with positivity I felt as if she was cheering me on. Truly I think I could make a quilt out of my old t-shirt that would spark joy not only for me but my family."
Nicole B.

"I love it! It makes a daunting project seem simple by breaking it down into easy to follow steps. I am new to sewing and to be honest I get most of my instructions from videos on the internet. I learn best by watching and copying, so the abundance of pictures in this book helped immensely. I also found the sections on color coordination/organization of the squares particularly helpful. Color coordination has never come easy to me. Again, the pictures were very helpful here. It was also nice to be reminded that there are many ways to do things and there is no "wrong way" if you still get the result you want. There are also some suggestions on how to fix mistakes, which I don't normally see in quilting books. I normally have to follow the instructions to a 't' or the whole thing doesn't work. Yet, somehow this book manages to make an exact process of sewing a quilt, relatively flexible. And that is exactly what I need as a beginner, flexibility and room to make mistakes. Thank you!"
Jessica J.

"The T-Shirt how to book is thorough, with lots of great images and step-by-step instruction on how to sew a keepsake t-shirt quilt. I've been utilizing her expertise for quilting with the longarm machine for several years now and am never disappointed. She goes the extra mile to make sure all is done well and as expected, going above and beyond expectations. So this how to book is extremely thoughtful and complete – a job well done."
Tari B.

Dedication

This book is dedicated to my parents. Without your help, I would not have embarked on this journey. Thank you for helping me discover my passion.

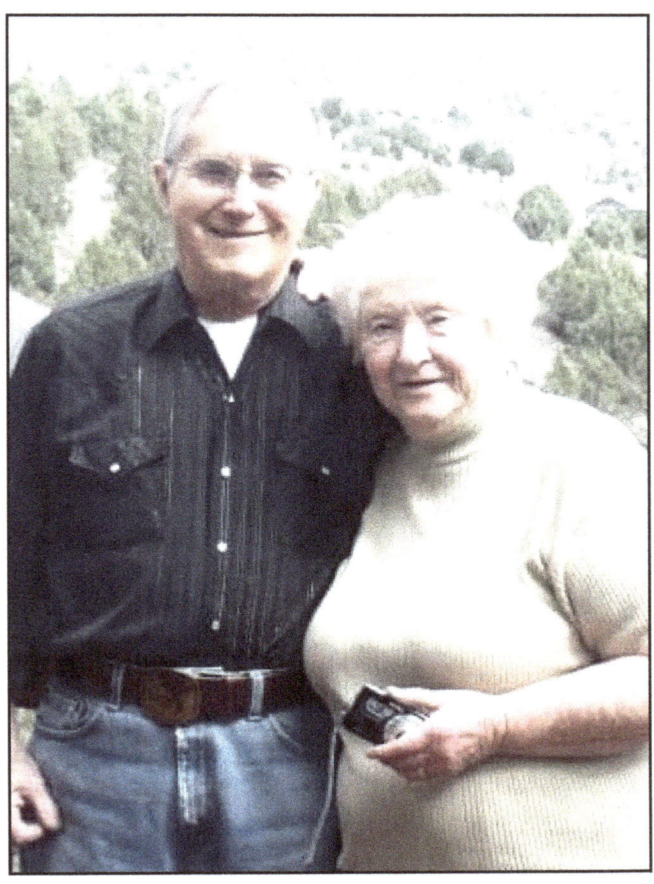

CONTENTS

FOREWORD

INTRODUCTION

CHAPTER 1 - CHOOSING YOUR COLORS AND FABRIC   1

CHAPTER 2 - PREPARING THE T-SHIRTS   7

CHAPTER 3 - ARRANGING THE T-SHIRTS   21

CHAPTER 4 - SIZING IT UP   25

CHAPTER 5 - CREATING THE BLOCKS   29

CHAPTER 6 - CREATING THE COLUMNS   51

CHAPTER 7 - BORDERS   63

CHAPTER 8 - THE BACK & BATTING   73

CHAPTER 9 - THE QUILTING   77

CHAPTER 10 - SQUARE IT UP AND BIND   83

CHAPTER 11 - FINISH WORK   103

CONCLUSION   106

ABOUT THE AUTHOR   107

FOREWORD

By Staci Wendland

I first met Marie about twenty years ago. My children were new students at her husband's family karate school, and over the next decade I watched her keep everything running behind the scenes while also   working toward a black belt of her own. I knew nothing of her quilting talents at the time, but I was always   impressed by her work ethic.

A few years ago, I joined my local quilt guild and discovered Marie was already a member. I learned she had a long-arming business and had established herself as a quilt artist. I've had the opportunity to see many of her quilt projects since then, and among my favorites are her t-shirt quilts.

As someone with a stack of sentimental t-shirts, I feel like Marie wrote this book for me. Decades of sewing experience of my own wasn't enough to convince me to cut into them. I needed this gentle nudge from   Marie to take the first steps toward turning them into a quilt I could enjoy, rather than continuing to let them sit on a dark shelf. While I saw a pile of mismatched t-shirts, she shows how they can be brought together into a cohesive and visually appealing keepsake.

To many of us, the idea of sewing stretchy knit shirts into orderly squares seems like a daunting project, but Marie breaks it down into manageable steps. In this book, Marie has translated her calm and kind demeanor to the page. It's as if she's there with you, walking you through the steps. Being a visual learner myself, I   appreciate the numerous photos that illustrate each step, in addition to explaining how it's done.

Marie is holding her hand out to you with this book. Grab it, and your stack of t-shirts, and let her help you make a memory.

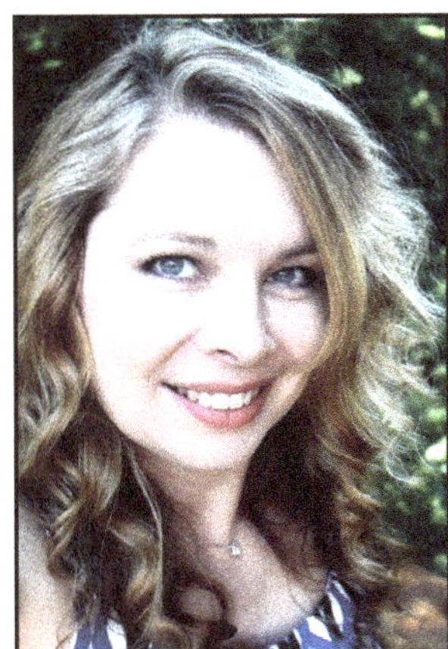

Staci Wendland is an Oregon craft artist who specializes in hand-made crafts, sewing and many kinds of home-made artistry. You can read her blog as well as find many tutorials   sewing patterns at www.craftystaci.com.

INTRODUCTION

Becoming The Artist

Part 1:

The family reunion was different this year. It was not that I had finally reclaimed the yard from the encroaching forest, or that I had managed to clean and paint my small cabin in the woods to the standards of my most discerning family member. Nor was it that we were expecting a record number of family   members - 70 in all. It was August 2008. My older brother had passed away from colon cancer earlier that year and it would be the first year that all of my siblings would not be there to celebrate my parents' anniversary.

We progressed through the weekend; people arrive, set their camp sites, the generation's pair off into their various age groups. Some will play at the creek, others will brave the sketchy waters of the "swimming pond," young adults go off to hike the cliff trails of the gorge while the rest of us sit and visit with the new babies and talk about the latest news having to do with the younger adults, past times, growing up-I think like any other family would.

On Sunday we all go up to the top of Larch Mountain. The day is beautiful and we gather in a circle around   a campfire and say our last goodbyes to my brother. We laugh, tell jokes and cry. We had forgotten tissue - someone had brought toilet paper. As various members of the family cry, the roll of toilet paper was thrown around the circle, adding an element of humor to the event. The day ended with clean up, the family leaving in their cars, safe travels wished and suddenly as fast as it happened, the weekend was over.

My parents always stayed an extra day to rest, settle up on costs for the weekend, take me and my husband out for dinner and thank us for putting on the event. My dad came over to talk while mom napped and asked if I would/could help with mom. She was not the same since my brother passed. She had no energy. The doctor wanted to put her on medications. I was devastated. My mom survived so many things over her 82 years of life. How could this be her? I needed a plan.

Consulting with my older sister who is a medical doctor, we put together a nutritional and therapeutic plan that would bring her back to physical and mental health. The plan included my traveling to Central Oregon every other weekend, a trip that would take 5 hours one way over farming roads, 2 mountain ranges, cattle country and government lands. We needed an activity to be a   center of the weekend – enter quilting classes every other Saturday for the next 3 months.

We settled into a routine: Friday afternoon, call my parents and tell them I'm on my way. Friday night arrive to a late dinner, drink and visit. Find out how much of our "homework" for quilt class we had completed and finish whatever we needed to for Saturday morning. Saturday we went to class 9-3pm. The ladies were fun, filled with small town gossip and opinions on everything.   Mom and I learned how to do a French braid quilt and we were in heaven. She came out of whatever dark place she had entered into and life was good. We both proceeded to make several of these quilts in a wide range of colors.

I continued my visits to Central Oregon, not because my mom needed me anymore but because I found a beauty in the country. The drive restored my inner peace and I truly found that I enjoyed my parents company. Mom and I continued to make quilts together – picking out colors together, shopping in quilt stores together and spending our weekends sewing.

My parents moved to the city as they got older and their doctor visits increased. I continued my visits all the way through the last weekend when we filled the final trailer with the last box and piece of furniture. Then we said goodbye to their home in cattle country.

   Part 2:
I'm in the car with my mom – I'm driving as she is 86 and we are going 2 hours east to her friend's house to quilt 4 quilt tops. Gwen has already flown south for the winter but she has graciously invited us to use her house, quilt barn and long arm for the weekend.

I walk into her shop and it has everything: 4 domestic machines, huge tables, a wall full of fabric neatly folded into color groups and on one side of the room is the frame and huge Gammill long arm that will quilt our king size quilts.

To mom and me, we had just entered heaven. For the next 2 days we sewed and completed our projects. On the way home, my mom said, *"We need our own long arm – I just don't have a place to put it."*

   I responded, *"I'd love to have a long arm too – I have a place to put it, I just don't have the money."*

   She smiled, *"OK! You do the research, you find it and we'll set up at your place."*
   Me: *"Great! Give me a budget."*
   Mom: *"I think I could do $5000.00."*

So I set out on my search. I went to shops in town, I went on the internet, I looked at reviews and there   wasn't anything that would do what we wanted for less than $15,000! The type my mom's friend had was now $30,000. I checked into used machines. I found 1 in Michigan – nearly 2000 miles away – for $10,000. We would have to pick it up with a UHaul, assemble it and learn to use it on our own. No warranty, no lessons, no tech support. My heart was sinking. My dream disappearing as fast as it had sparked.

I broke the news to mom and I fully expected her to say *"Well we can't do that."* But instead she told me to find a shop in town that I liked that sold what I wanted.

I research through the shops, I find the place and the day comes – we walk in the door and the owner is there. She has two   machines set up ready for us to sew on and proceeds to show us them. We sew for about an hour. I have decided I should be   practical and settle for the less expensive of the 2. The owner catches my drift and starts talking about all of the advantages of the less expensive machine. Out of the blue, my mom pipes up and says: *"I don't want that one. I want that one!"* while pointing to the most expensive machine.

The sales person nearly drops her jaw but pulls it together and says *"Cash, check or charge?"*

My mom pulls out her check book and says *"Check."* and proceeds to write a check for $21,000.00. I didn't even know you could write a check for that amount, let alone that my mother was prepared to do so.

We settled up on the details and headed back to their apartment to give dad the news.

>Dad: *"How did you do?"*
>Mom: *"We did well!"*
>Dad: *"How much?"*, looking at me.
>Me: (pause) *"$21,000?!?"*

He smiled, laughed and said, *"So how does it feel to have spent your siblings inheritance?"* I was speechless. My heart sunk. He went on, *"You will need to have a business and pay us back."* My heart sunk further, my stomach in terror. I have never had my own business. I had to decide to take on this new roll or give it all up.

So on my dad's counsel I put up a sign, I got cards out to fabric stores, I made a Facebook page and a web site. I started making things – small and simple at first. I joined a quilt guild and found out who the best quilters in the area where. I found out who did free motion and who had computers. I started practicing   and making things for friends at a discount rate. I found out who I could call for advice and help. I watched YouTube videos.

   Part three:
Then one day a woman who I knew to be an award winning quilter brought me a quilt top to quilt. It was a cute little baby quilt, nothing complex, I was terrified. We discussed thread color and then I asked *"What do you want on it?"*

She looked at me and said, *"I don't know, you're the artist!"*

I was like, *"I am?!? I guess I AM the ARTIST!"*

She proceeded to school me on her philosophy – it was her job to create the best top and mine to enhance that top with the best quilting. It was collaboration. I had to decide again, do I become the artist or do I stay small?

I decided to become the artist!

That is what I wish for you with this book. You are the artist of your home, your job, your next quilt project, your whole life.

Embrace it. Be daring and adventurous with it. Take some risks. Using the techniques I show you here, you will be able to create numerous designs to match any décor. Have fun with it! I have written this book for you so that you can take your own   journey of creating a work of art that satisfies a need to remember good times while honoring those that helped create those times.

My Purpose

The timing could not have been worse. The customer needed the quilt done before Christmas. It was already mid-November. She wanted to make a quilt using some of her clothes that her daughter specifically liked. In addition, she did not have the funds to have the quilt made professionally. Being a person who likes to think in solutions, I asked if she knew how to sew.

"Yes," she replied, *"I took home ec in high school. But I haven't sewn since then and I don't have a machine."*

Me: *"Would you like to make the quilt yourself?"*

Customer: *"YES! That is what I really want to do! Then it is completely from me!"*

It was settled. I coached her through the exact same steps that you will learn in this book: How to cut the clothes, what types of fabric need a fusable web backing, arranging the blocks of fabric, sewing them   together, putting on borders, then quilting and binding for the final project. In the end, she had a beautiful quilt that was made by her for her daughter. It was a true gift of the heart made with love.

This book is for all of you who want to make a quilt for yourself or a loved one. You want to design it yourself for a one of a kind look. You want to learn a concept of putting a quilt together that allows for imperfection and in fact embraces the unconventional. This book is *not* for those that want to follow an exact pattern. I teach you a concept of how I go about making quilts whether it is from old clothes, t-shirts, pictures printed on fabric or squares of fabric that you like.

We will cover different designs: Every square is the same width with sashing the same so that the columns are the same width (left picture). All the squares are different and sashing is different (right picture).

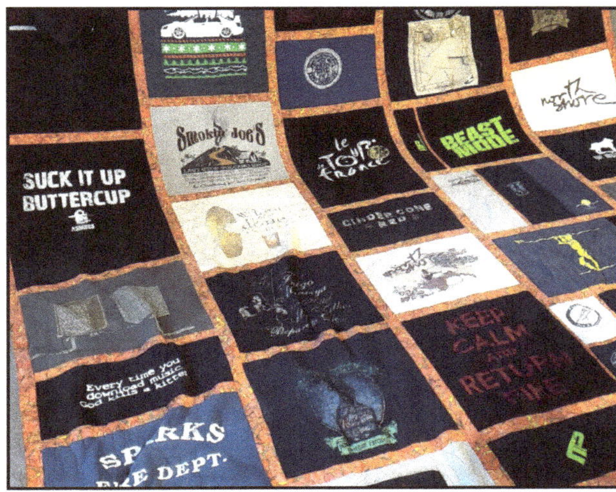
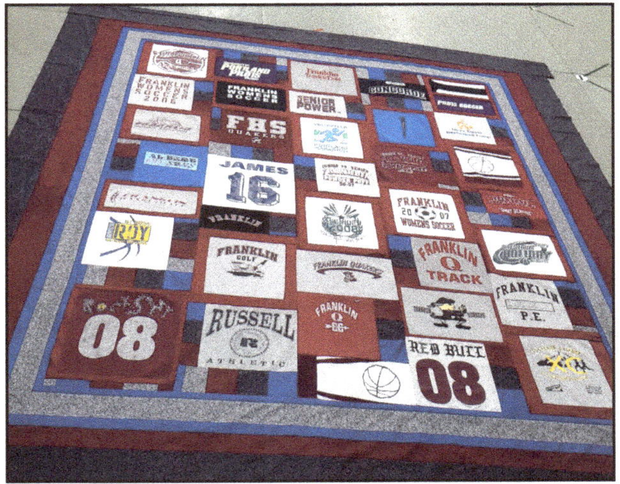

No sashing (left picture). The squares are different sizes (right picture)

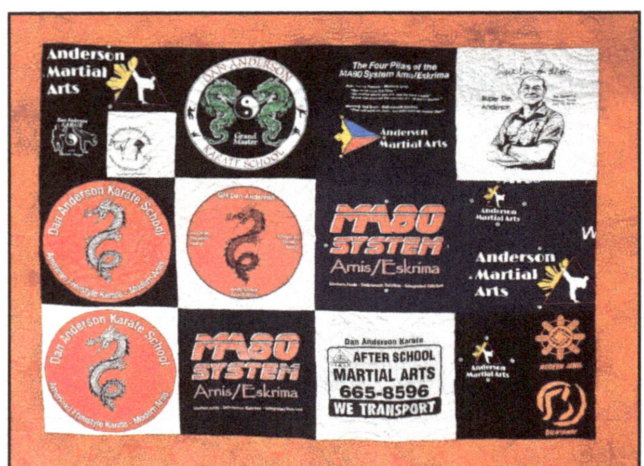 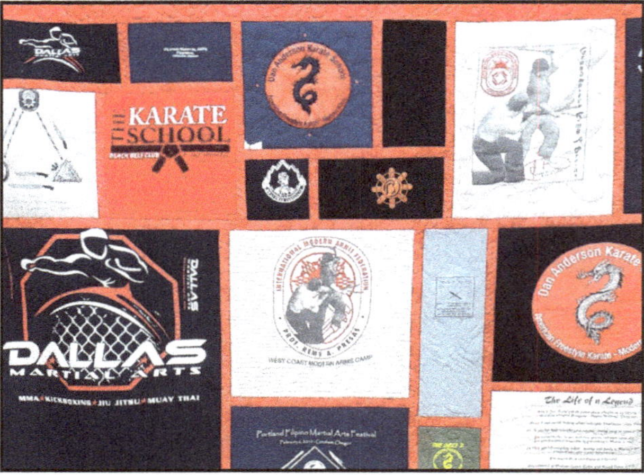

My dream for you:

By following these simple concepts you will be able to create your very own memory quilt with a minimum of math, design headaches and redoing seams. Let's have fun!

Chapter 1
Your Colors & Fabric

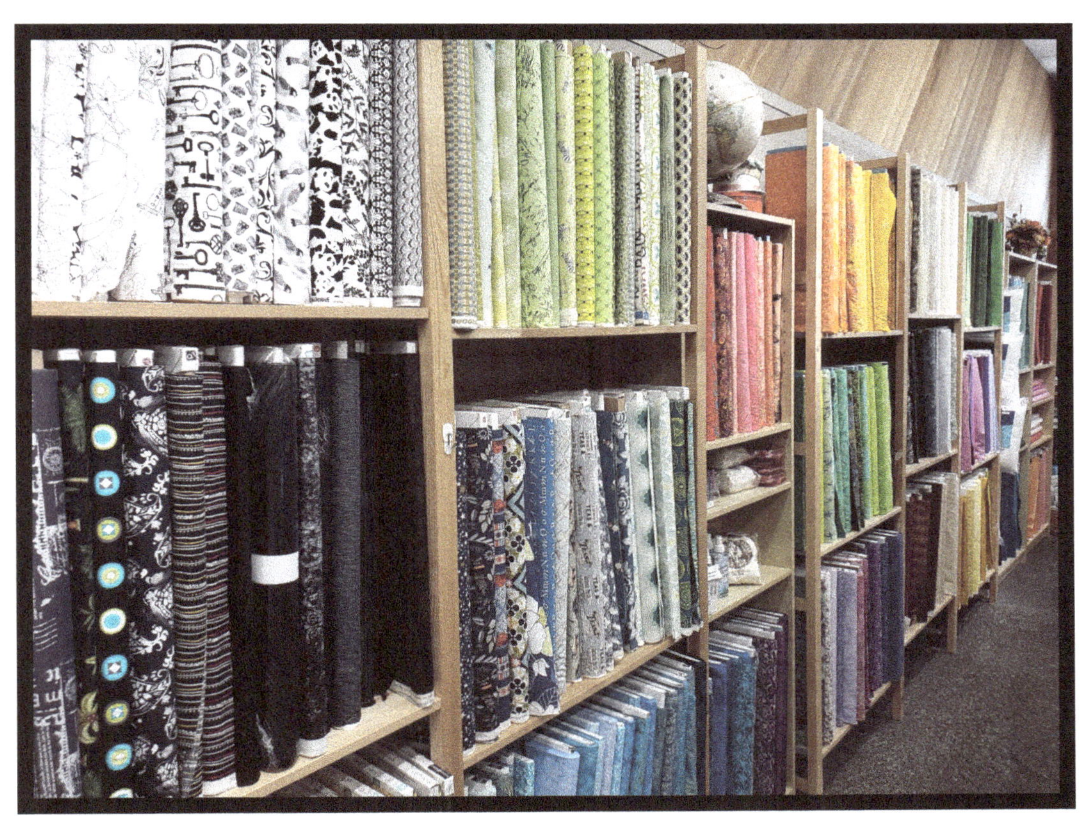

CHAPTER 1 - YOUR COLORS AND FABRIC

Colors: How to do the colors? I use to worry about getting the right colors on a t-shirt quilt but it is actually simple. Take the shirts to the fabric store.   Find 4 colors that match closely the colors in the shirts.

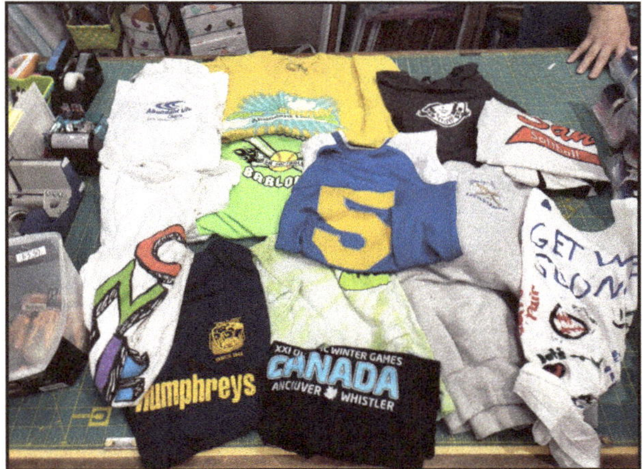
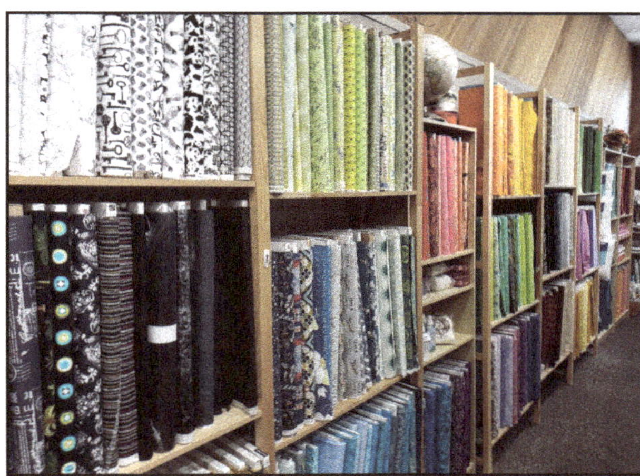

It is a good idea to lay out your t-shirts at the fabric store so that you can visually find the right match on location.

The shirts will have accent colors in them from the logos. If you pick a color that matches or is very close it will pull that color forward and make it stand out. Notice the blue, yellow, green and red –all of these would be great, if we can find colors to match.

You can use the color a lot or a little. You can also pick a color that is not in the t-shirts but compliments the colors that are. Keep in mind that not all reds go together, not all blues are complimentary, etc. The good news is that with the wide range of fabrics, it is not hard to find a color that is very close to the colors in the t-shirt logos. In this case I chose green, yellow, blue and white. The fabric colors matched those in the t-shirts well.

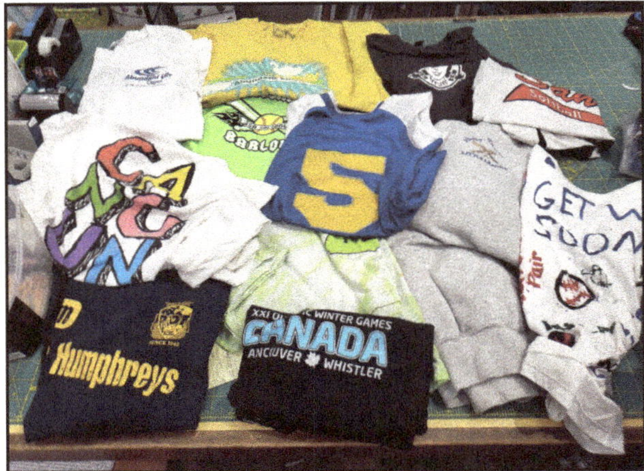
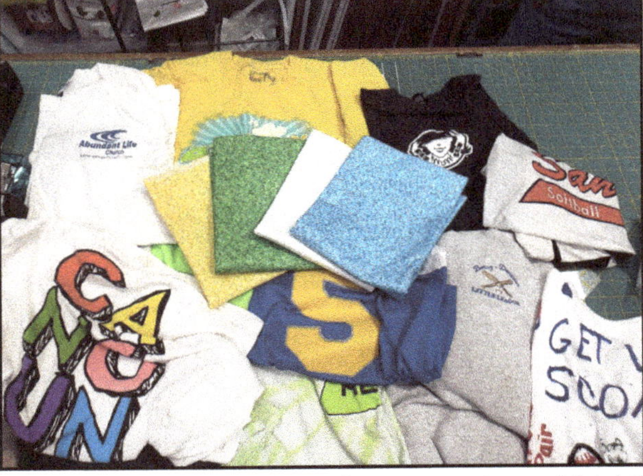

You see the wide range of colors in the shirts (left). The colors I picked compliment this color range quite well (right).

Now take a look at the other colors we looked at. The red fabric was the closest red we could find and it was not a good choice. The pink/mauve fabric may go with the pink "C" in Cancun, but it doesn't go with the rest of the quilt (below left).

Take a look at this other red with the yellow, blue and green and the t-shirts. This might have worked if the pattern of the red fabric was the same as the other colors. For the sake of a little more continuity, I went with the white (below right).

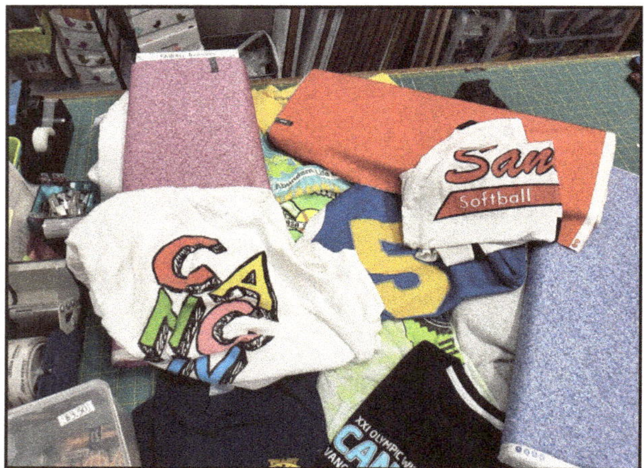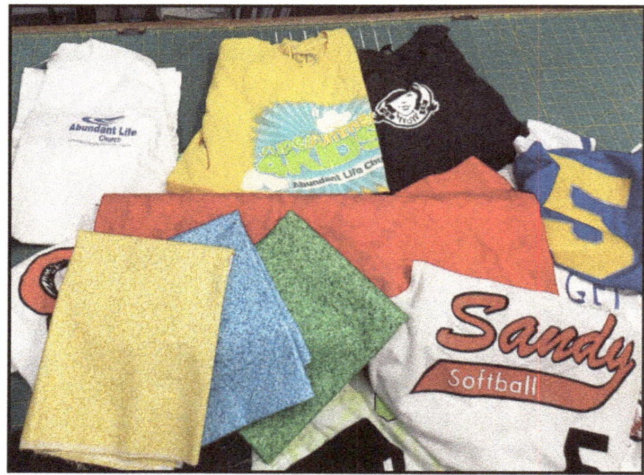

Here are a few pictures with the wrong color green. They are gorgeous fabrics! Just not with this project. Also, one of the greens looks like Christmas fabric – wrong theme.

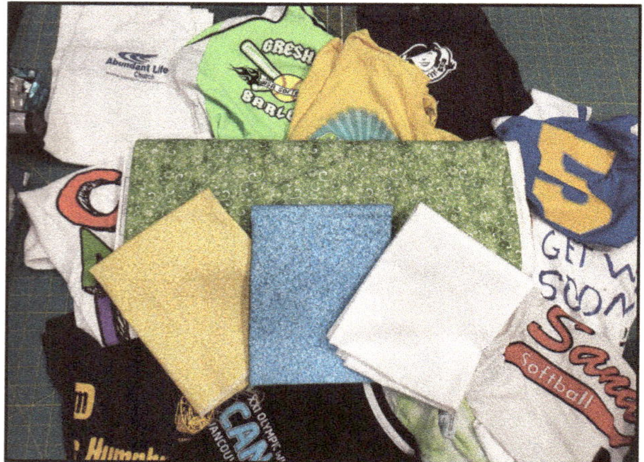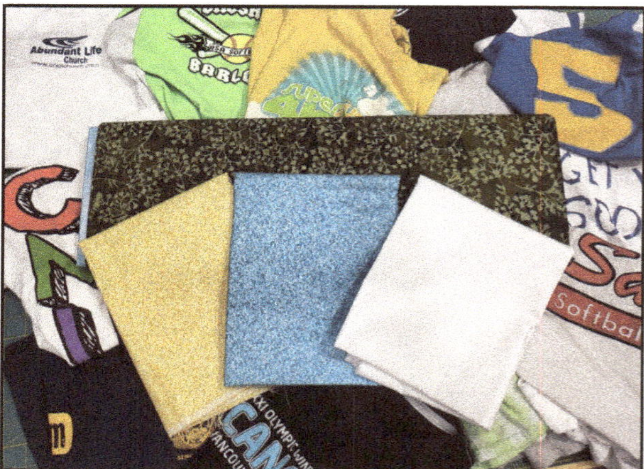

As you can tell from the above photos, the fabric can be fabulous but not match your project.

At this point I want to show you what you will be doing with your 4 color choices. In the example I am going to show you I was given about 35-40 t-shirts. Most of them were a stained white or gray color (old soccer shirts). Very few had any colors at all. There were a few t-shirts with the school colors: maroon, blue and   yellow and a few work shirts that were green. I found fabric that matched in color for the maroon, yellow, blue and green.

Here are the t-shirts laid out without the accent colors.

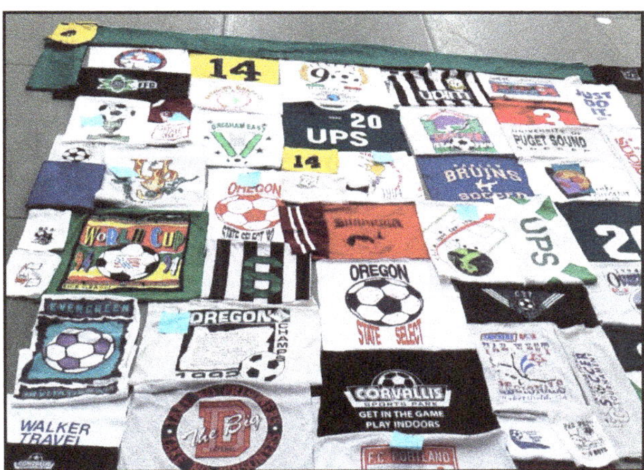

Here is the finished quilt with all the accent colors in place.

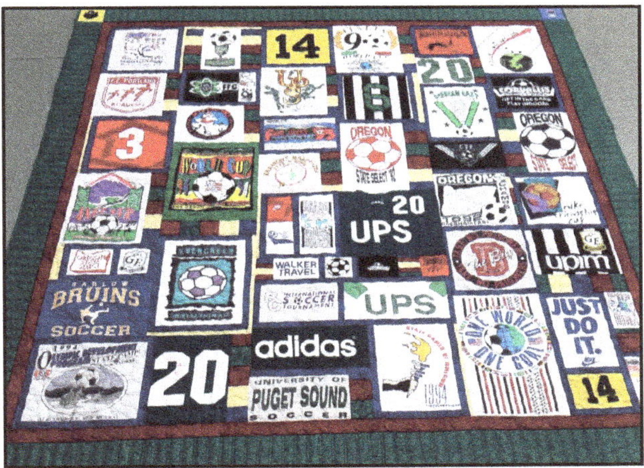

The accent fabric adds color to the quilt and brings out the color in the t-shirts.

Now that you have picked out your colors, buy 1 yard of each of your accent colors and 2 yards of your   border color. This would be for a small quilt – about 20 t-shirts or 60"x60".

Buy 2 yards of each color for accents and 3-4 for borders for a large quilt about 35-40 t-shirt or 90"x100".

What if you buy too much fabric? Is that possible????!!!!! Ok, just kidding. Save the fabric for another project or make yourself matching pillow covers after the quilt is done. What if you don't buy enough fabric? You have a couple choices: Go buy more OR use the left over back t-shirt fabric as your accent fabric. I will go over how to do this in a later chapter – but here is a picture to give you a sneak peek.

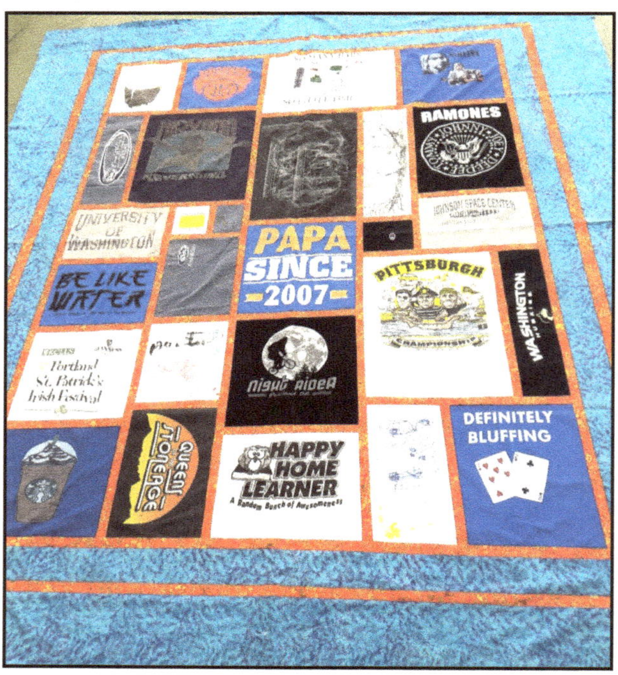

Chapter 2
Preparing The T-Shirts

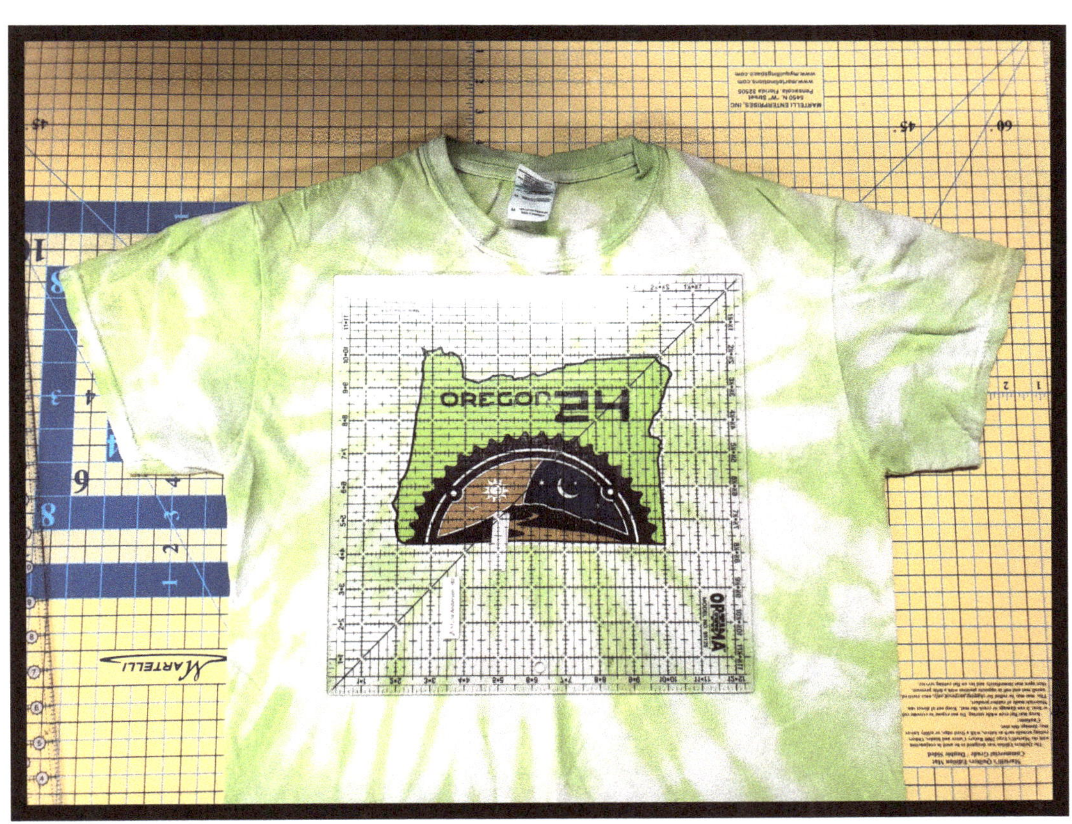

CHAPTER 2 - PREPARING THE T-SHIRTS

Your next step is to cut out the t-shirts. I like to use a rotary cutter and a cutting mat. I don't use scissors   unless I need to cut up seams carefully or if I am using a logo from the front and the back of a shirt and I need to be careful not to cut the back side logo.

I use a 12 ½ inch square ruler and a 6 ½ inch by 24 ½ inch ruler. These 2 cutting rulers seem to work for nearly everything I do. In most cases, I center the 12 ½ inch square ruler over the front t-shirt logo and cut the shirts.   In this case, there is no logo on the back of the shirt, just a cool tie-dye design. I decided to cut both front and back and use both pieces.

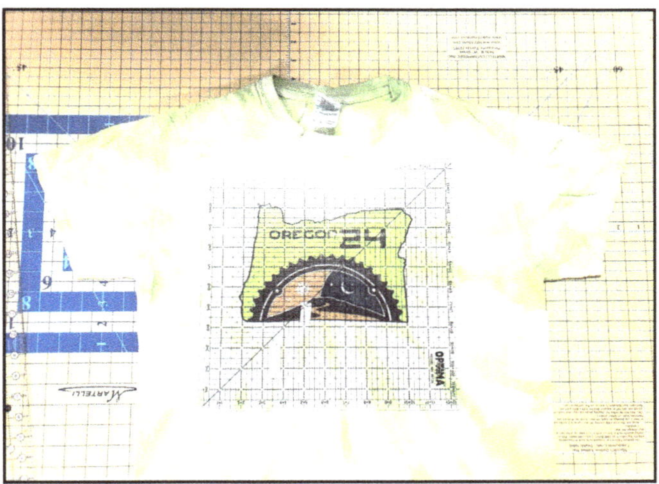

Cut the sides and top of the logo. Leave the length of the t-shirt for a longer piece in case we need it later.

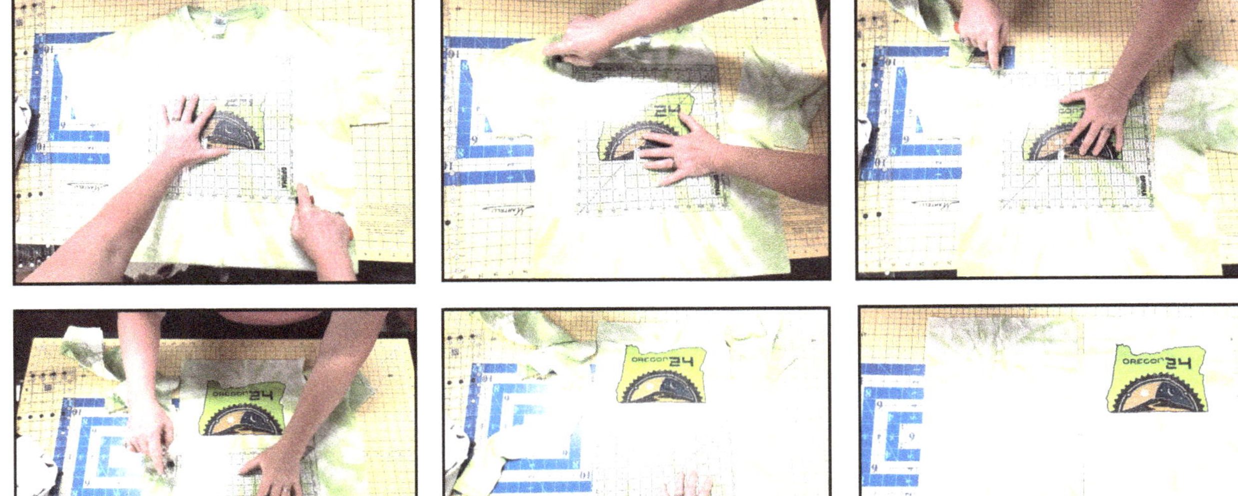

My tie-dye shirt is now ready for the quilt.

When I have a logo on the front and the back AND the shirt is big enough, I cut up the side seams and the shoulders of the shirt using my ruler and rotary cutter.

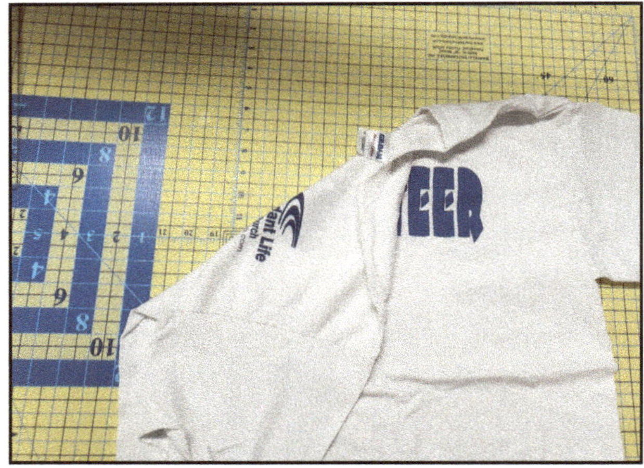

Notice the logos on the front and back.

Smooth out the shirt, place your 24 ½ " ruler near the side seam and cut up the side.

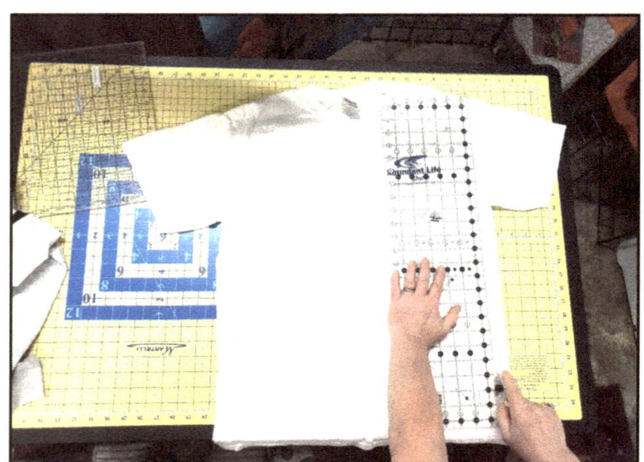
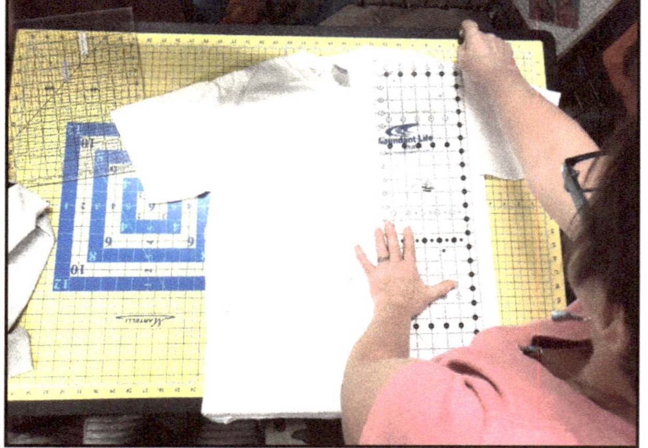

Cut across the top of the shirt near the shoulder seam.

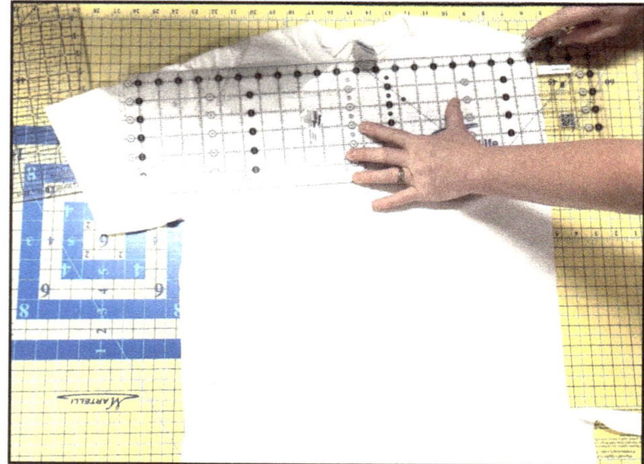
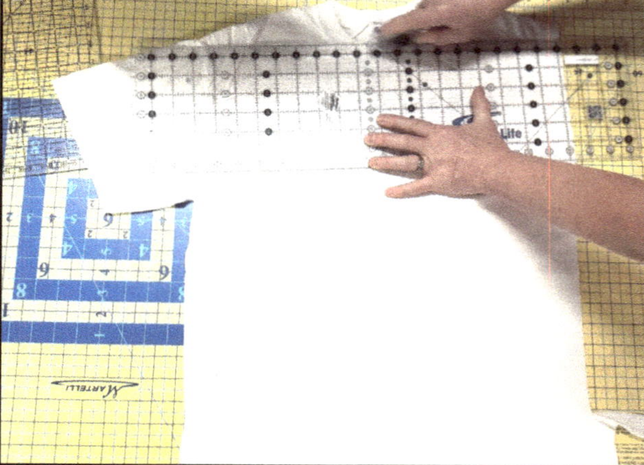

Cut down the other side near the side seam of the shirt.

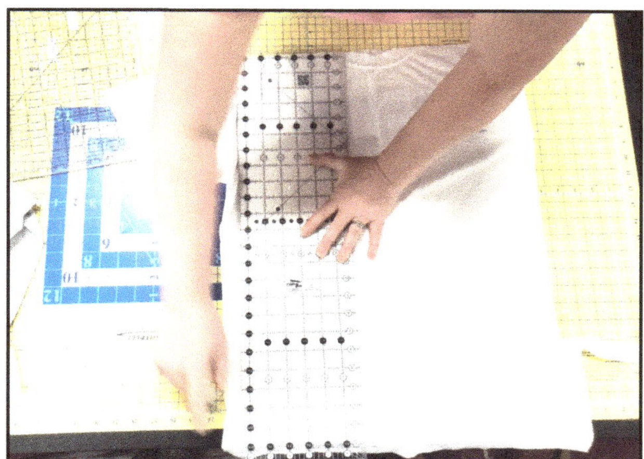
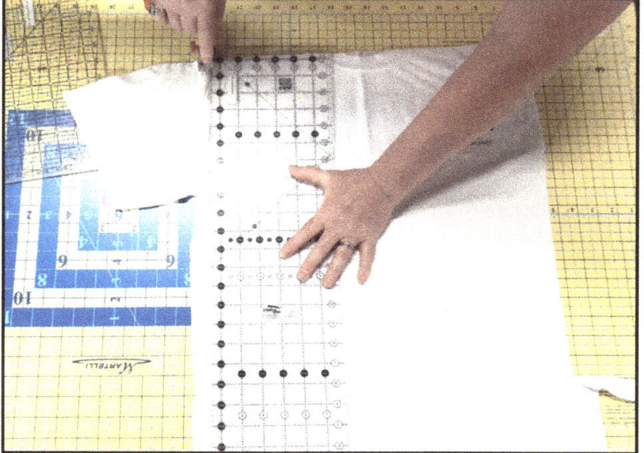

Now that the front and back is separated you can center the logos and cut them individually.
I like to save even the small logos, don't worry about different sizes. The more different sizes
the better.

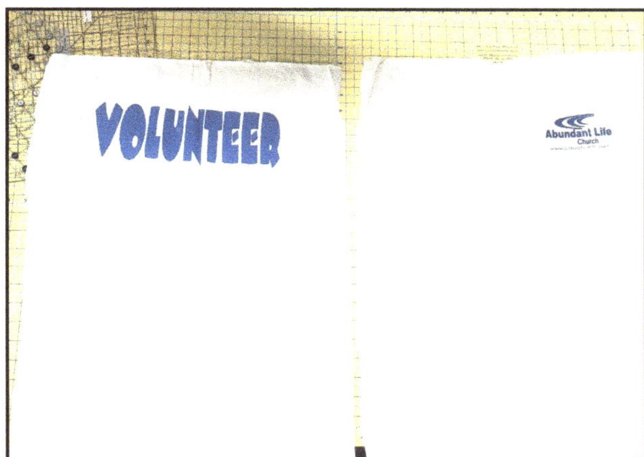

I decided to cut this one down to 6½ inches height and left the length in case I needed it.
I decided to cut the back logo the same way.

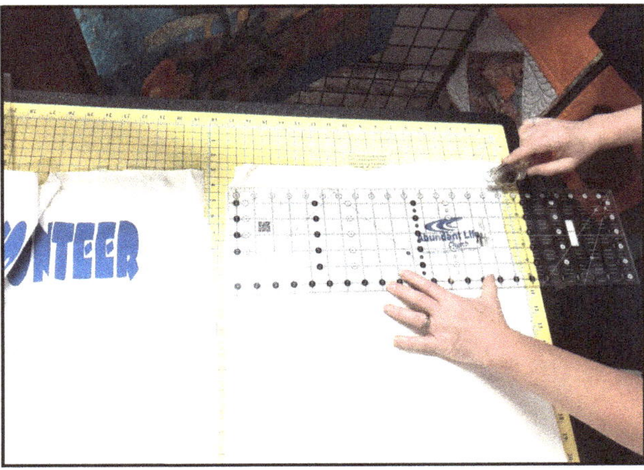

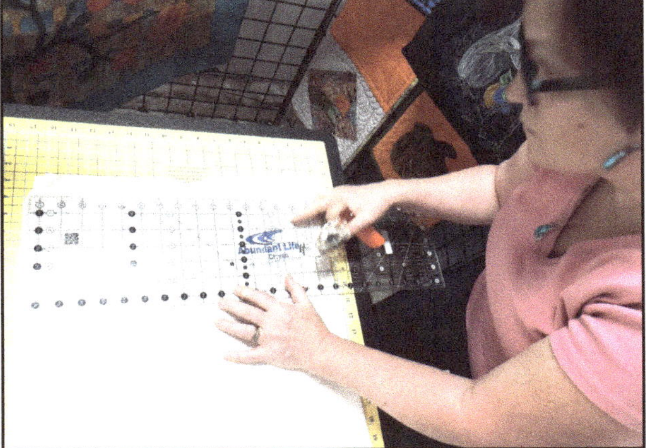

Remember to center the logo before you cut. There is 1 ½ inches above the "volunteer" and 1 ½ inches below the "volunteer".

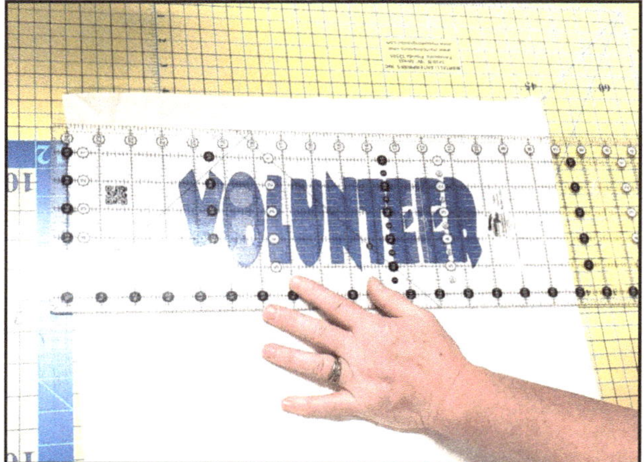

I do not cut the sides yet as I am not sure what width I am going to make the block yet.

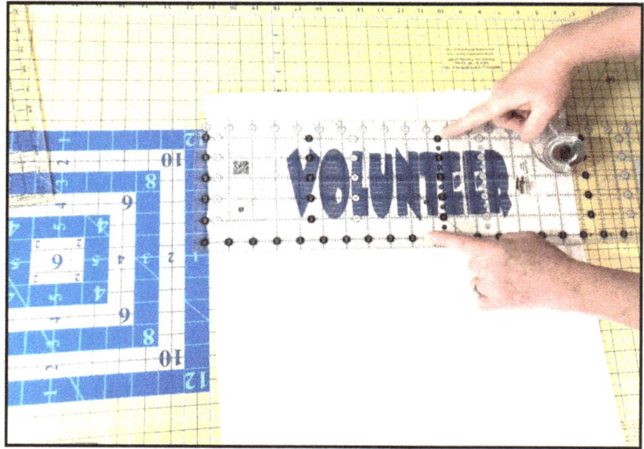

Sometimes I get a shirt with a design all over.

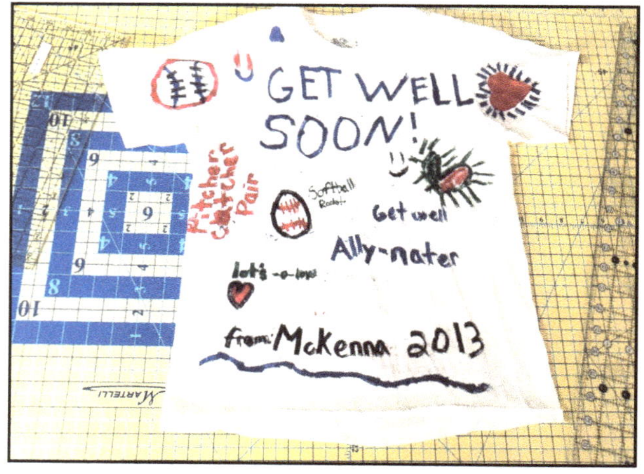

Front

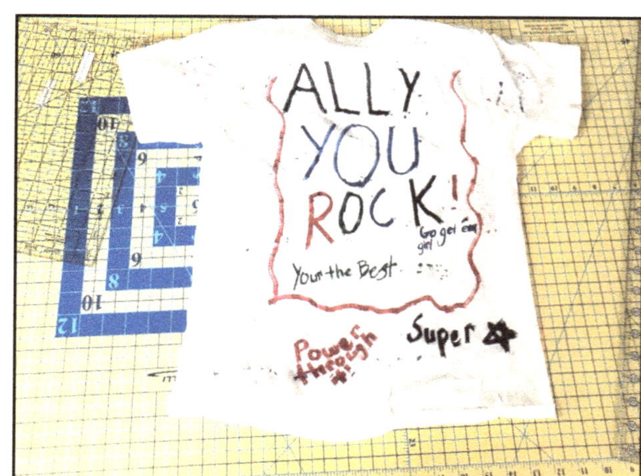

Back

Using scissors cut up the side seams and through the arm pit on both sides.

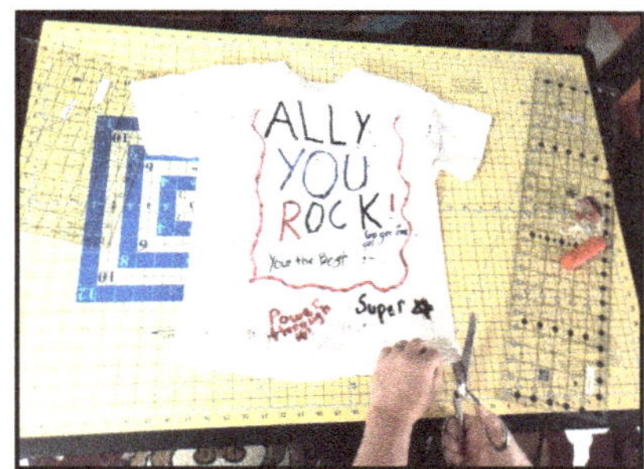 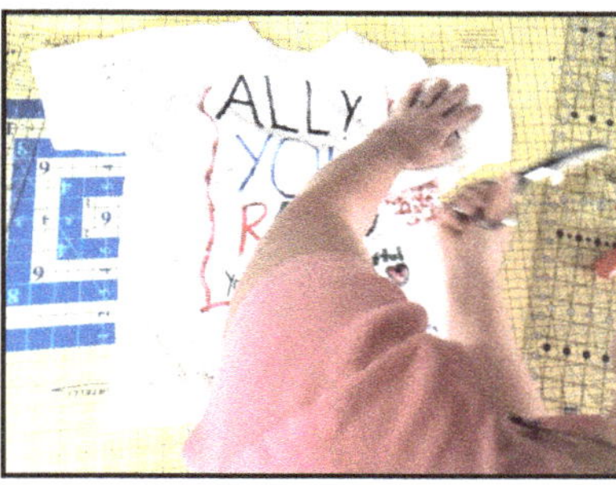 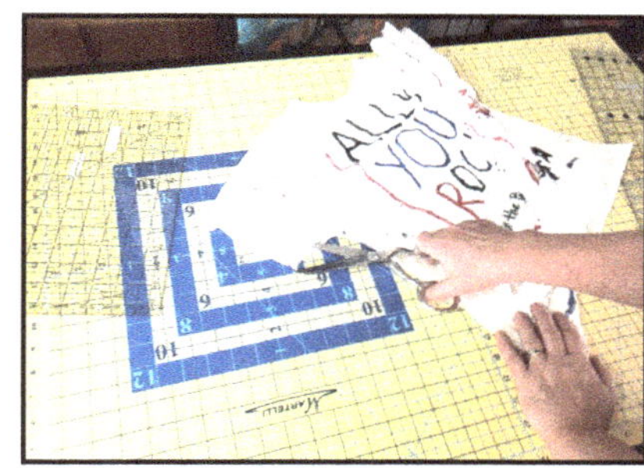

Open the front and back and cut through the sleeves seams.

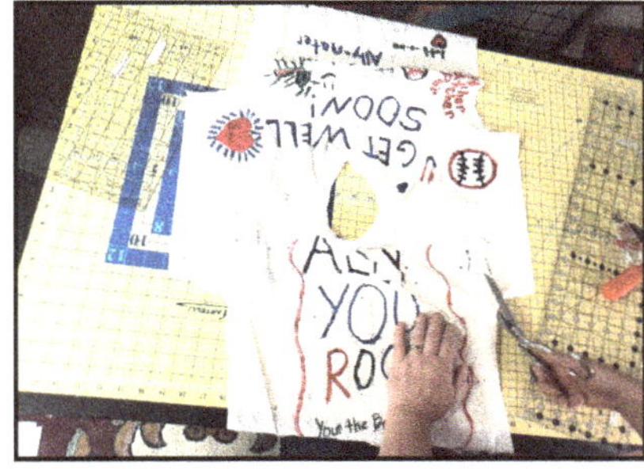 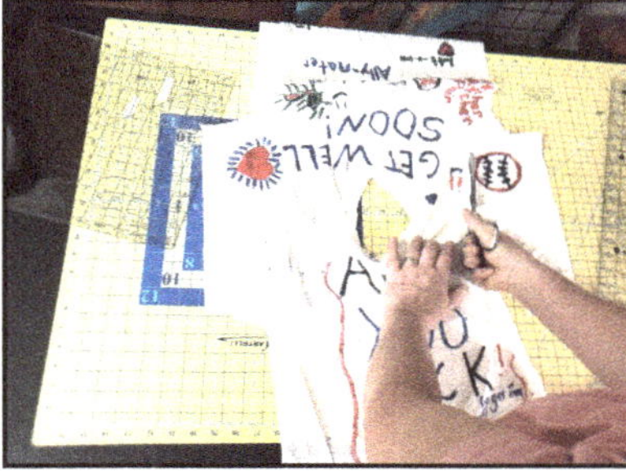 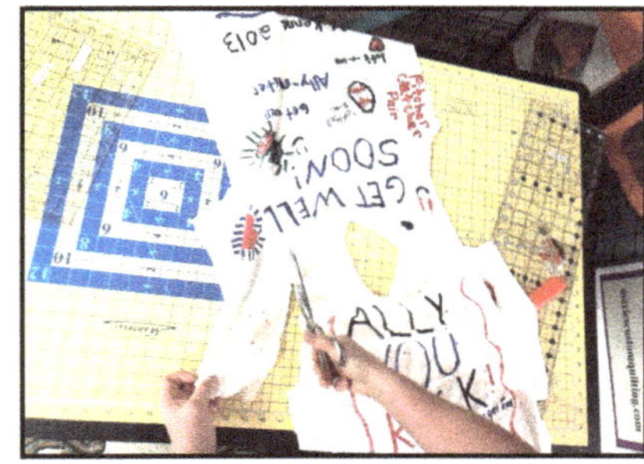

Cut the remaining shoulder seams to fully separate the front from the back.

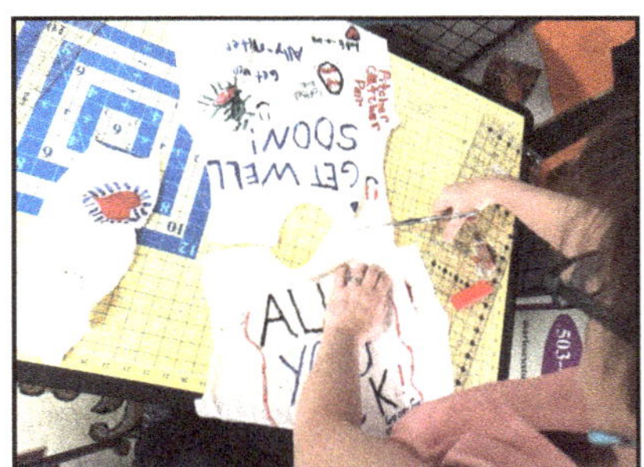 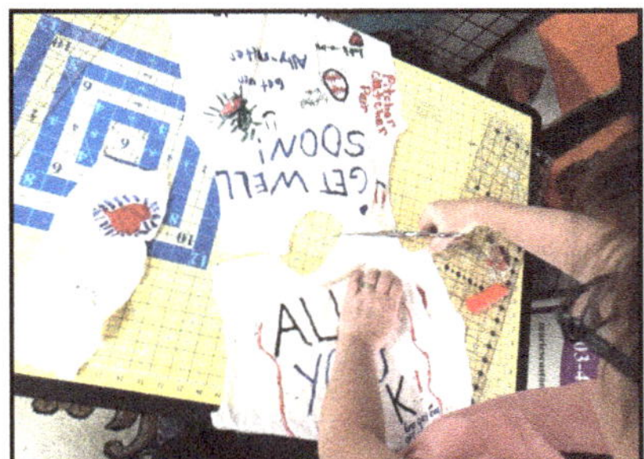

If the logo is longer than most, leave it long. The different sizes and shapes of the t-shirts will add interest to your quilt.

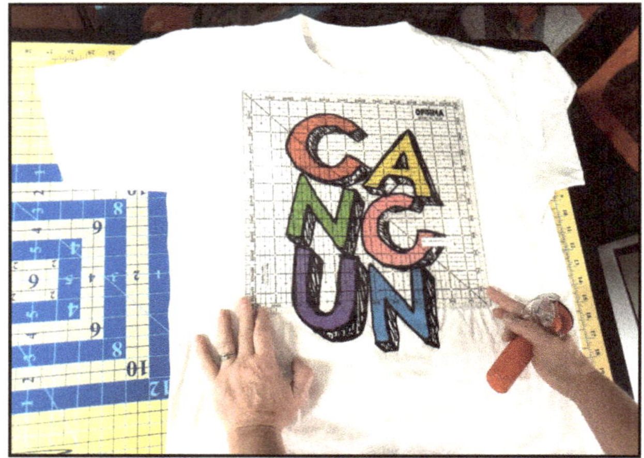
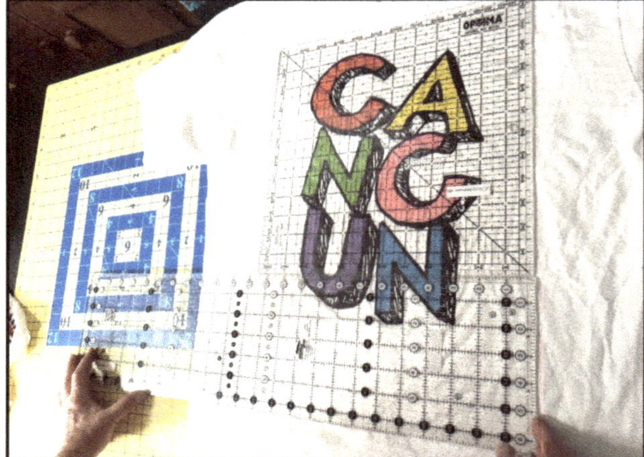

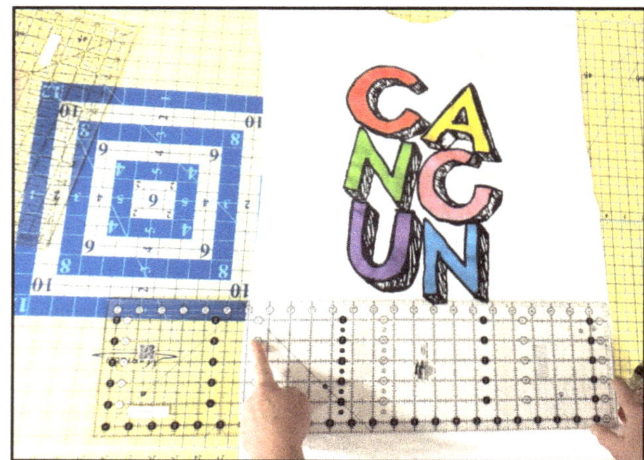
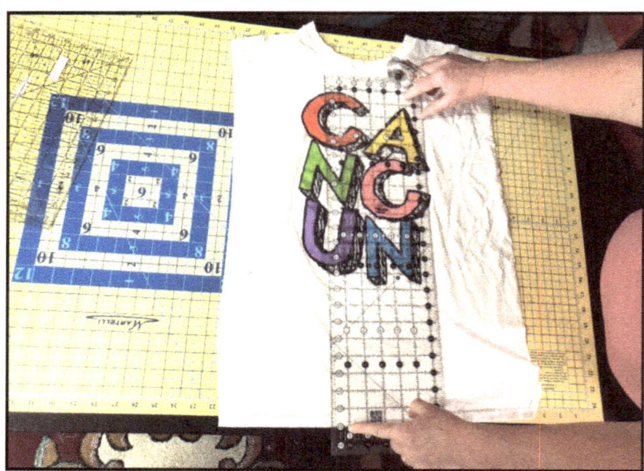

When you are cutting odd shaped t-shirts sometimes using scissors are the only way to go.

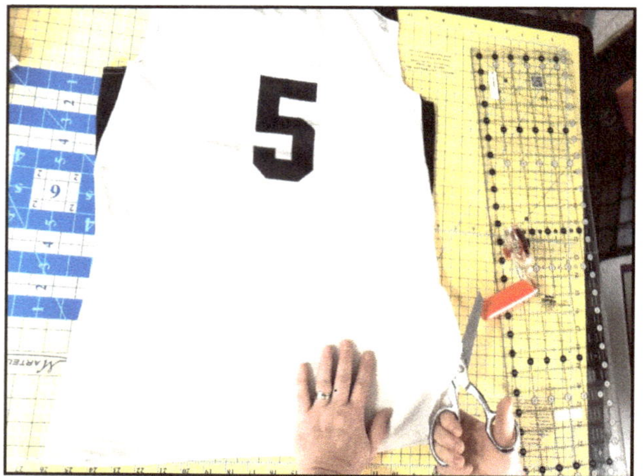
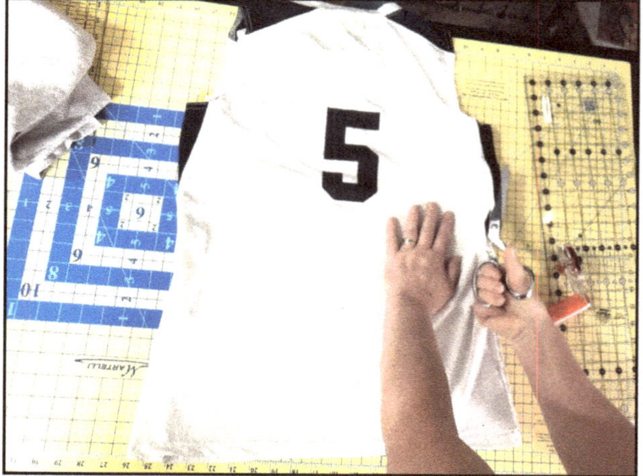

Sometimes you can use the rotary cutter without the ruler.

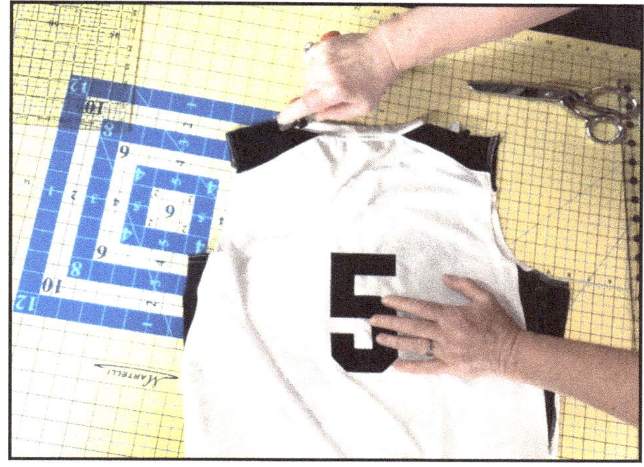

Open the shirt and cut up the side or decide to cut your 12 1/2 " square right now. Since it is a plain shirt, I decided to cut the 12 ½ inch square. Remember to center the logo top, bottom and sides.

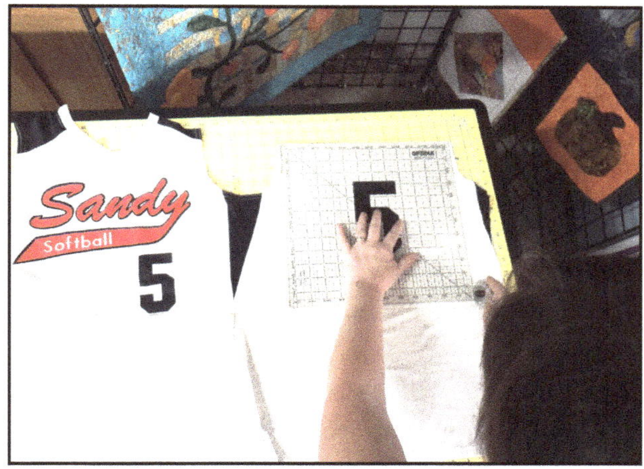

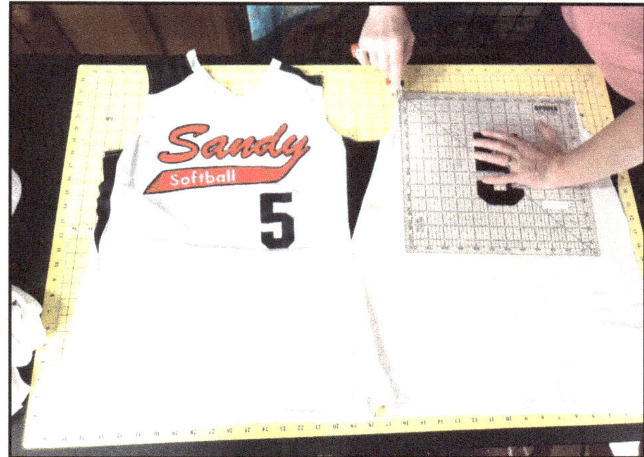

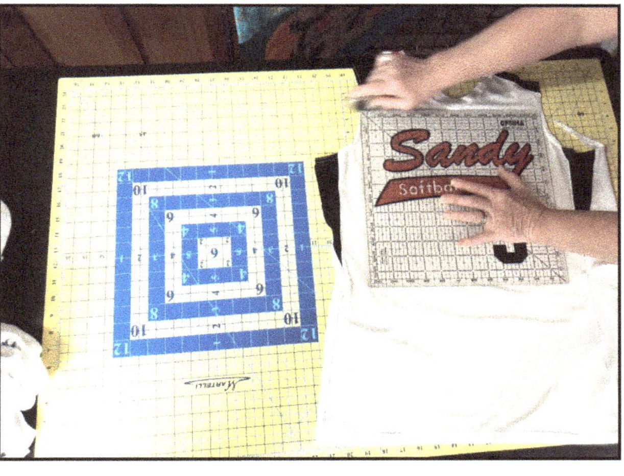

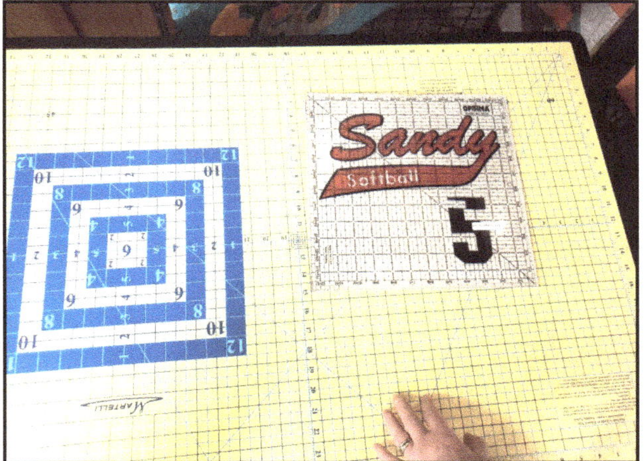

Just cut up the sides, around the arm and shoulder seams and across the back if you want to use the hoodie or collar. I am keeping the piece long in case I need it long.

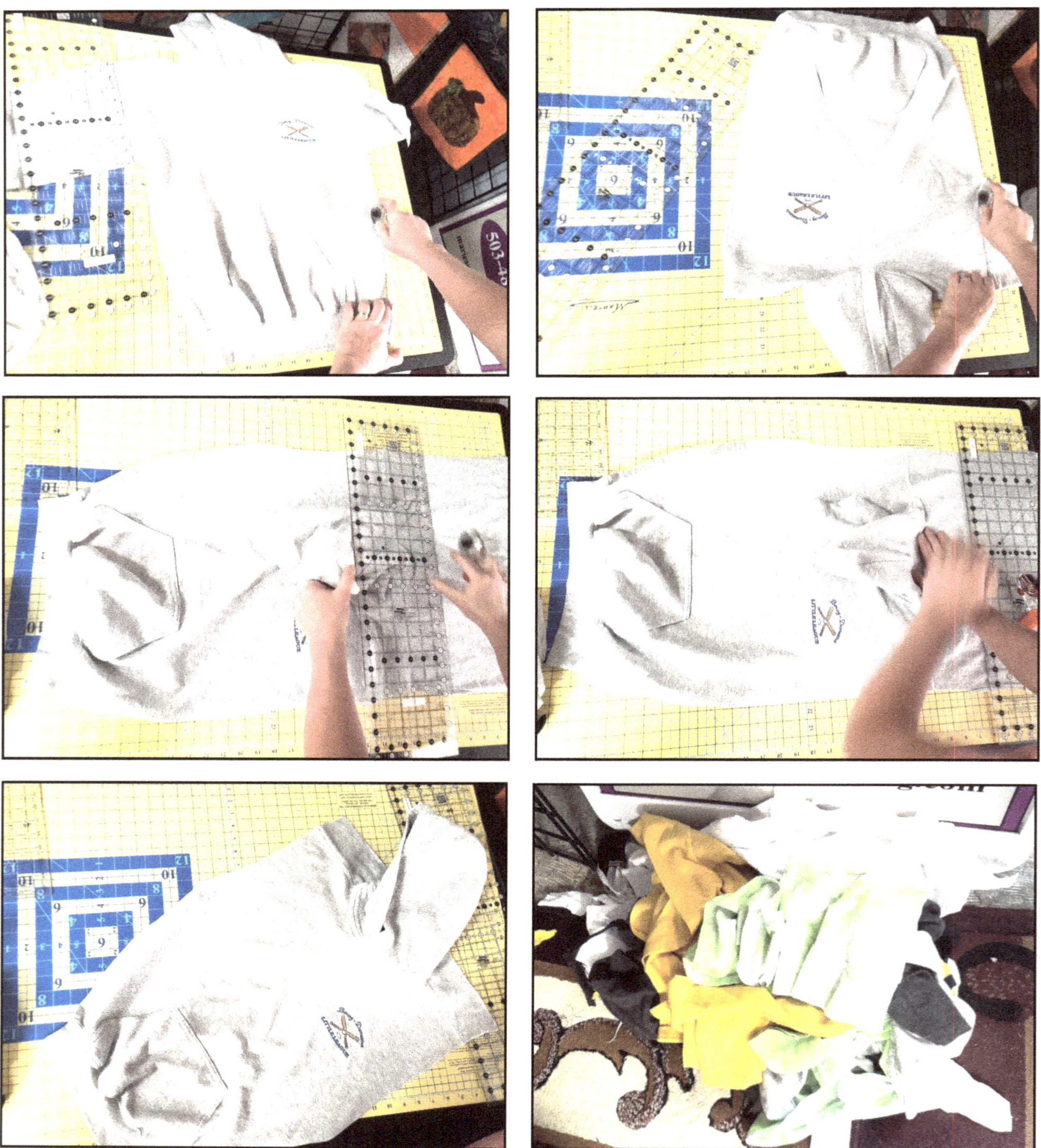

When you are done cutting – save all the scraps because you might need them for accent squares or full squares (photo above right).

Your next step is to iron on the fusable web to the back of the t-shirts. I use a lightweight woven fabric that has an adhesive on one side.   Fusable web comes in black and white. I always use white because you can use white on a black or dark t-shirt but you can't use black fusable web on a white or light t-shirt . Black   fusable web will show through on a white or light colored t-shirt.

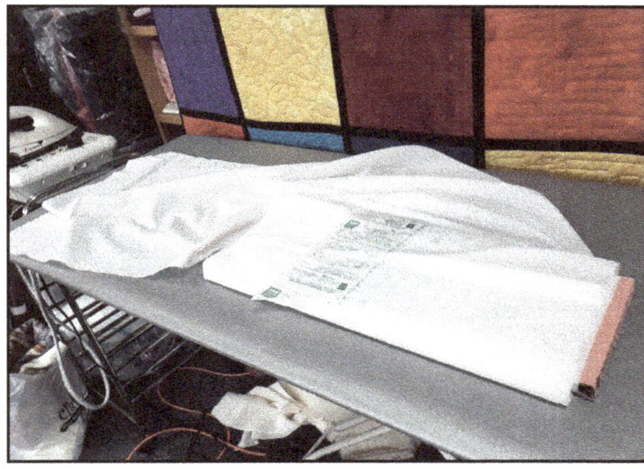

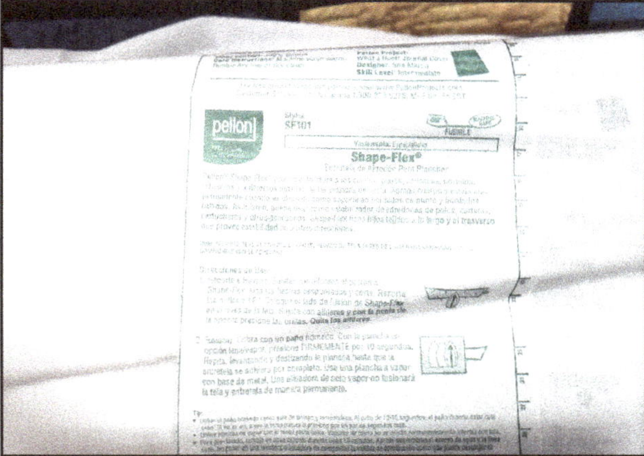

Ensure whatever you use that it is lightweight. The type I use weighs less than 1 pound for king size quilt. When attaching the fusable web to the t-shirts I have some steps to make it go faster. Place some towels or pillow cases over your ironing board to keep it clean.

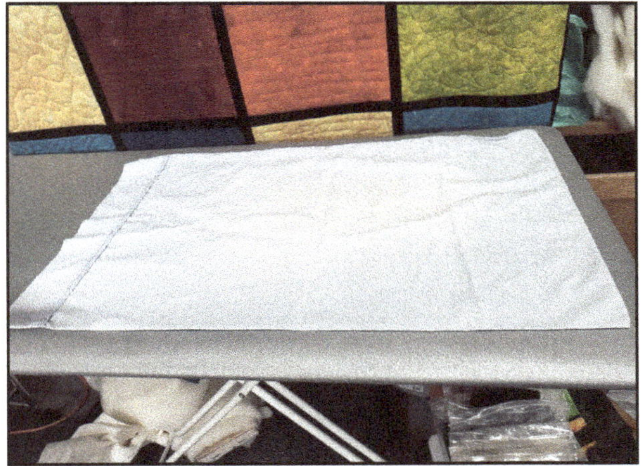

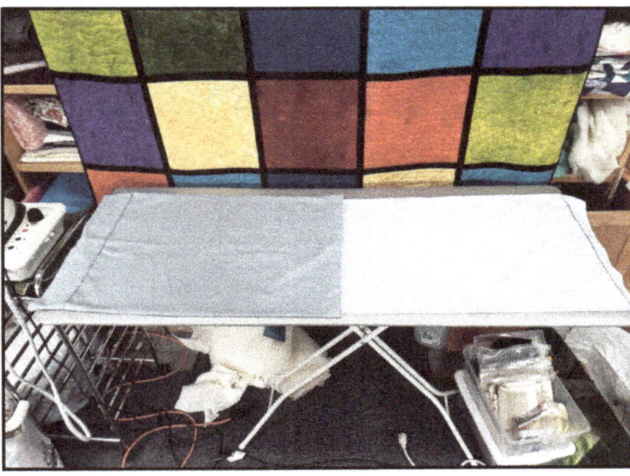

Place t-shirts face down on the covering on the ironing board.

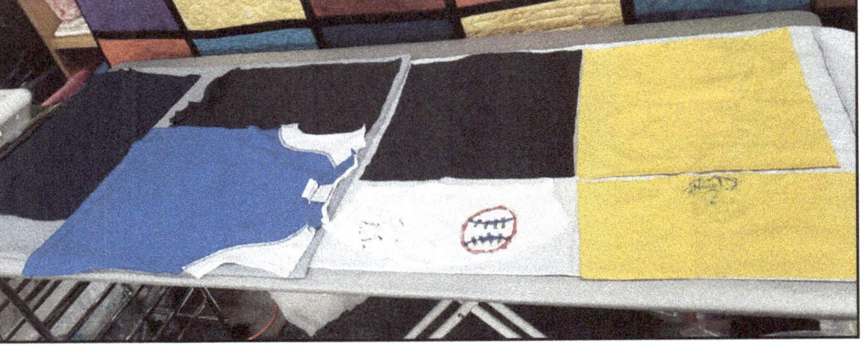

Position the fusable web over the top of the t-shirts with the sticky side down. Iron per the instructions on the package.

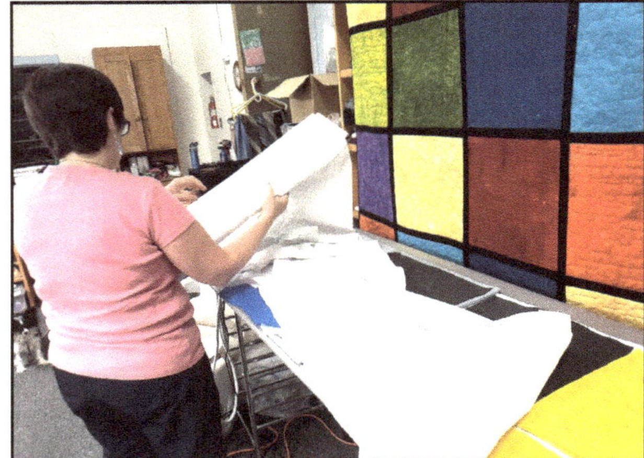
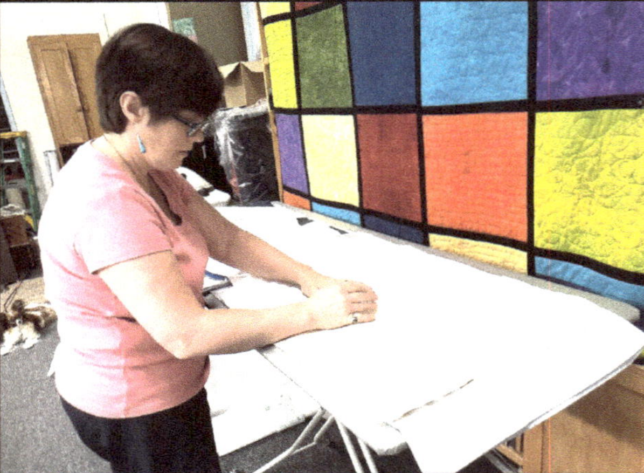
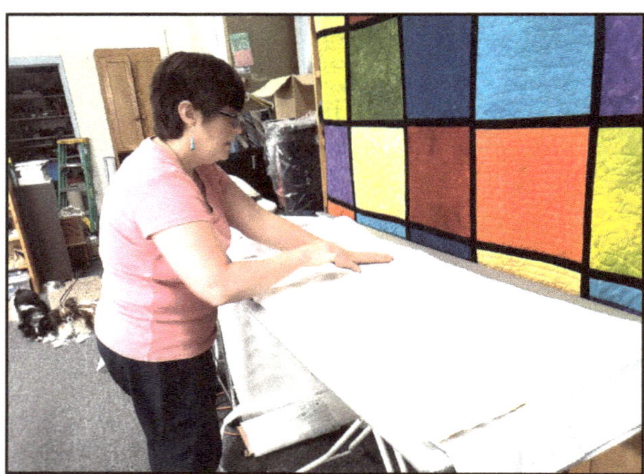
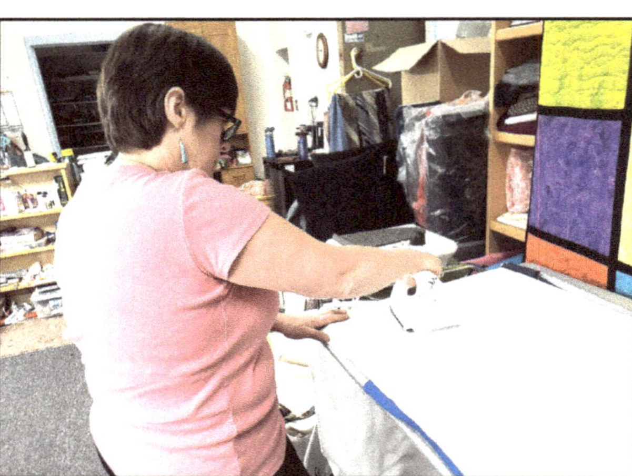

When you are fusing odd shapes, think of how you will attach them to a flat surface. With a hoodie, make the front and back flat. For the pocket cut off the band and iron flat.

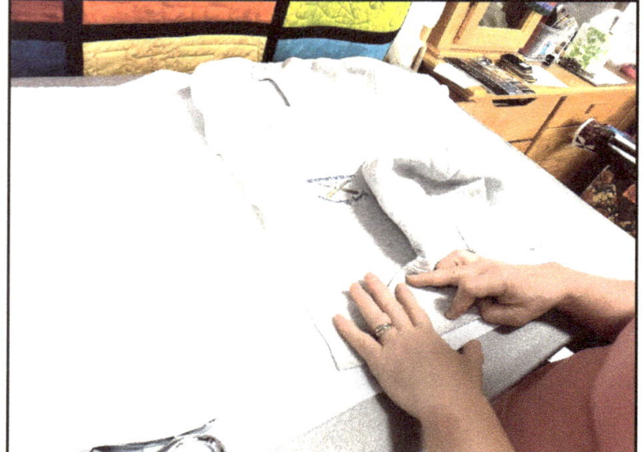
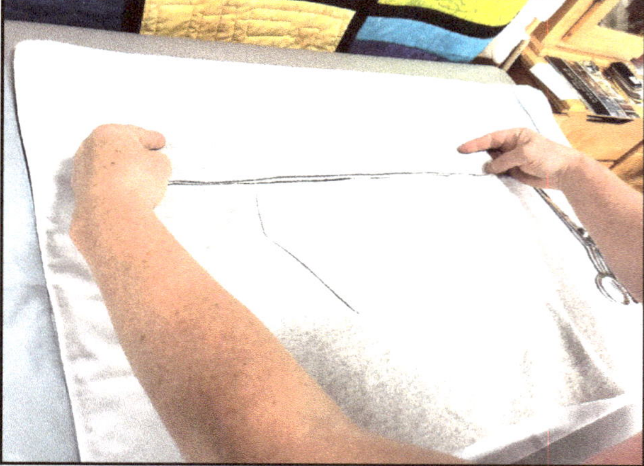

Cut the webbing so that the t-shirts are separated.

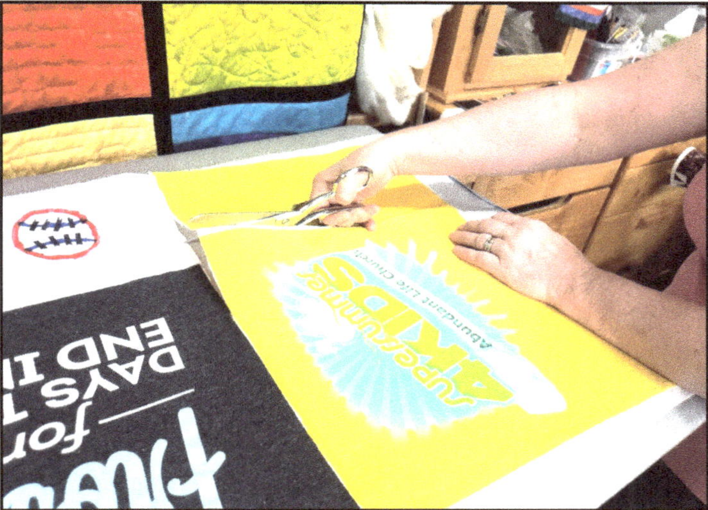

Now it's time to take all of your pieces and begin to arrange them.

Chapter 3
Arranging The
T-Shirts

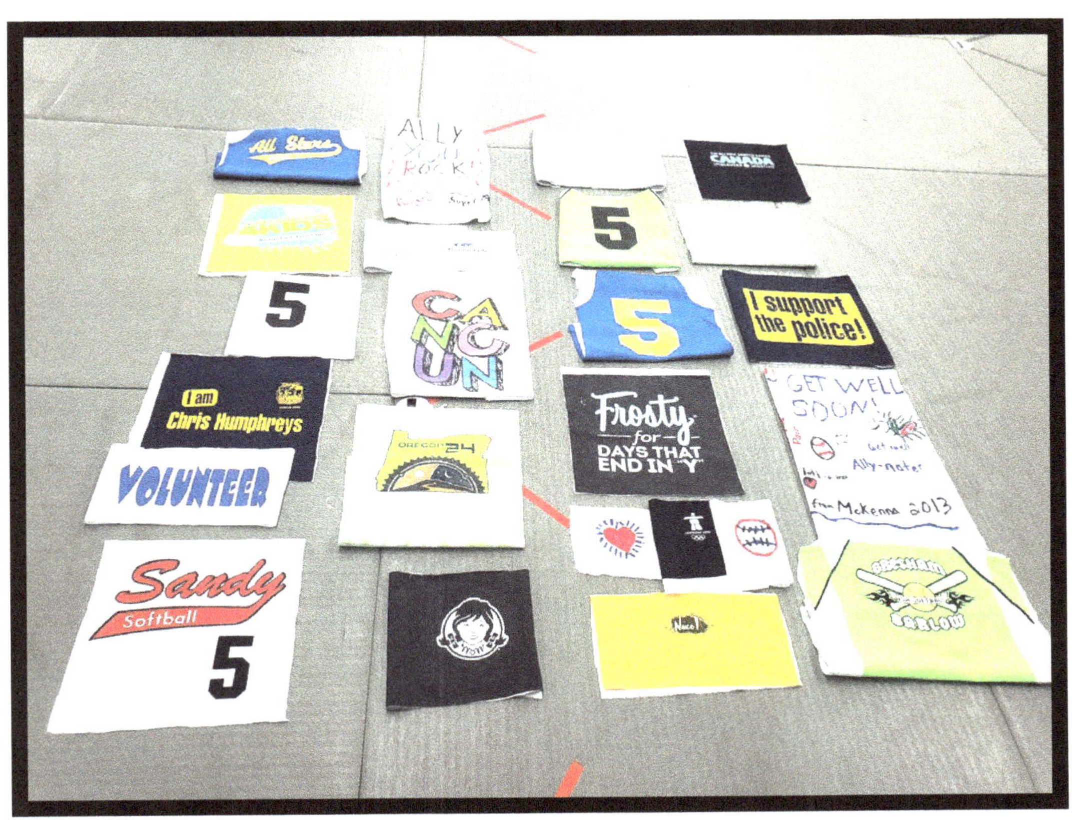

CHAPTER 3 - ARRANGING THE T-SHIRTS

Lay out each of the shirts in the order you want them (a). Don't worry about sizes, fold the t-shirts to the size you want them. Think more of colors. Do you want an even balance of color (b)? Alternating colors? Balance the colors with 2 or 3 black t-shirts scattered among the gray or red? Notice how the black or red jumps out at you? Spread out the bright or dark valued colors among the more muted colors. Or do you want an ombre' effect? Going from light to dark values in a range of hues (c)?

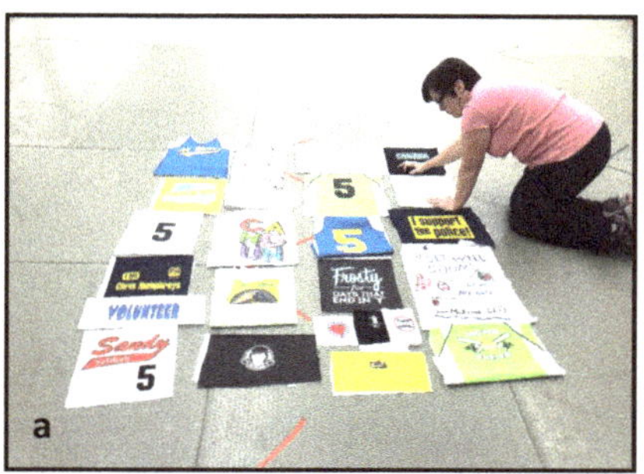
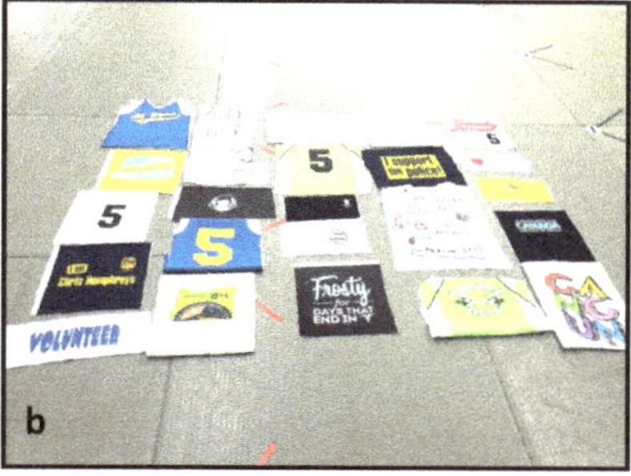
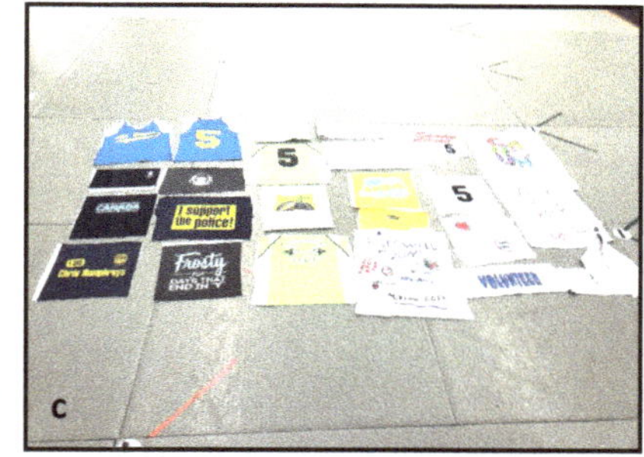

Arrange the shirts in a line that leaves "holes" where the shirt is not big enough. Think with alternating patterns of striped edges, solid borders, multiple borders, etc. You will be filling the "holes" between the   t-shirts with strips of fabric, borders other t-shirt pieces, etc. Keep extra t-shirts to fill in, in case you decide to make some of the shirts smaller.

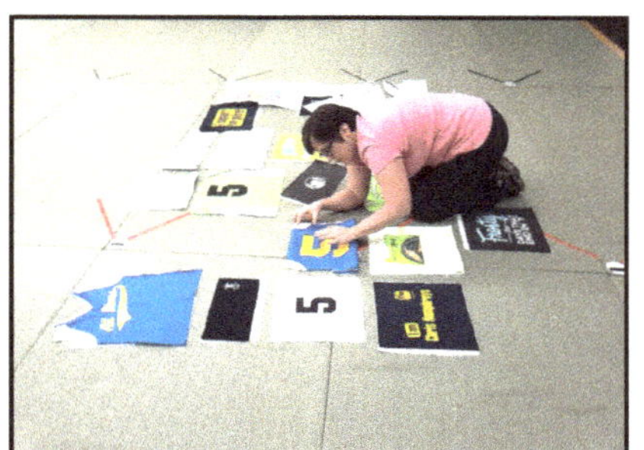
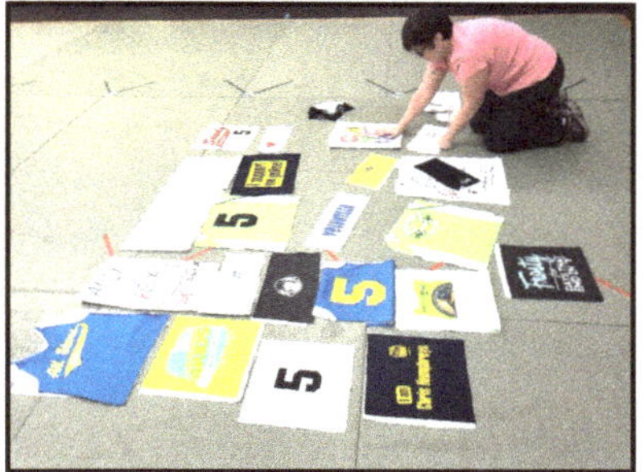
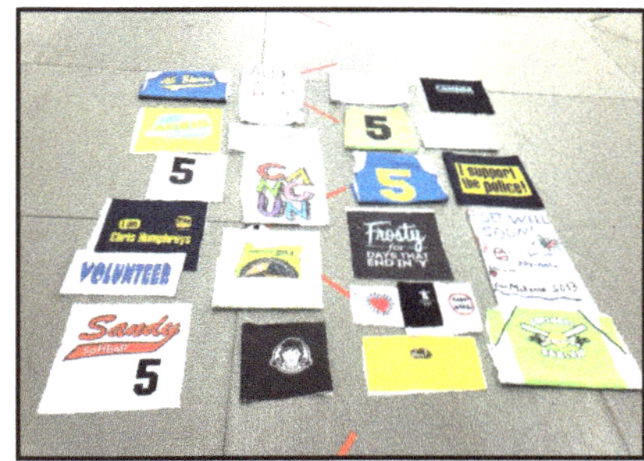

Below are a couple examples of different layout possibilities for a quilt I made and the finished product.

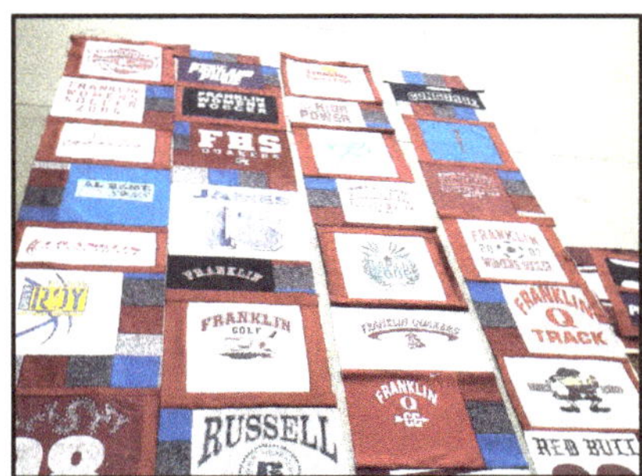
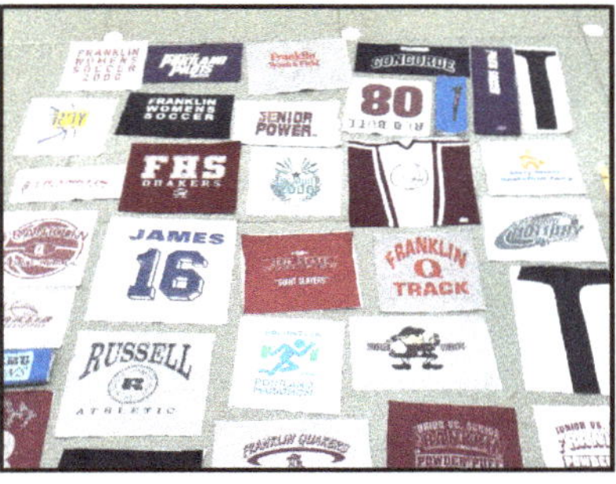
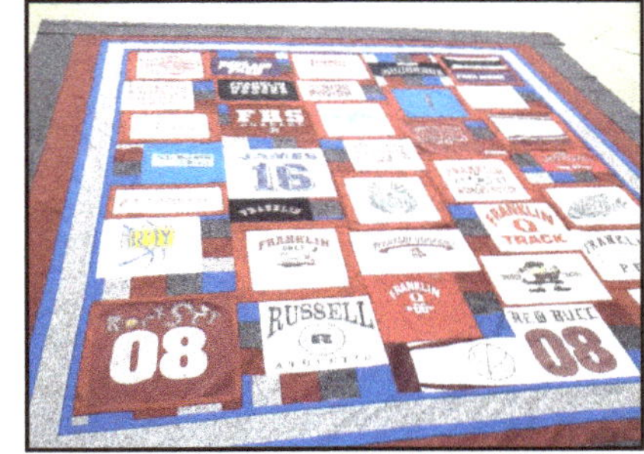

Chapter 4
Sizing It Up

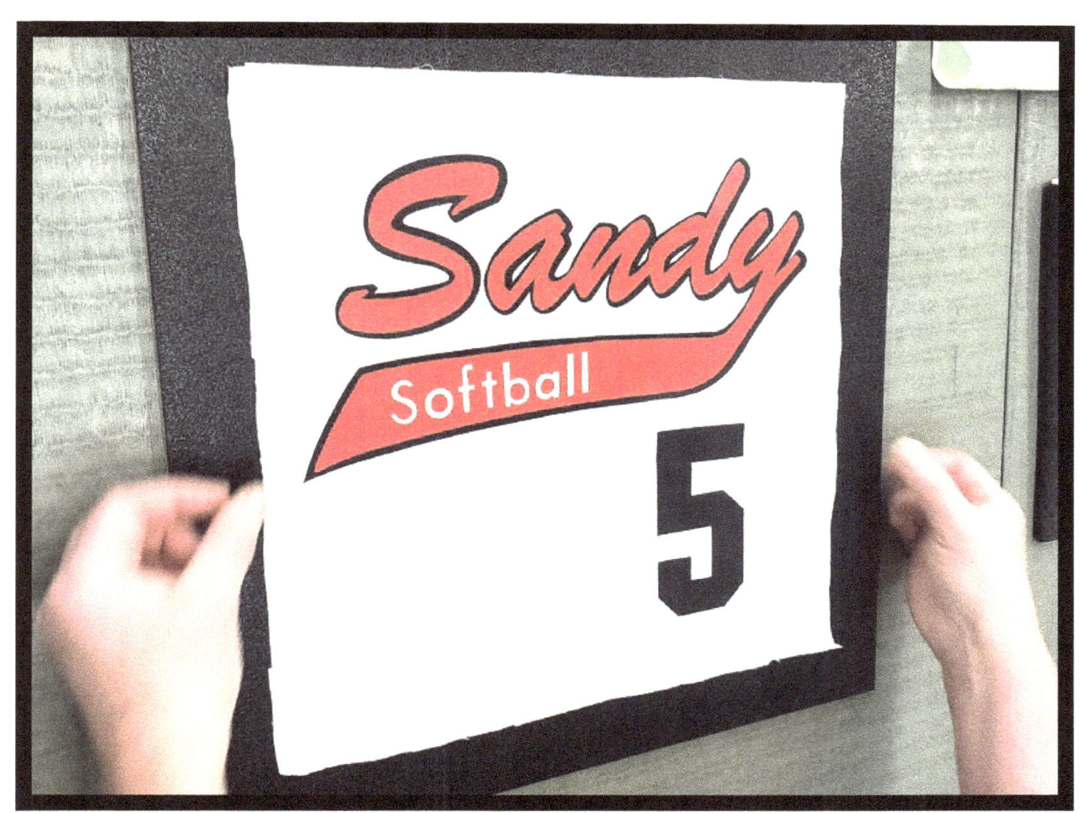

Decide how big you want each square to be. If your t-shirt is about 12x12 inches then maybe you want the finished squares to be 16x16. I have made the squares as big as 18 inches wide when my finished quilt was supposed to be 110x110 and I only had about 40 t-shirts.

The quilt I am making, this time, needs to be about 60x70. I just got this cool template that it 15.5x15.5 so I am going to use it.   If you have 24 t-shirts that are 16x16 and you have 4 across and 6 down your center of quilt will be 64x 96. This logo will make a perfect centered 15.5x15.5 block.

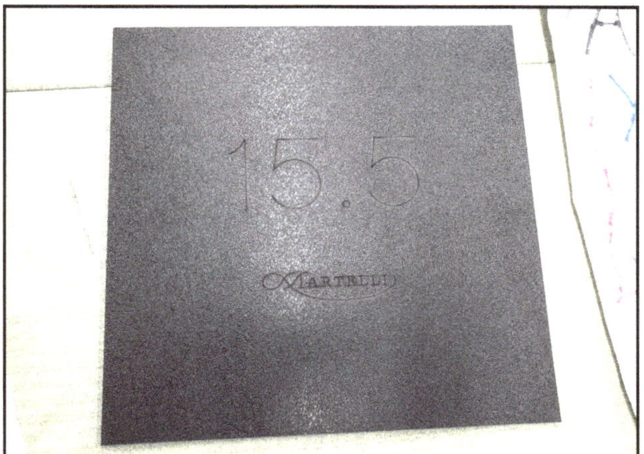

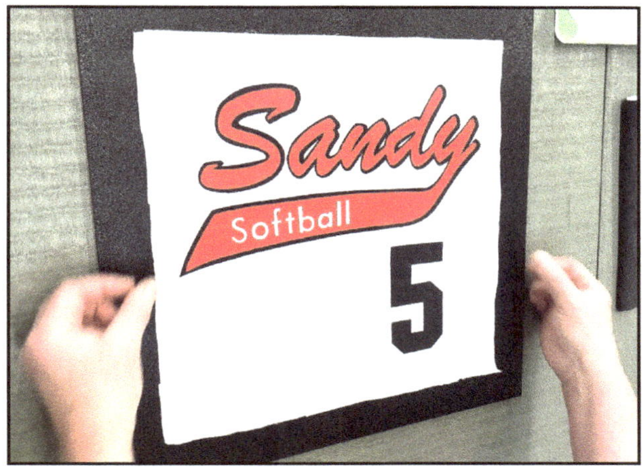

Most of the time, the logos are not 12x12 though. They are often 12 wide and 4-8 inches high so your finished quilt will end up being 64x75. You can choose to make a finished block with more than one t-shirt in it (below left). Another option is to have a finished block that is 15.5 wide and 4-6 or 8 long (below right).

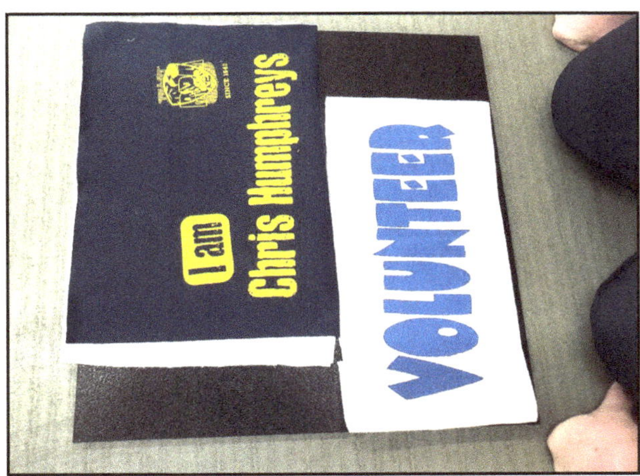

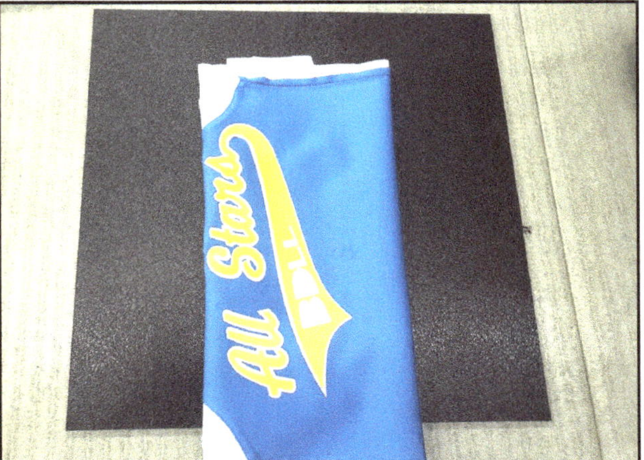

If you have shirt logos that are short they can be scattered around the quilt. If you have some very long and narrow logos they can be used to create a single block (below left). This works well for logos on pockets or on shirt sleeves. You can also use plain fabric from the back of a t-shirt. (below right)

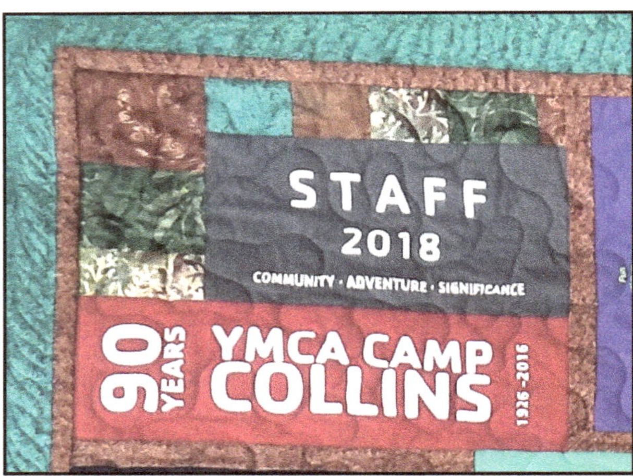

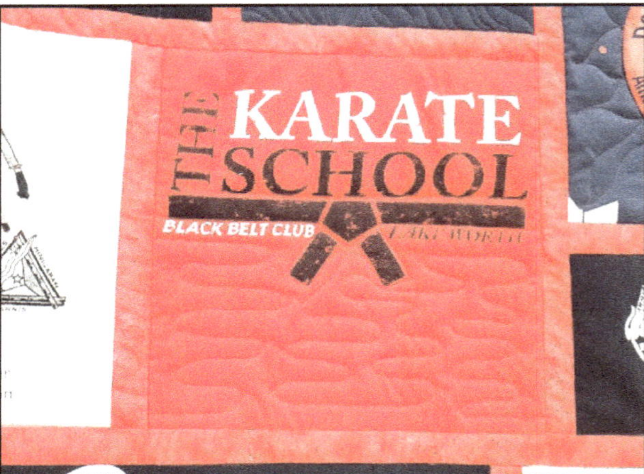

The plain fabric gives the quilter an opportunity to quilt in a special design or motif. For this particular quilt the quilt theme was "water and fire." The back and forth design is not the fanciest, but the overall effect of having "water" or "fire" in the quilt pattern was cool.

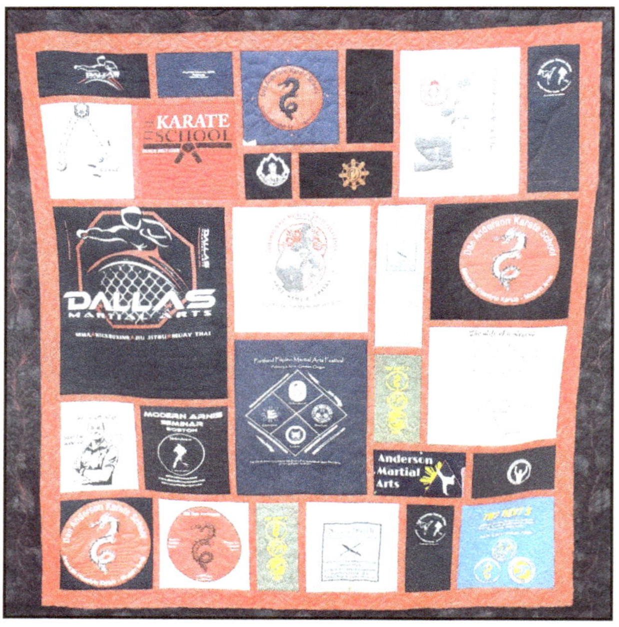

Chapter 5
Creating The Blocks

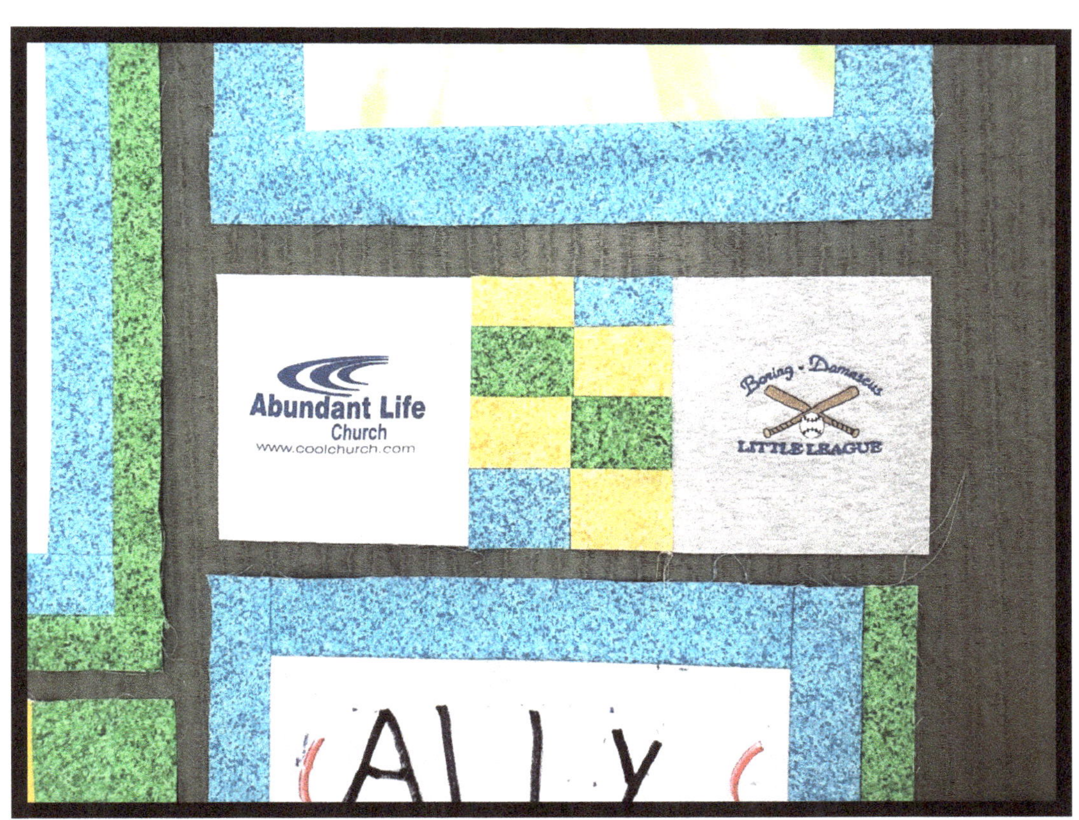

CHAPTER 5 CREATING THE BLOCKS

PART 1:

Arrange your accent strips so that you can cut one strip from each all at once.

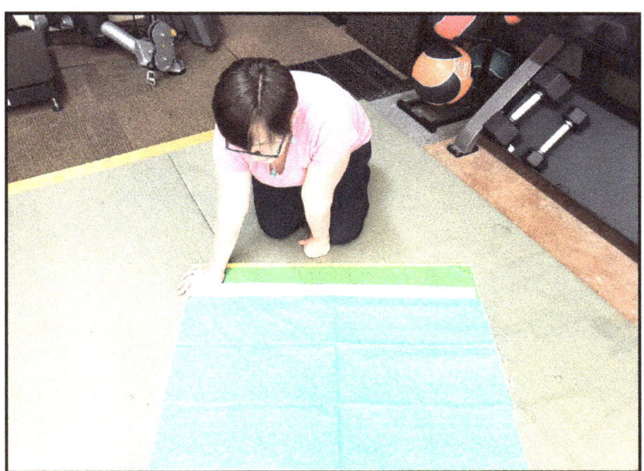

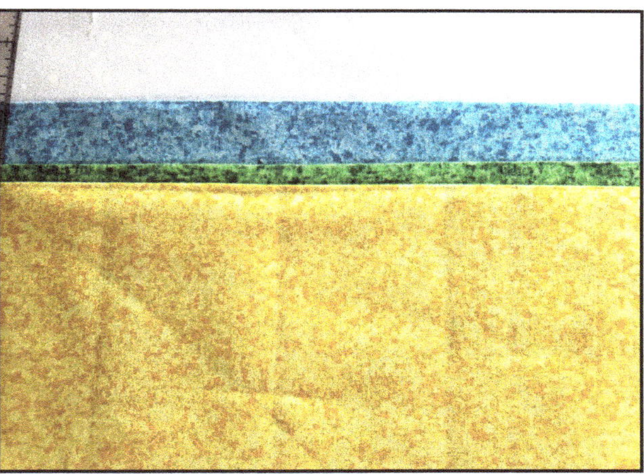

Take the accent fabrics and cut to about 3-4 inch wide strips that are as long as the width of your fabric.   Notice the fabrics are stacked one on top of the other. Notice all the center folds are closest to me (below left). I use two rulers to cut: one to measure from the right hand side and one that is as long as my fabric or longer (24.5") on the left to cut along. Notice how the right hand ruler measures out 3" for me (below right).

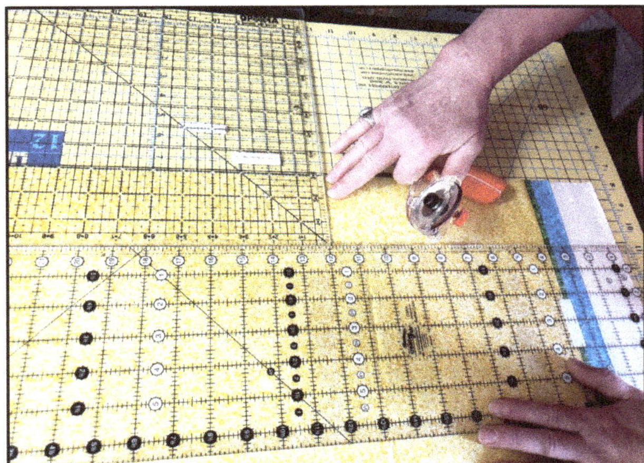

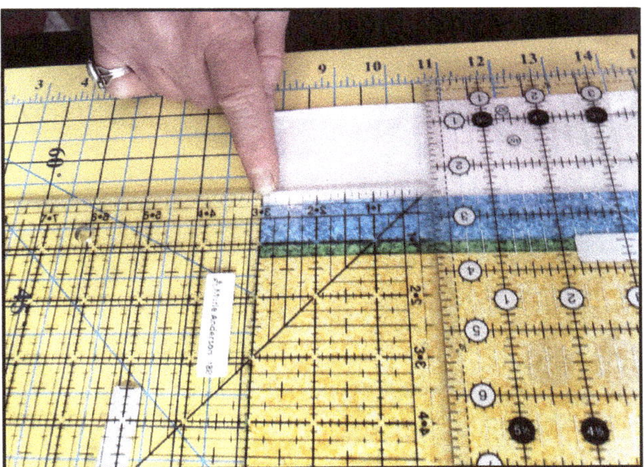

Using your rotary cutter, cut the strips. It helps if the blade in your cutter is sharp. My cutter will cut many layers at once but my hand doesn't enjoy the activity so I never cut more than eight layers at one time. You may only want to cut one fabric at a time because you may want several different widths of strips. As long as you use the same four colors of fabric you can change the colors around and change the size of the strips and your quilt will still look great.

Caution: Keep your left hand, fingers and thumb away from the edge of the ruler. (If you have to make a trip to the ER for stitches you won't get your quilt done in a weekend!) Move your left hand up the ruler so that it doesn't slip. Rulers have non-slip grips but they don't always hold while cutting so just pause, reposition your left hand and continue cutting.

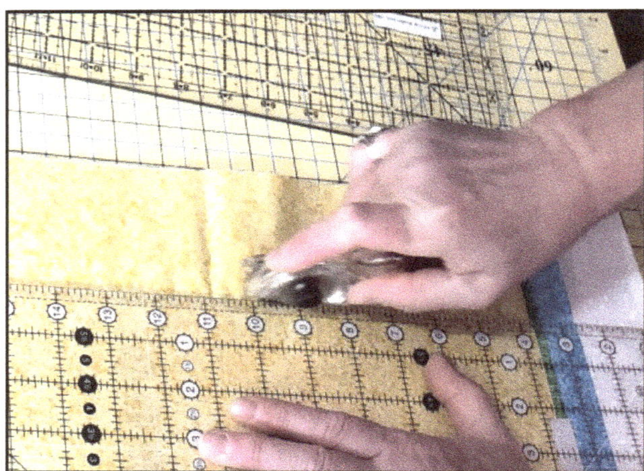
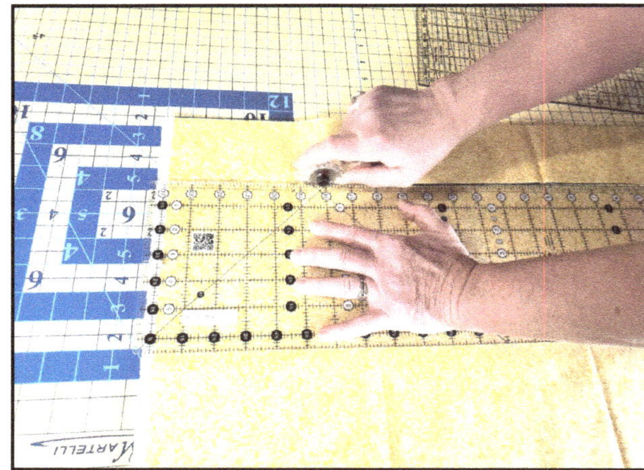

In using a rotary cutter (left), notice how far I keep my left hand away from the blade (right)

Sew the strips, right sides together, with ¼ inch seams. To do this I place a long wide piece of painters tape on the ¼ inch mark of my machine. The tape should be 6-8 inches long.

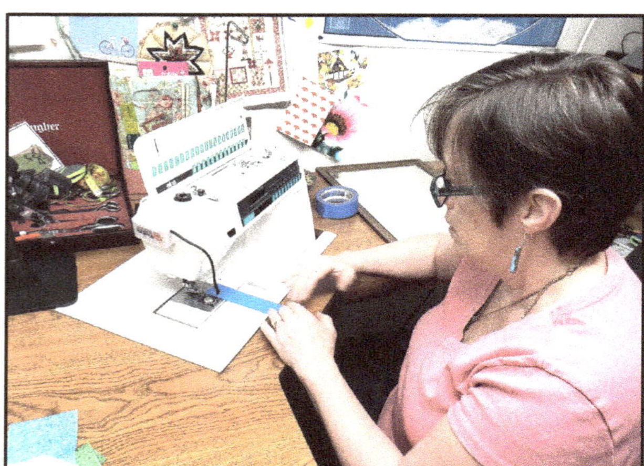
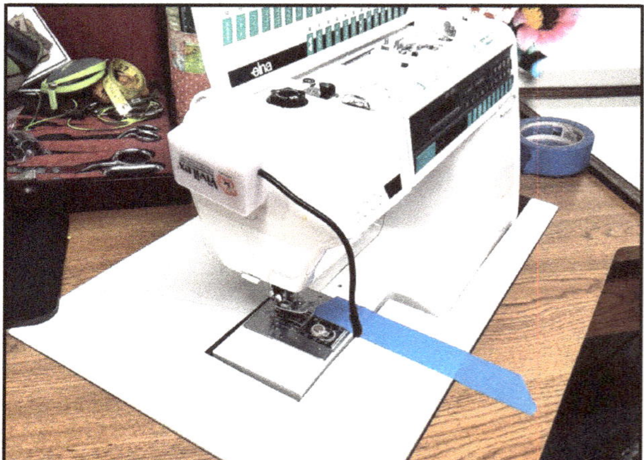

Line the fabric up with the length of the tape and sew.

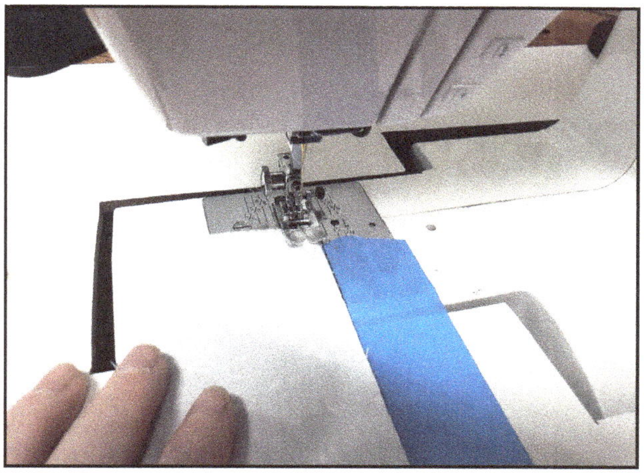

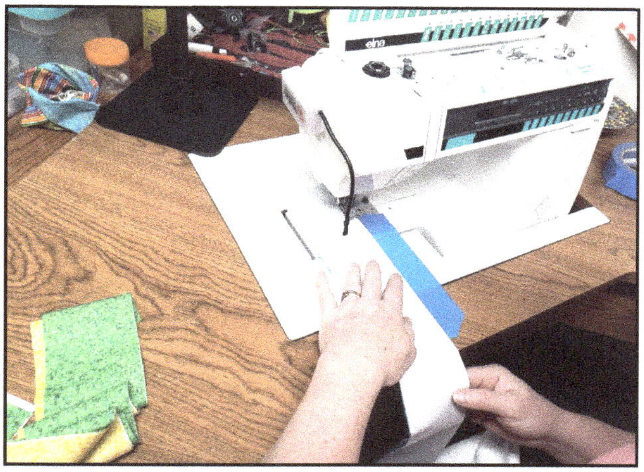

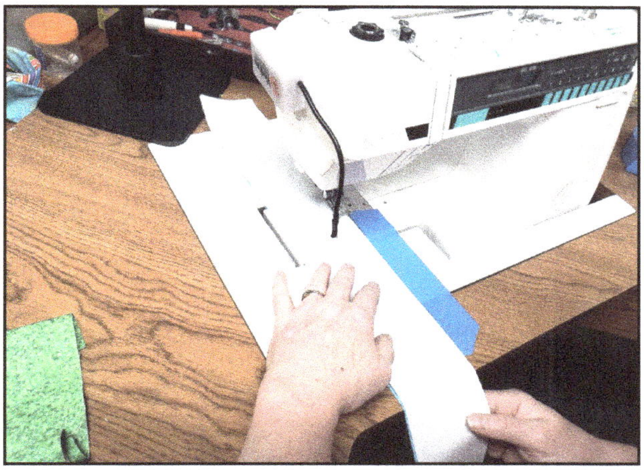

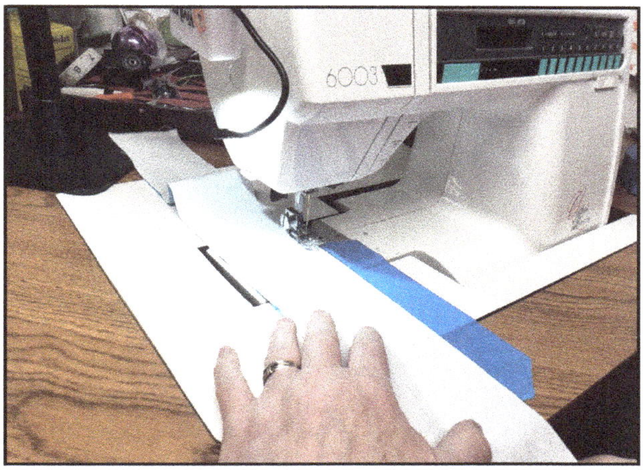

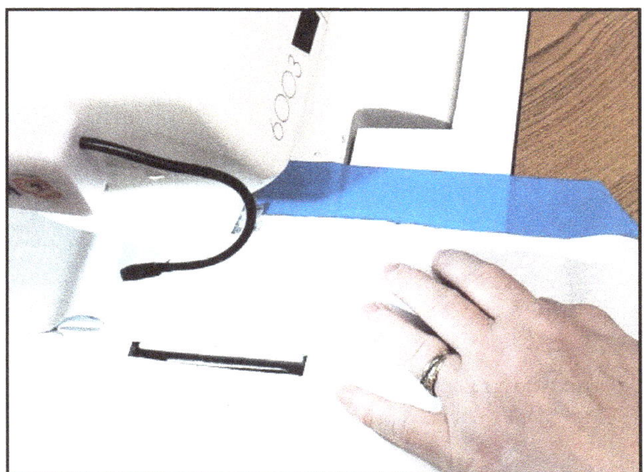

Notice how I am lining up the left side edges of my fabric with the right edge of the tape.

I use my thin metal ruler to confirm that my seam is ¼ inch. If it wasn't, I would reposition my tape and sew another strip until it is ¼ inch. If you are off a bit, don't worry. As long as the seam is at least a ¼ inch it won't matter.

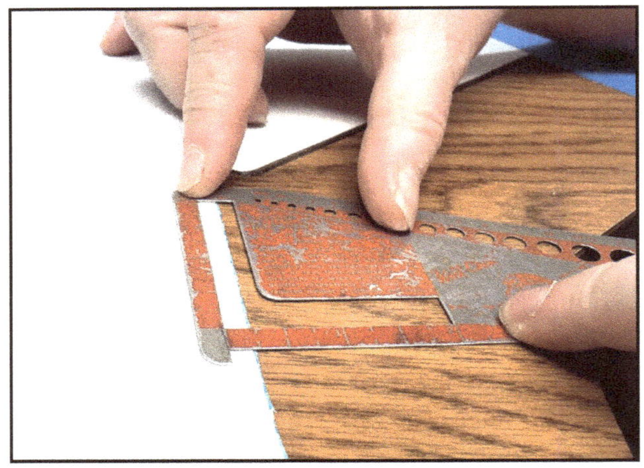

Iron the seams of the strips is a two-step process:

Step 1. "Setting the seams" is ironing the fabrics, right sides together, so that the fibers mesh and the seam flattens.

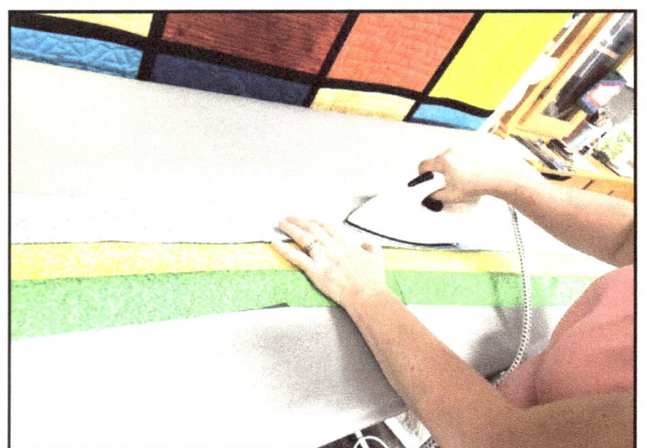

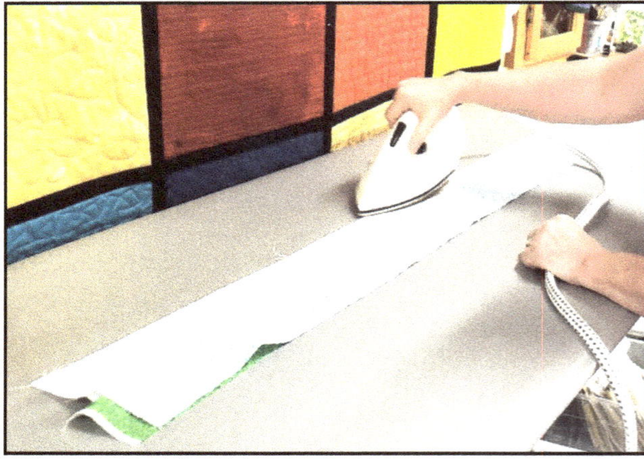

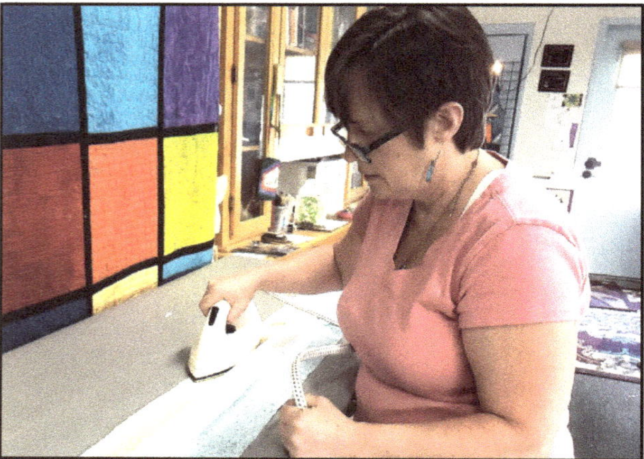

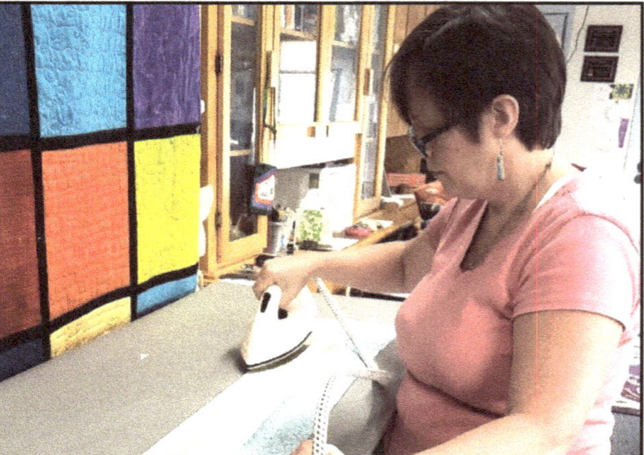

Step 2. Open the fabric so right sides are up and iron them open and so that the seam goes to one side. Don't press so hard that the fabric gets distorted. When you do this two-step process, your seams lie flatter and look better.

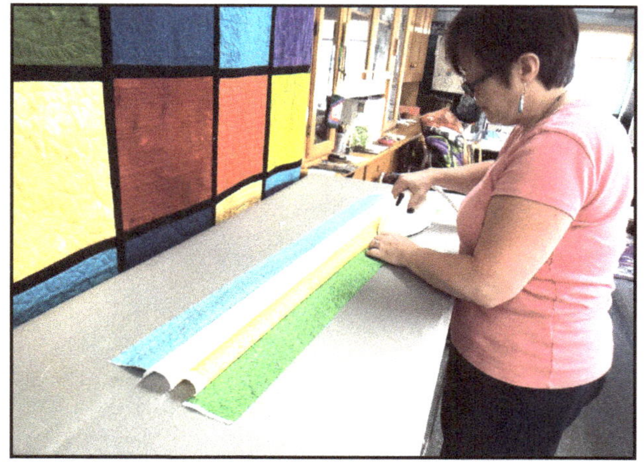
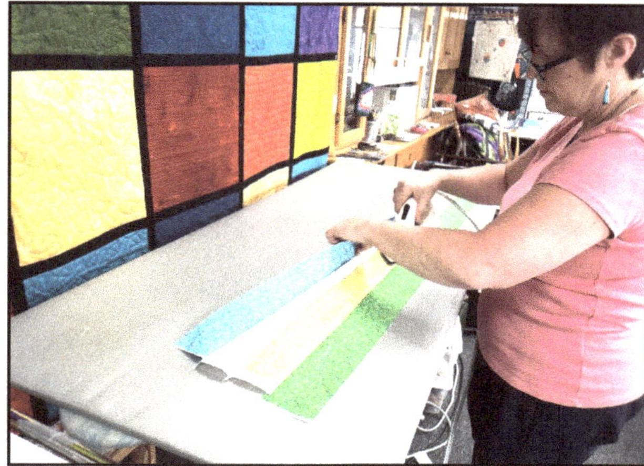
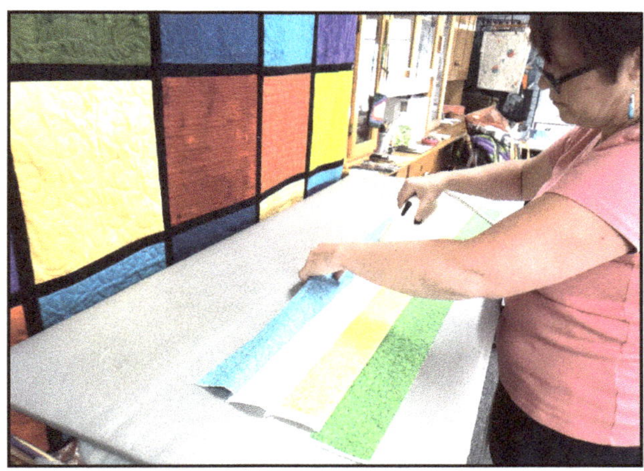
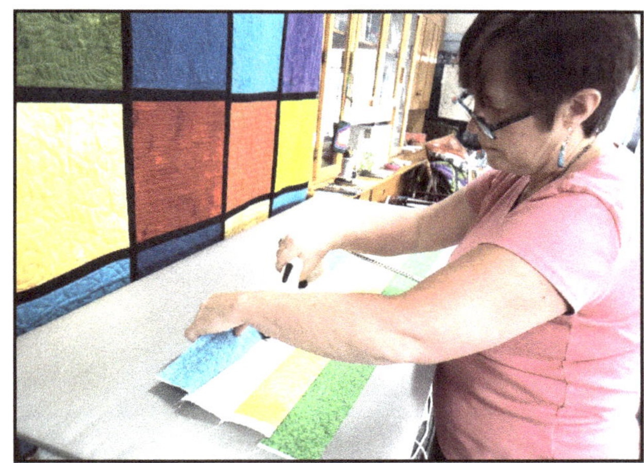
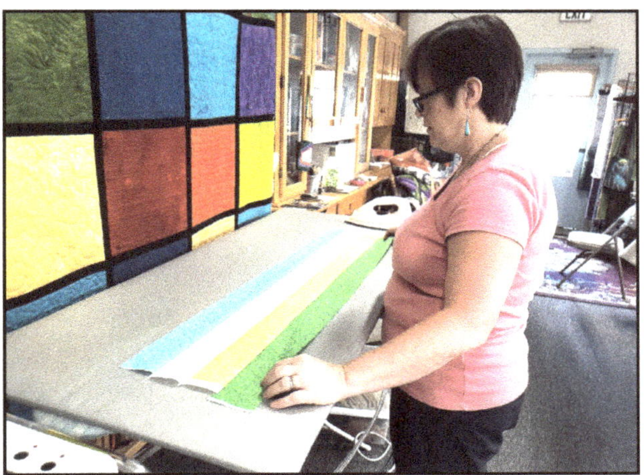

The seams are now set and pressed.

Turn the strips over and press again. Ensure all the seams are pressed to the side. Again, don't press or push so hard that the seams get distorted.

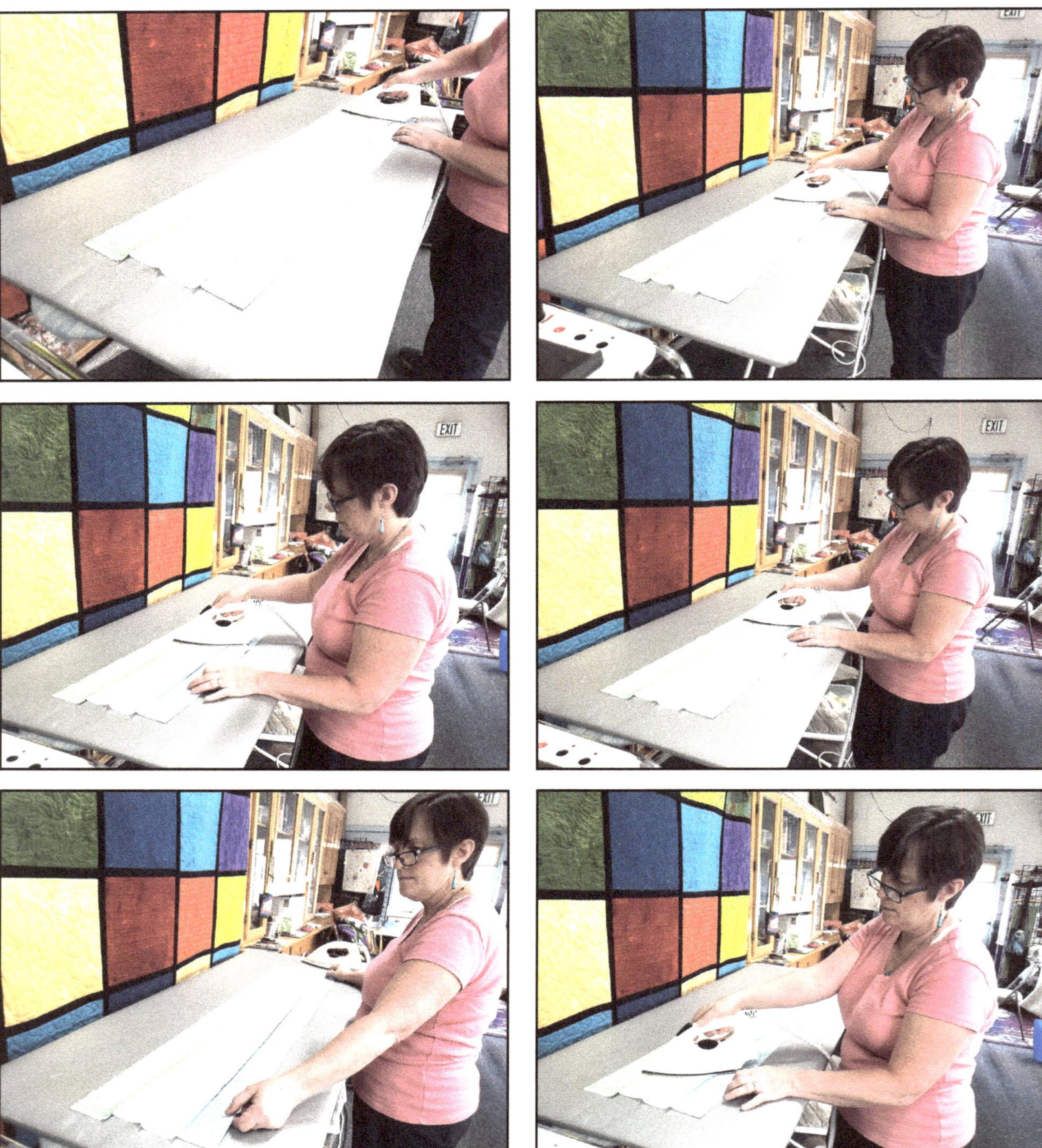

I then turn it right side up one more time and press to ensure that my seams are pressed fully open. This step is very important in making your quilt look well-made and in getting it to lay flat without puckers and tucks.

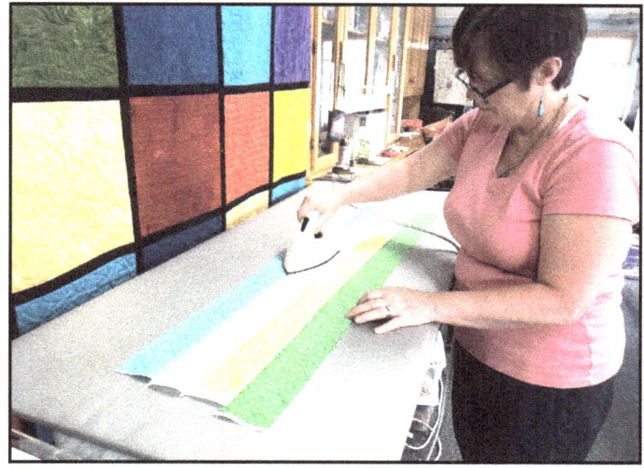
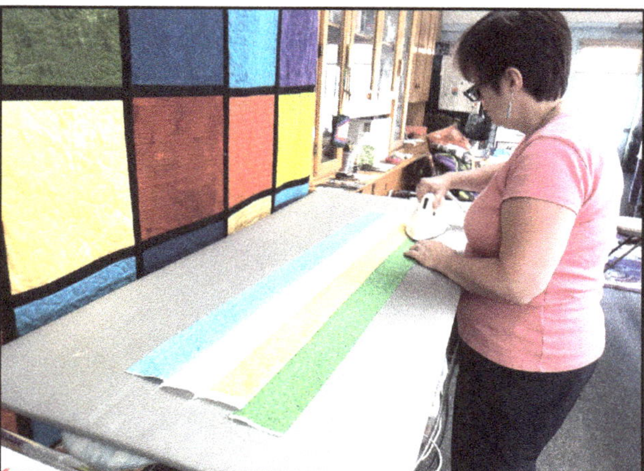
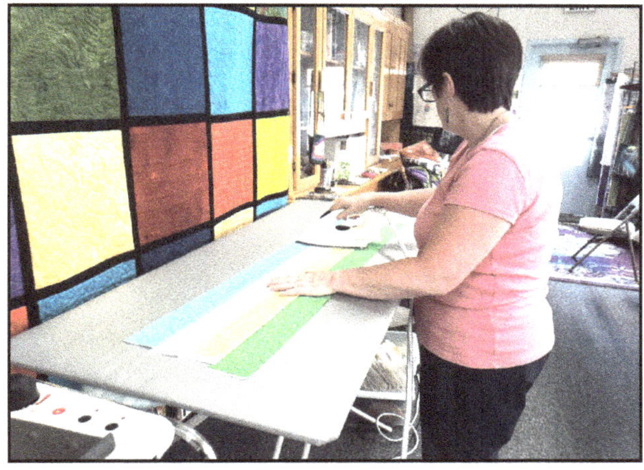
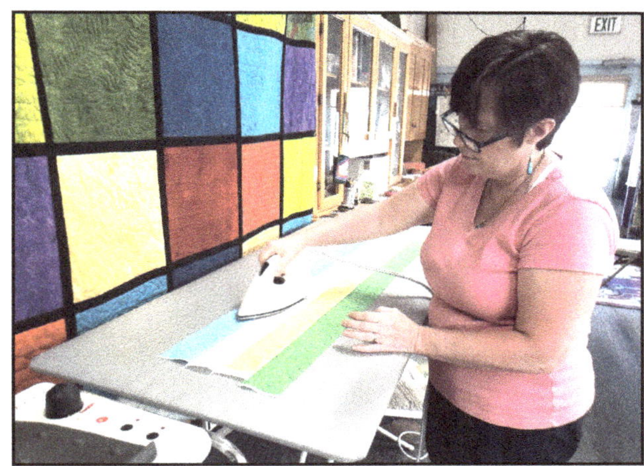

Cut off the selvage ends of the fabric.

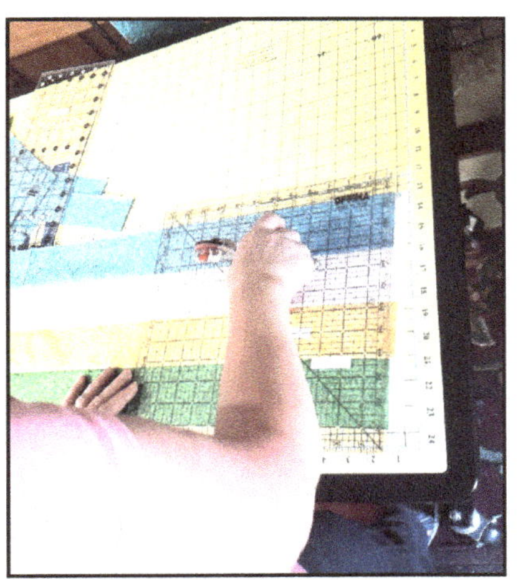
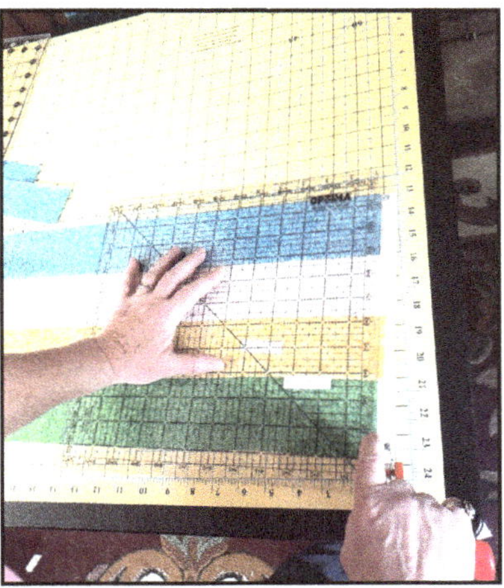
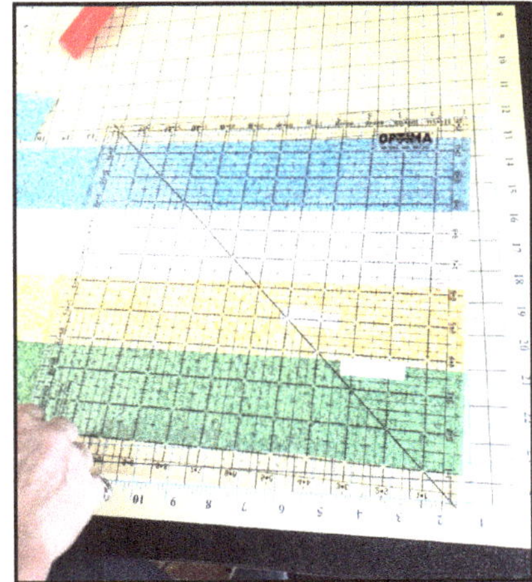

Go to your quilt layout and start with your first block. I have my 15.5 template underneath it for reference. Up to this point, I have folded the t-shirts so that I can position them. Now I start looking at how I am going to cut them into the shape I want them. I can see that if I cut "All Stars" and sew the strips to the side of   "All Stars" it will look nice.

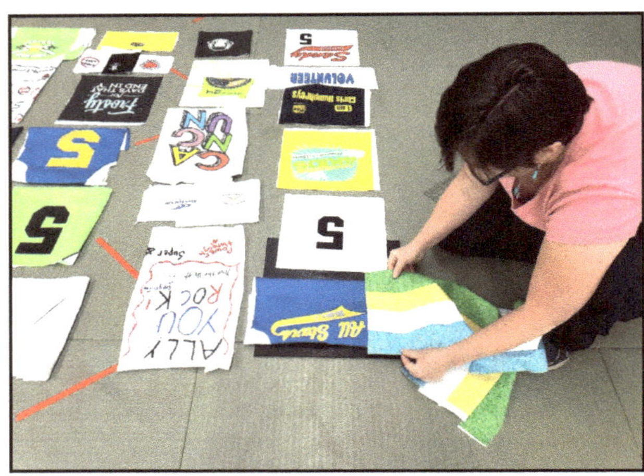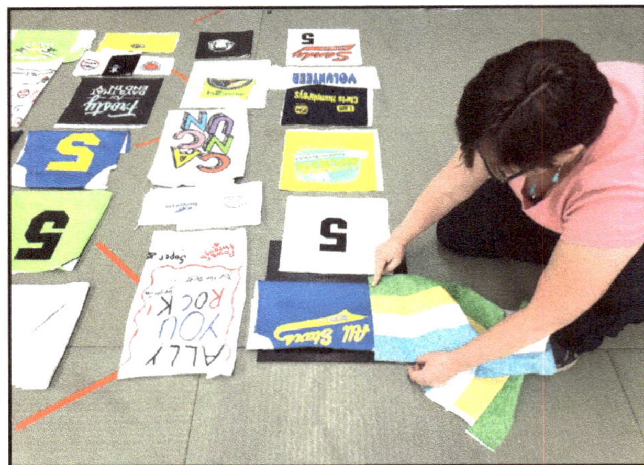

Cut the t-shirt.

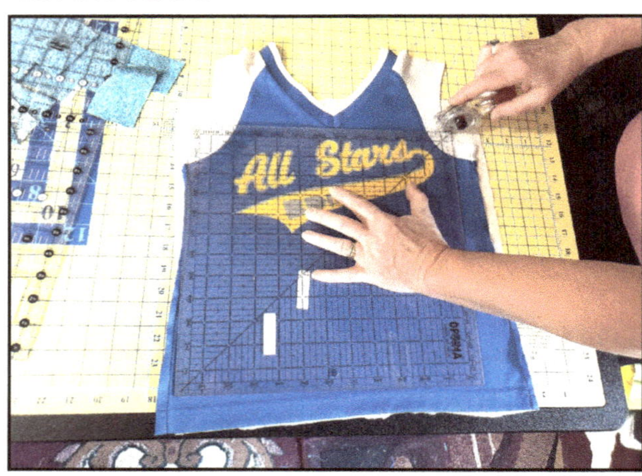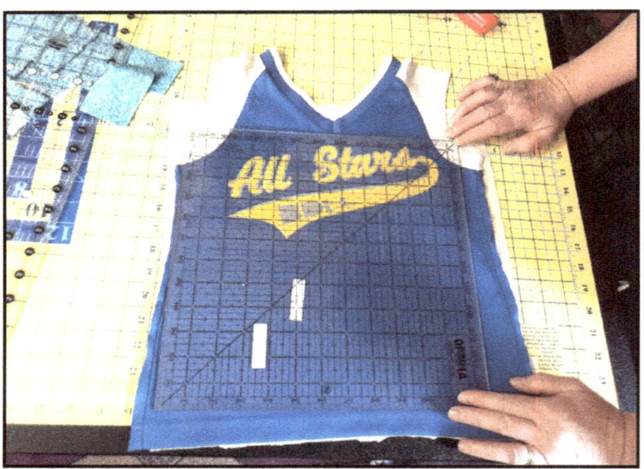

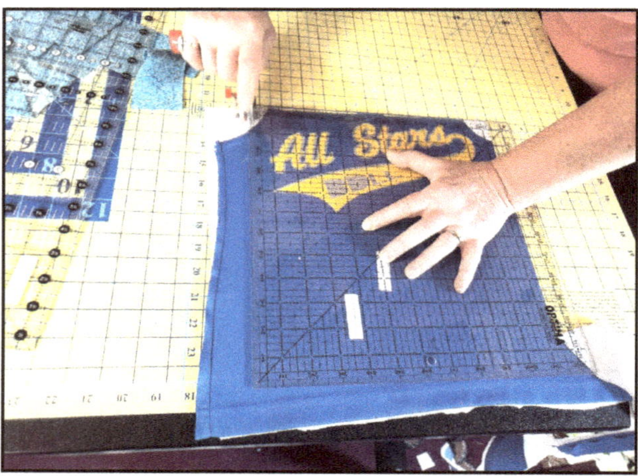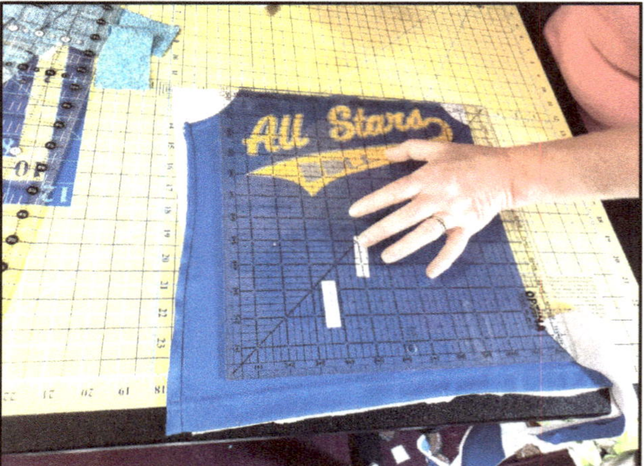

Notice at the bottom of the shirt I leave some length. This is so I have room to adjust the length of my column later – I can cut off an inch and the block will still look good. Or I can leave it and quilt in some cool motif (photo top left).

Sew the strips onto side of the T-shirt (photos a, b & c).

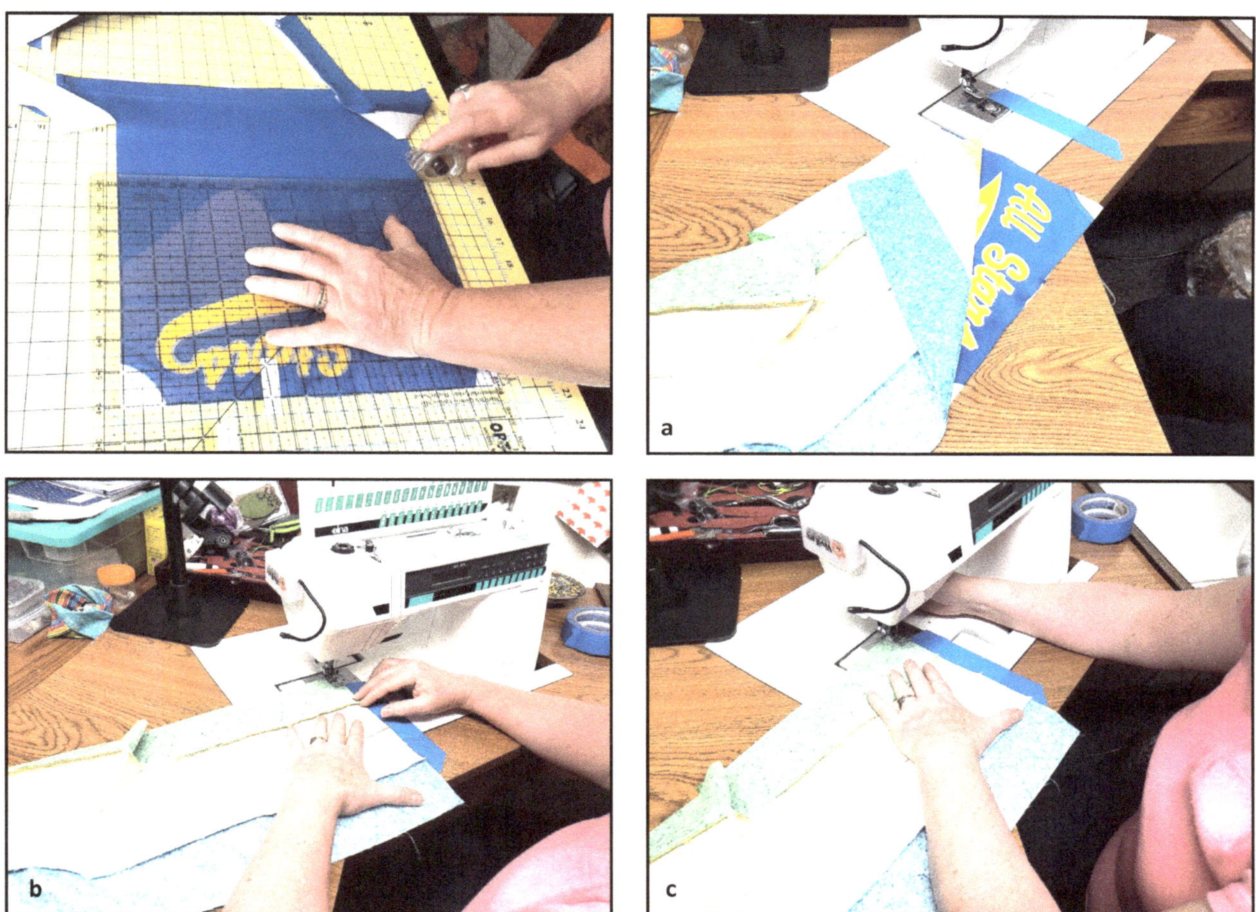

Set the seams by ironing the seam flat, opening the 2 pieces and iron the seam open with the edges to the side. Do this just like you did the strips. Caution! Do NOT IRON the logos! They melt and will stick to your iron. The melted logo might smear on your fabric and then you will have to invent a new way to cover that up. The stuff does clean off your iron with some old t-shirt backs and some scrubbing - but it isn't really fun to do.

See the photos on the next page for examples.

Example photos of sewing the strips onto the block.

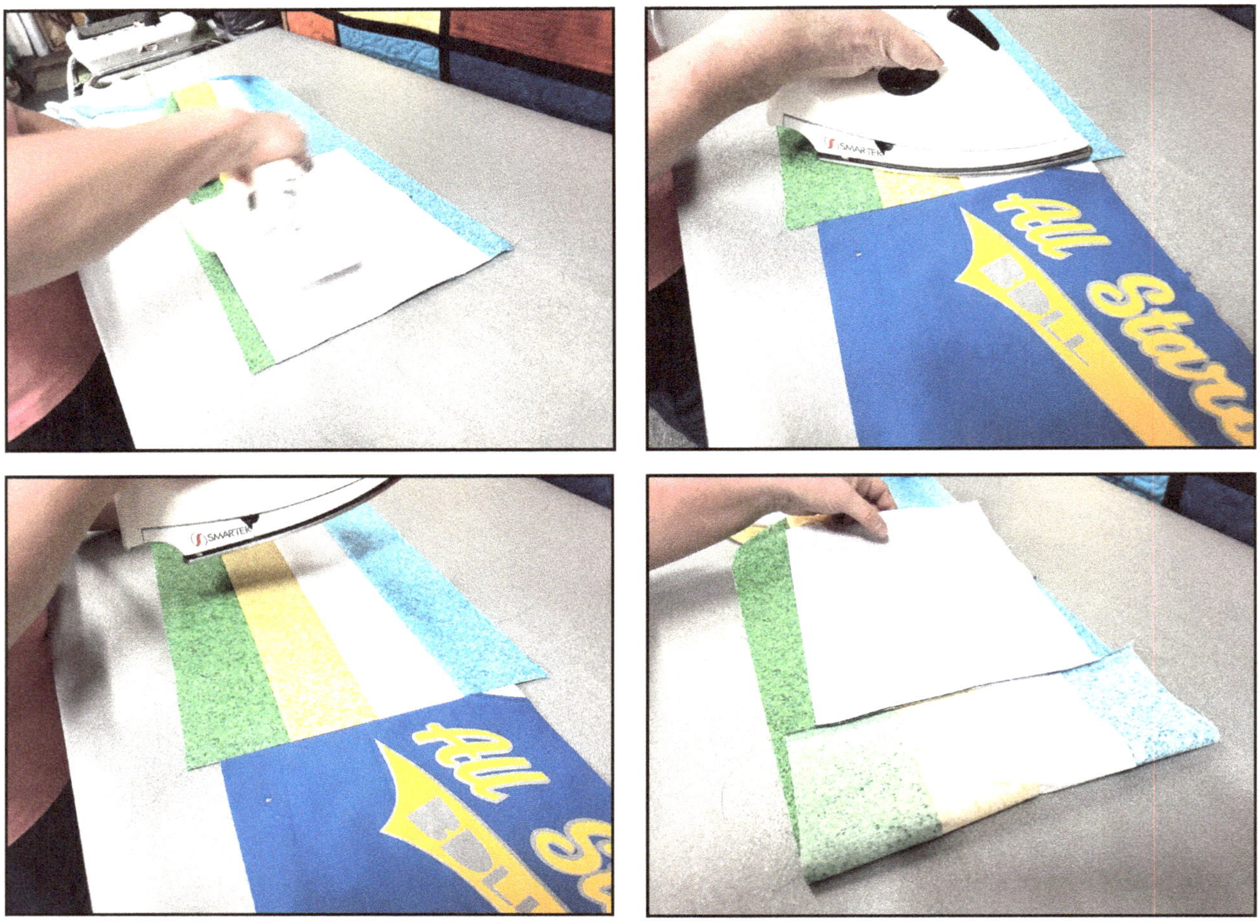

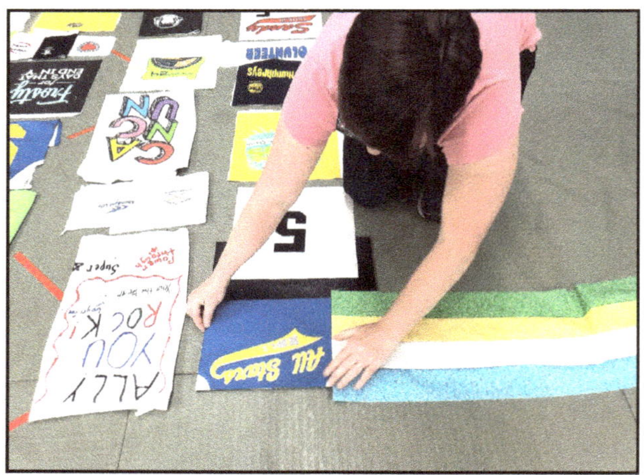

Take the block back to your quilt lay out and see how it looks. Note I have the template underneath to check out the width.

Using the template, cut off the excess strips so that your block is 15.5 wide.

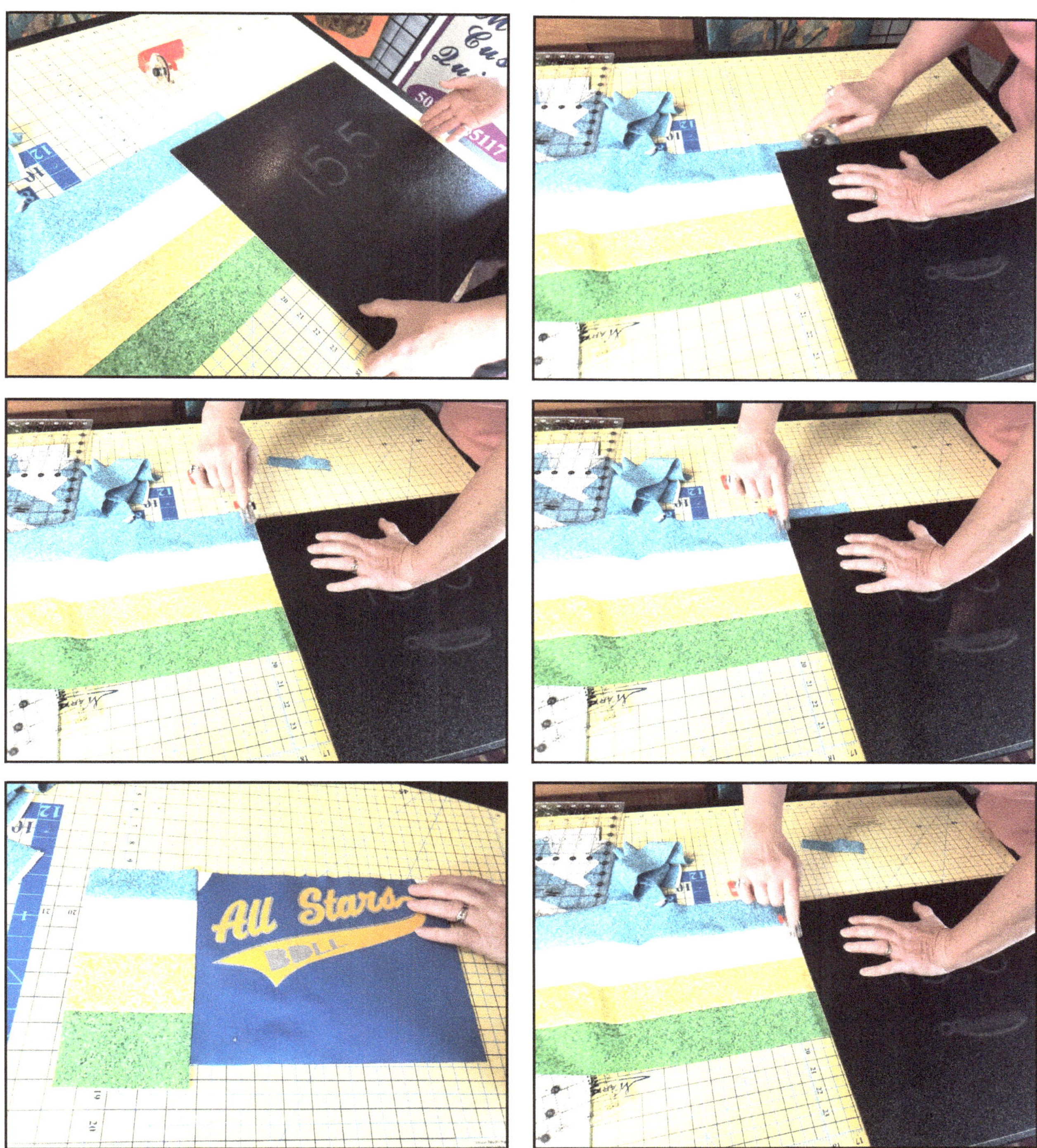

Cut off the strip excess from the top and bottom.

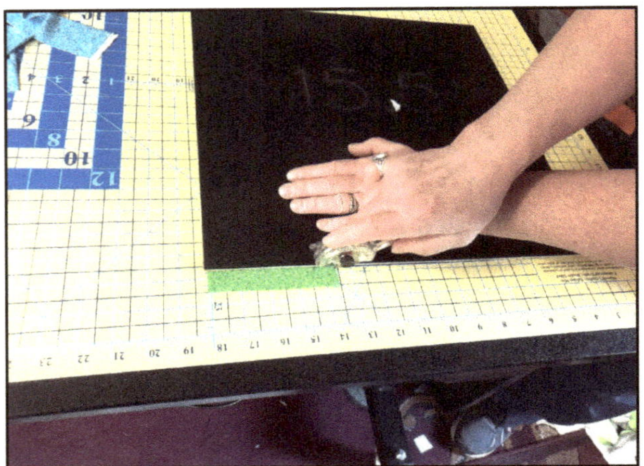 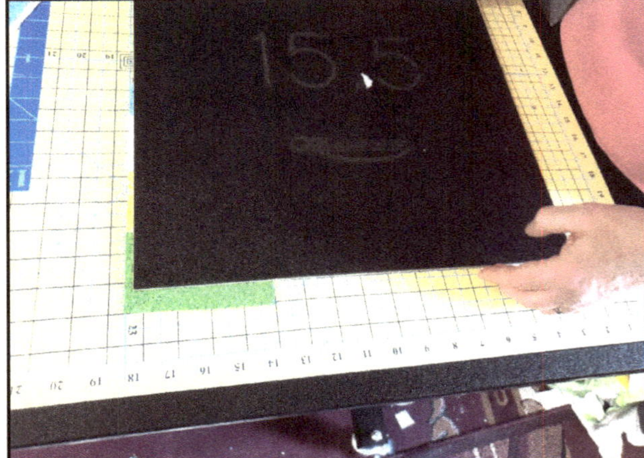

Part 2:

Some of your blocks will have strips, some will have single borders or double borders. Part 2 shows you how to make borders for a t-shirt logo.

Chose one of the fabrics that you would like to be in the quilt more than the other colors. For this quilt, I chose blue. Cut strips that are 2 - 2 ½ inches wide from this fabric. I chose to make it 2". I cut 2 - 3 strips. (I know in advance that some t-shirts are bigger and some are smaller. Some shirts will need 2 inch strips some will need 2 ½ inch strips some will only need 1 inch strips.)

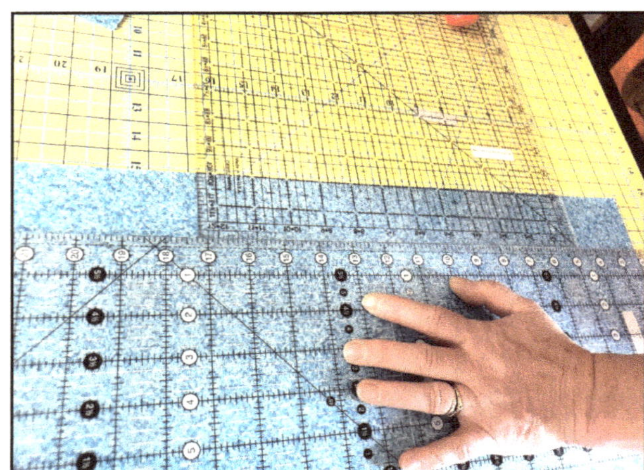 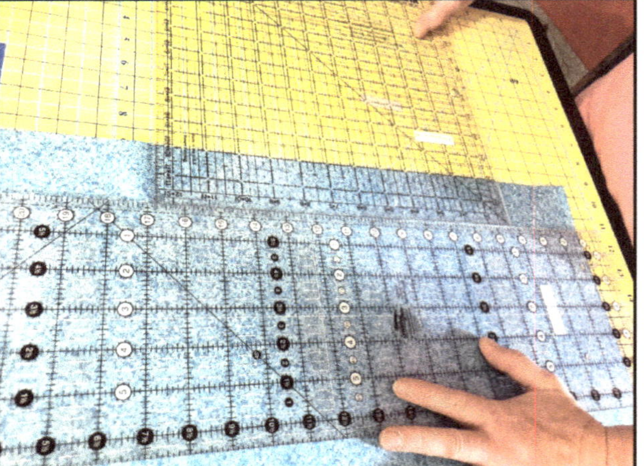

Sew the plain 2 inch strip (right sides together) to the side of the next t-shirt.

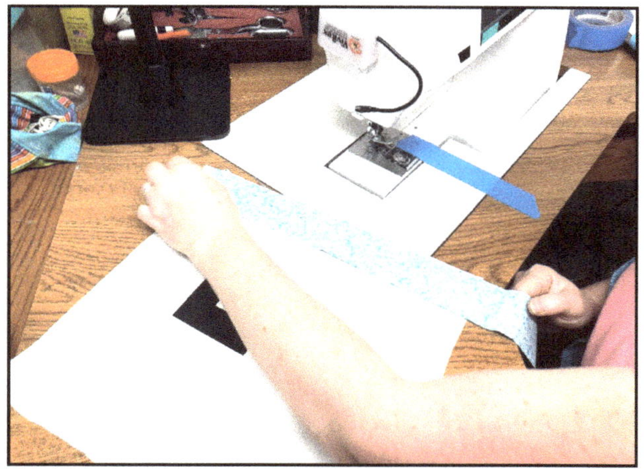

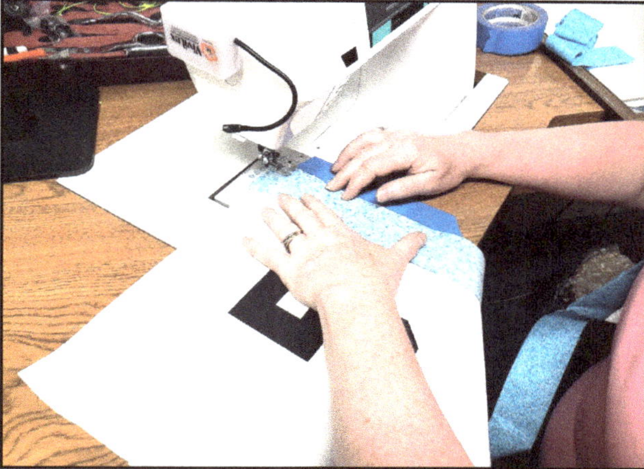

Cut the end of the strip off (a). Sew on the other side (b, c). Cut the end of the strip off (d).

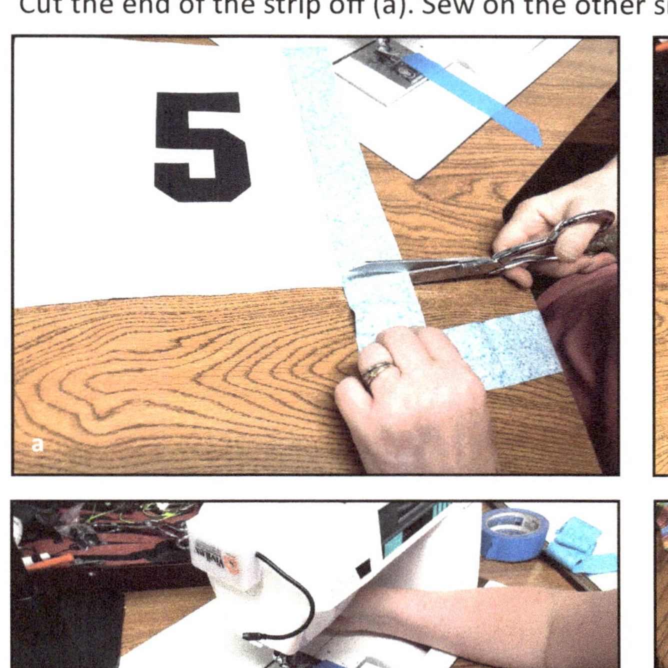

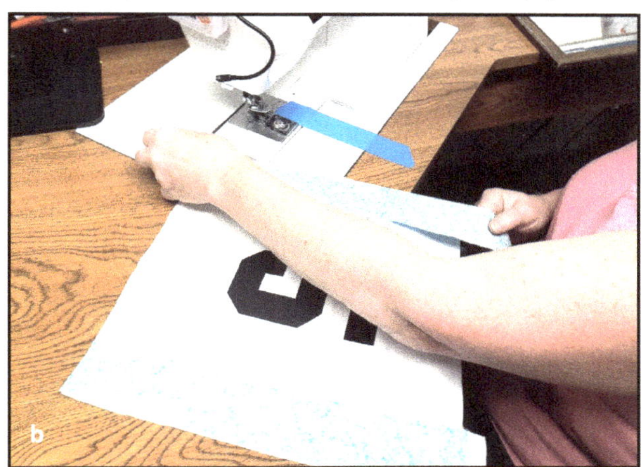

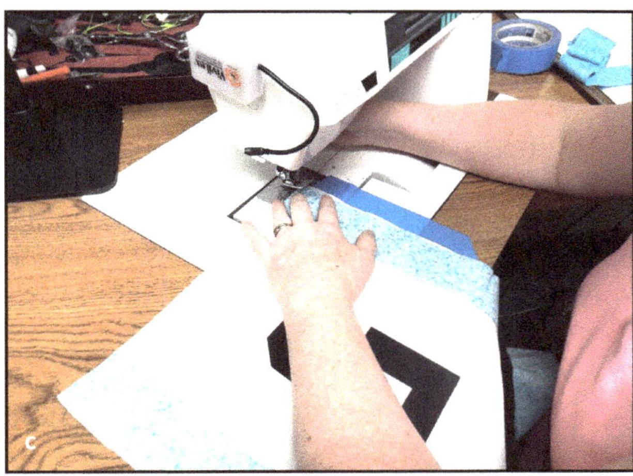

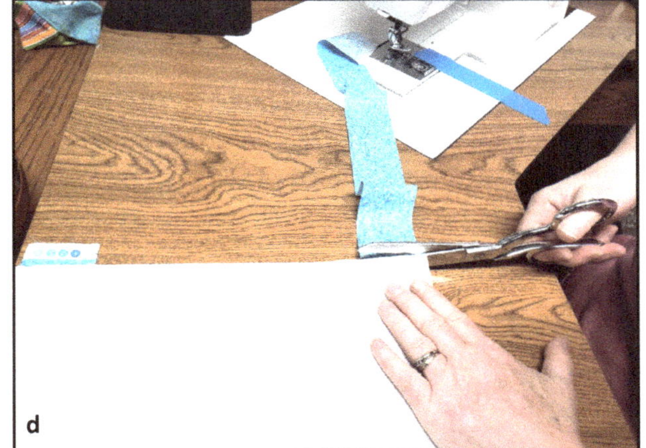

Set the seams by pressing. Again do not iron the logos. Also watch for t-shirt fabric that is man-made. It may melt like the logos so either let your iron cool off or only iron from the backside where the fusable web is.

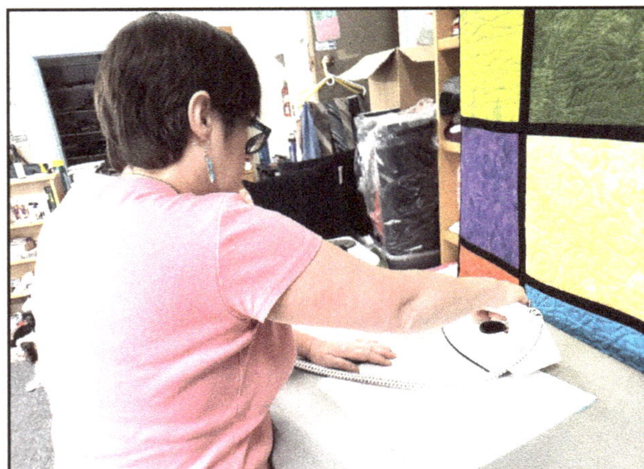
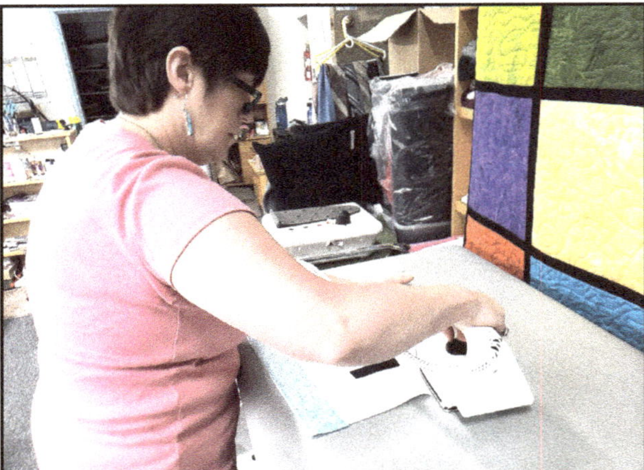

Open the fabric and press. The seams should go out toward the border.

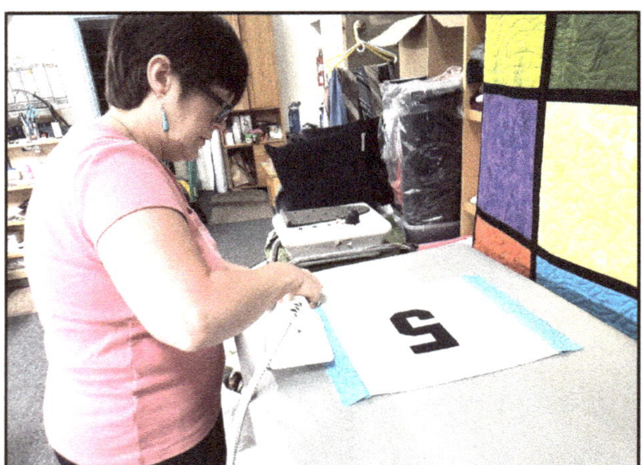
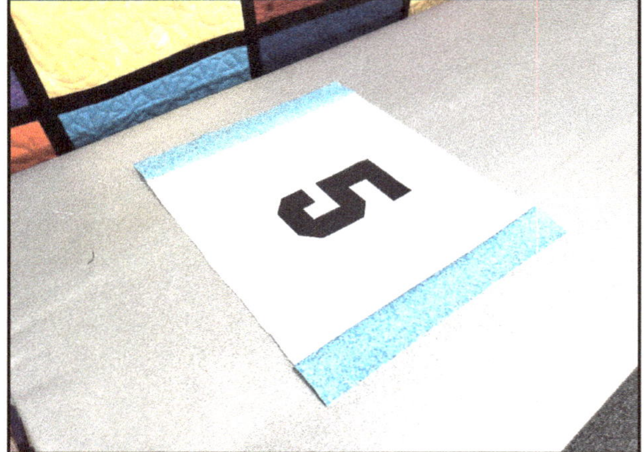

Note how the block is 15.5 inches.

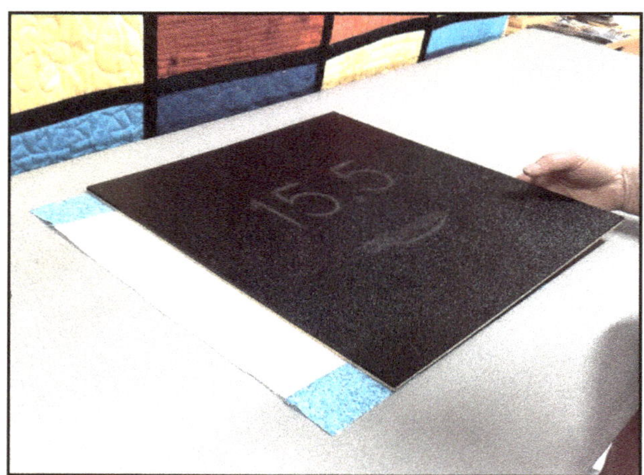

Add the top and bottom strip to the t-shirt.

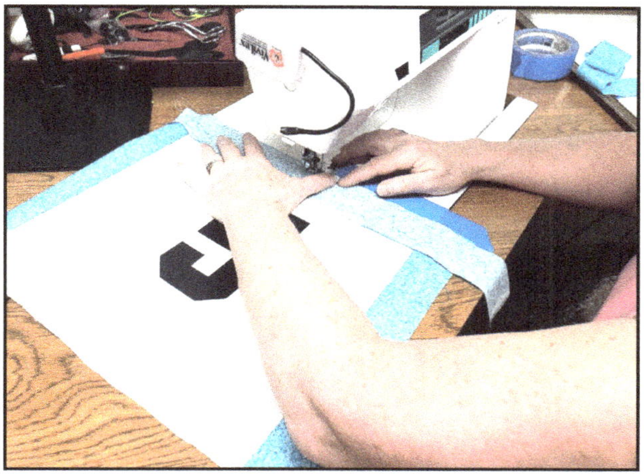

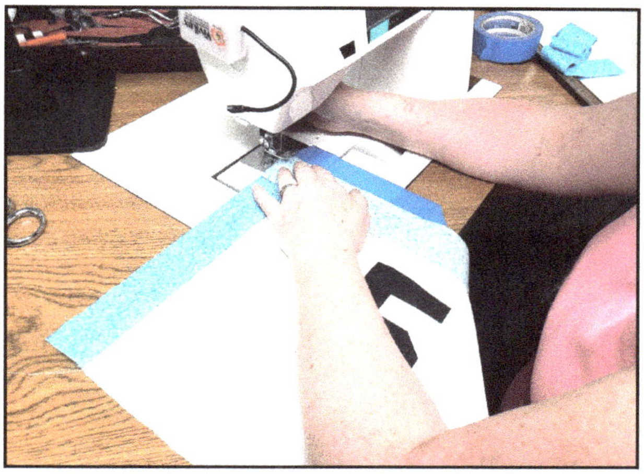

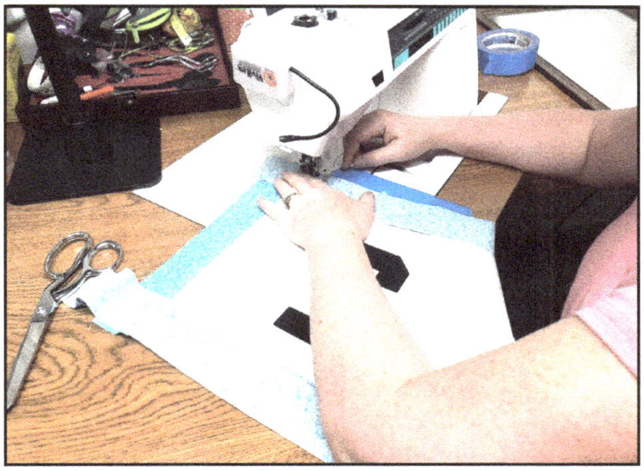

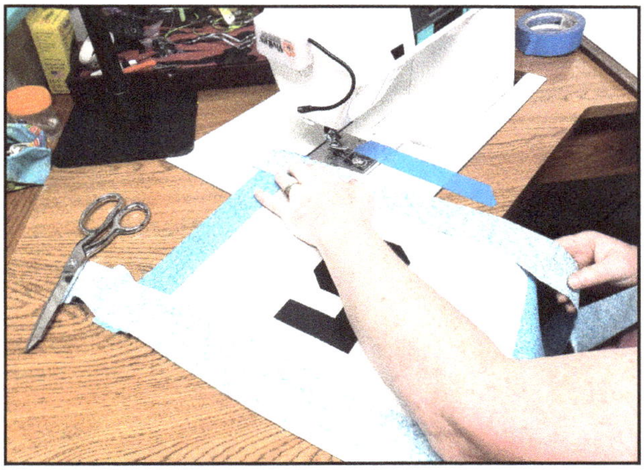

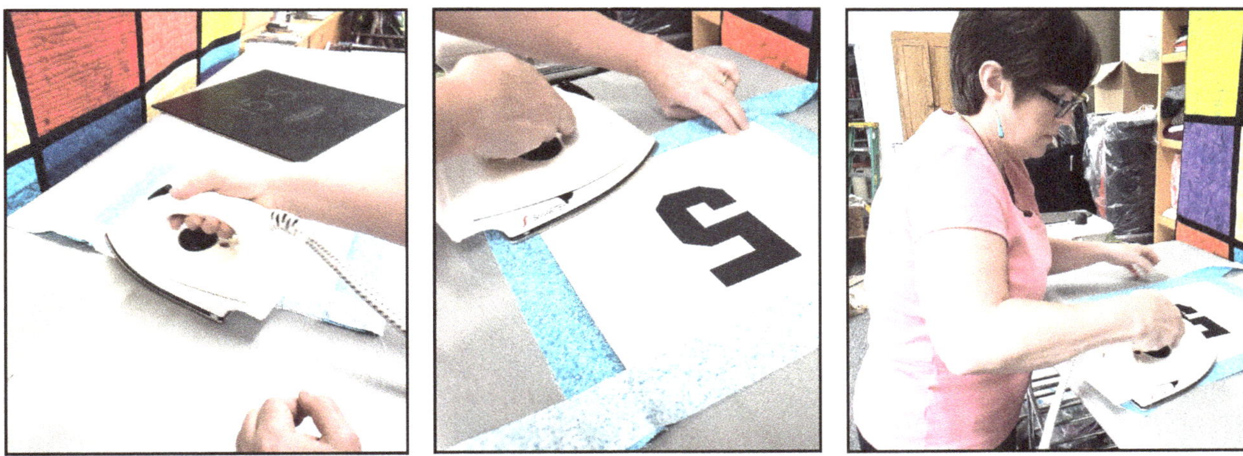

Set the seams by pressing.

Cut off the tag end of the border strips.

Fixing mistakes:

What would happen if my finished block was only 15 inches wide! Ugh! So think of this as a design opportunity – a way to make your quilt unique!

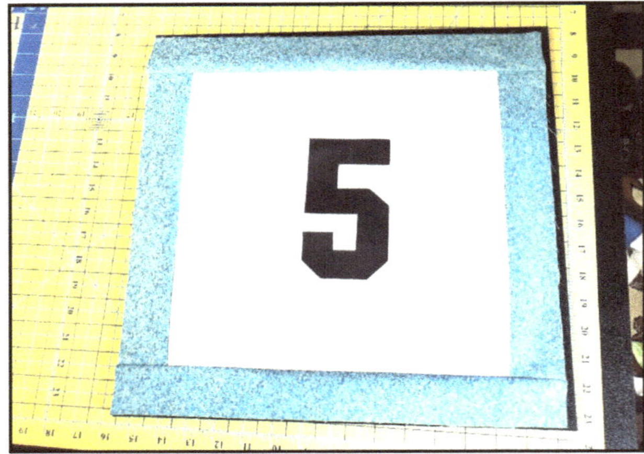

Take one of the other fabrics and make a second border. Make the strip big enough so that it will make the block big enough. I made this strip 1 ½ inches.

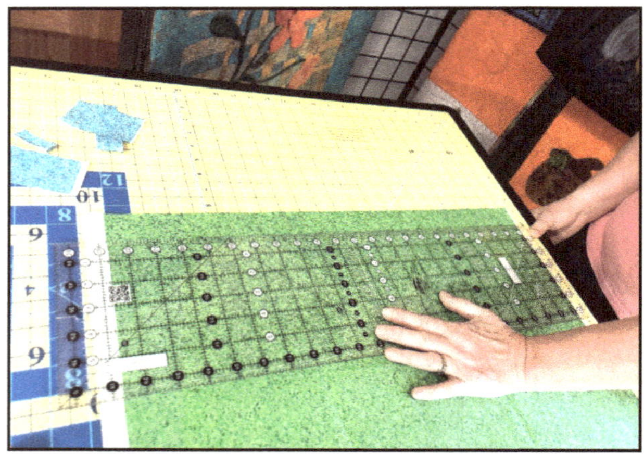
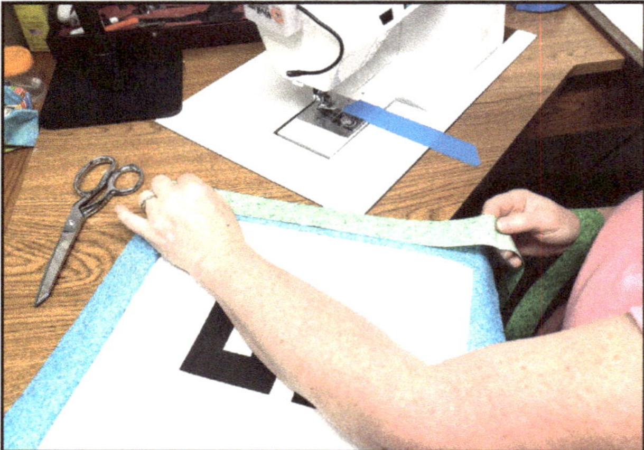

Sew the strip to the right side of the block (below left). Sew the same size strip to the bottom (below right).

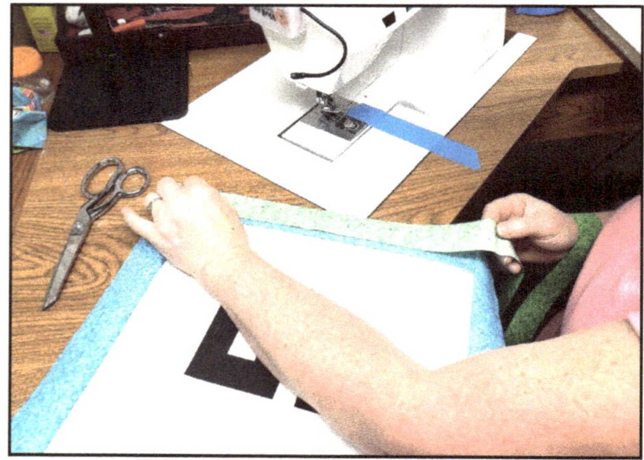
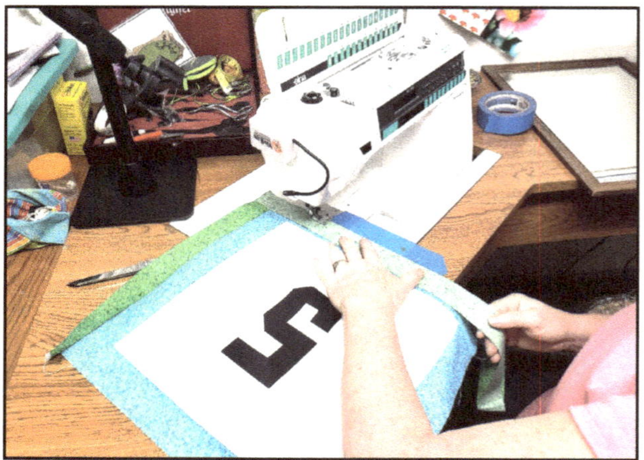

Set the seams.

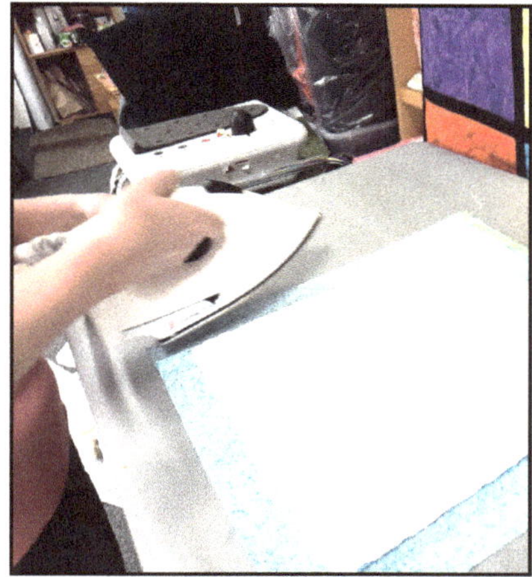 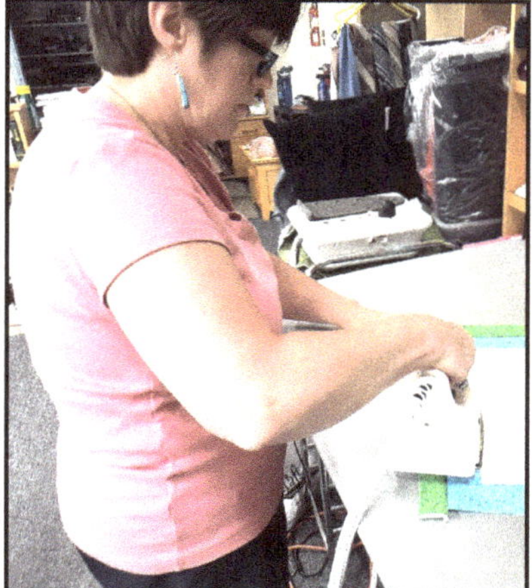 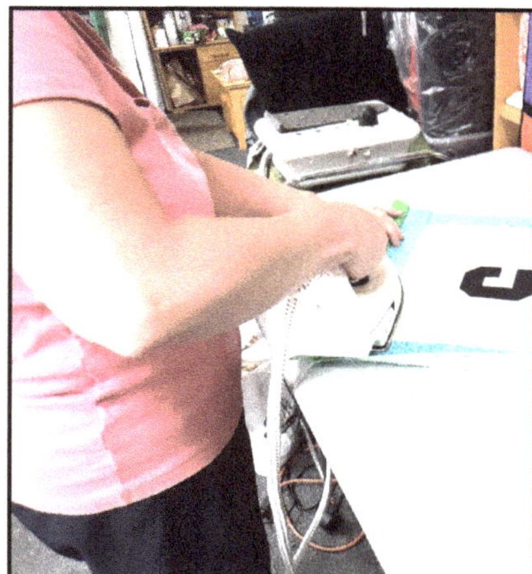

Using the template, cut off the excess.

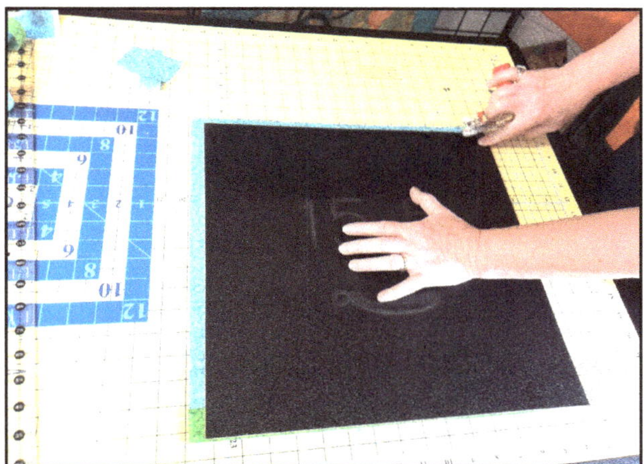 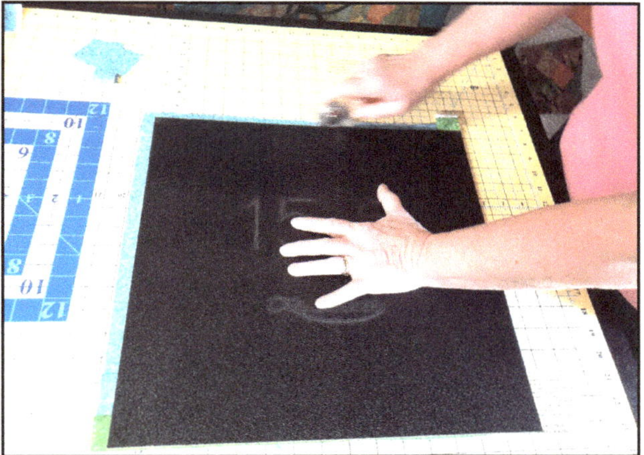

The mistake is now a successful design modification.

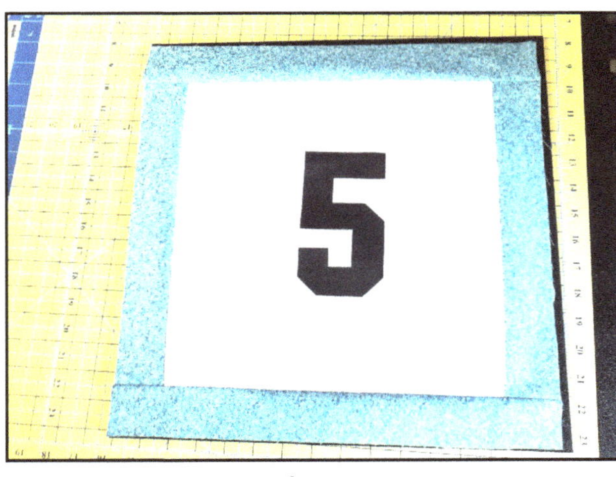 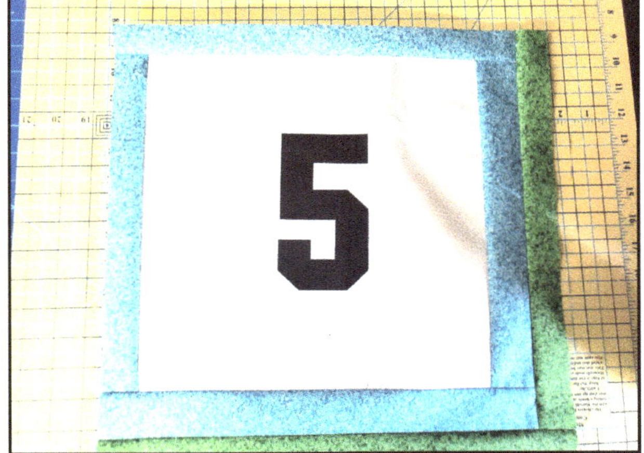

Before   *After*

Go to your next block in column one. Add strips to the opposite side from the first block – the right side.

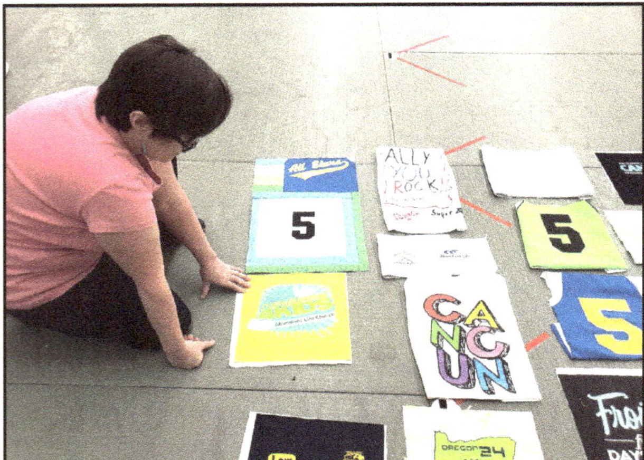 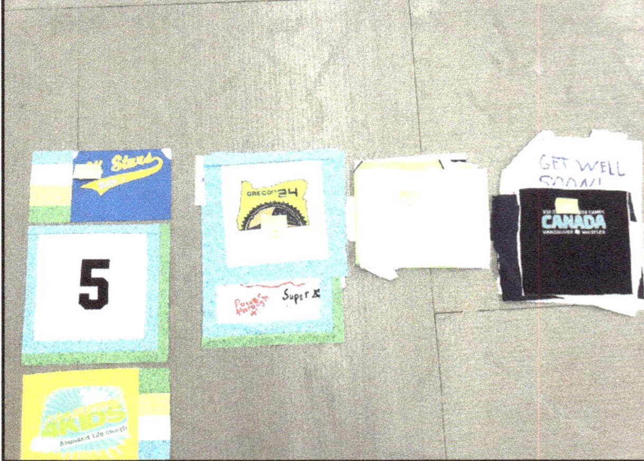

Go to the next block and do a border on all four sides.

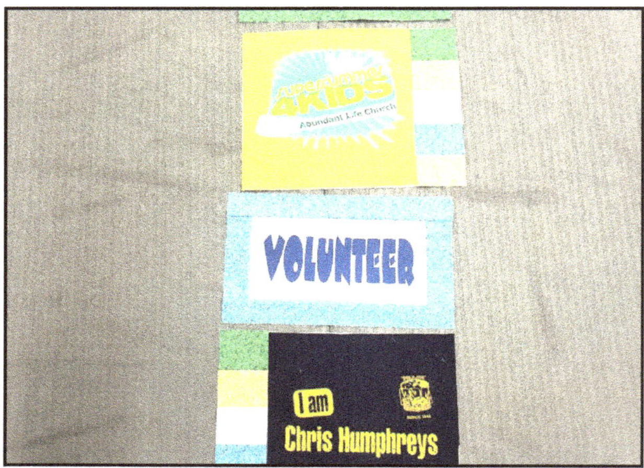

Continue down the column filling in the holes as you go. Notice that some t-shirts can be cut smaller. The logo is more like 12" wide and 8" tall. Go ahead and cut the t-shirt down to 12x8, add the extra fabric for stripes or borders.

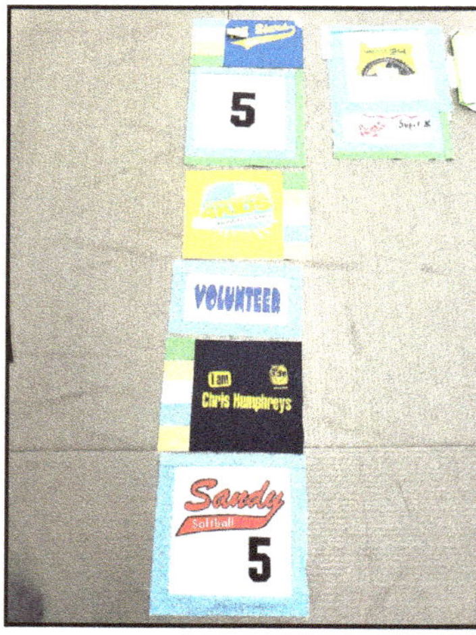

Now you can add in three 4x4 logos to the column or two 4x4 logos with some extra fabric. Make your first column as long as you think you want your *quilt center* to be (the *quilt center* is the main body of the quilt inside the border - see below). Then go to the second column.

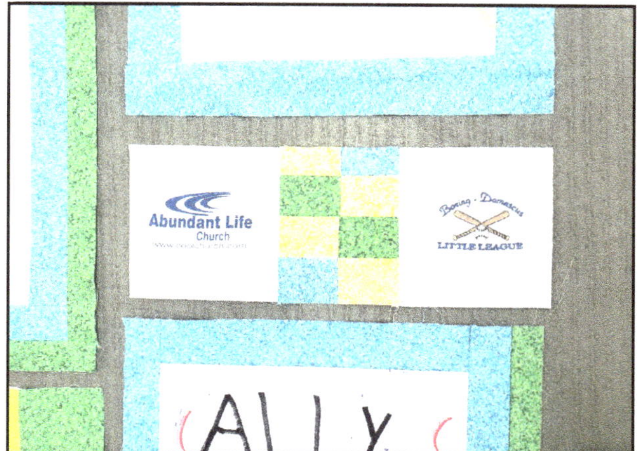

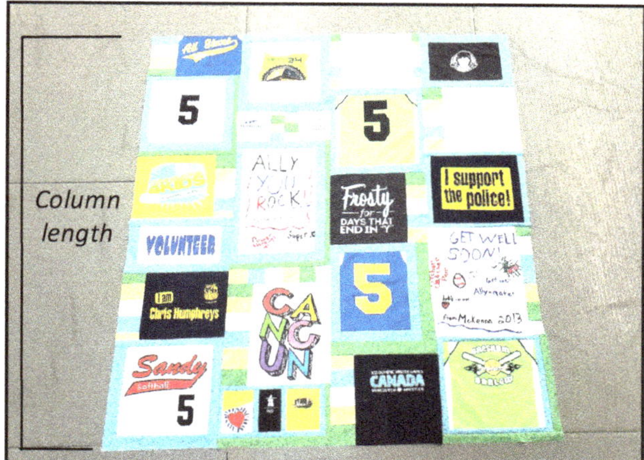

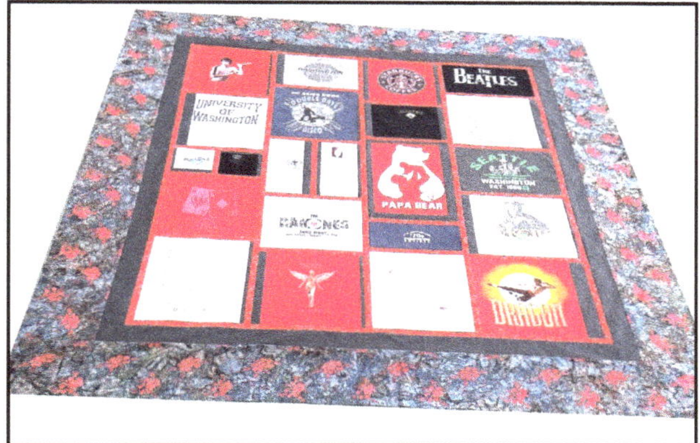

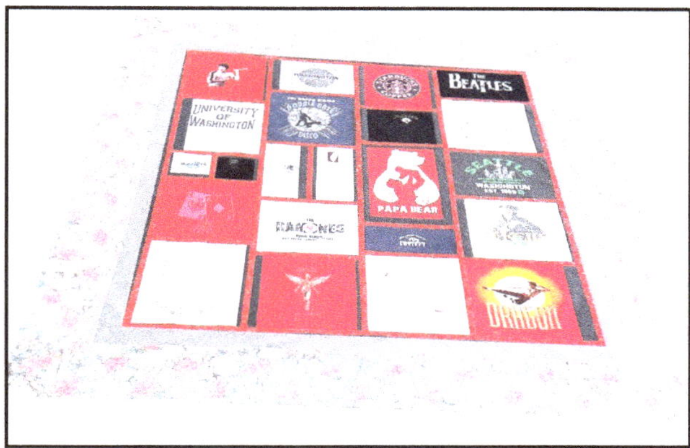

I lightened the border on the right side photo to highlight the quilt center, the main body of the quilt inside the border.

Chapter 6
Creating The Columns

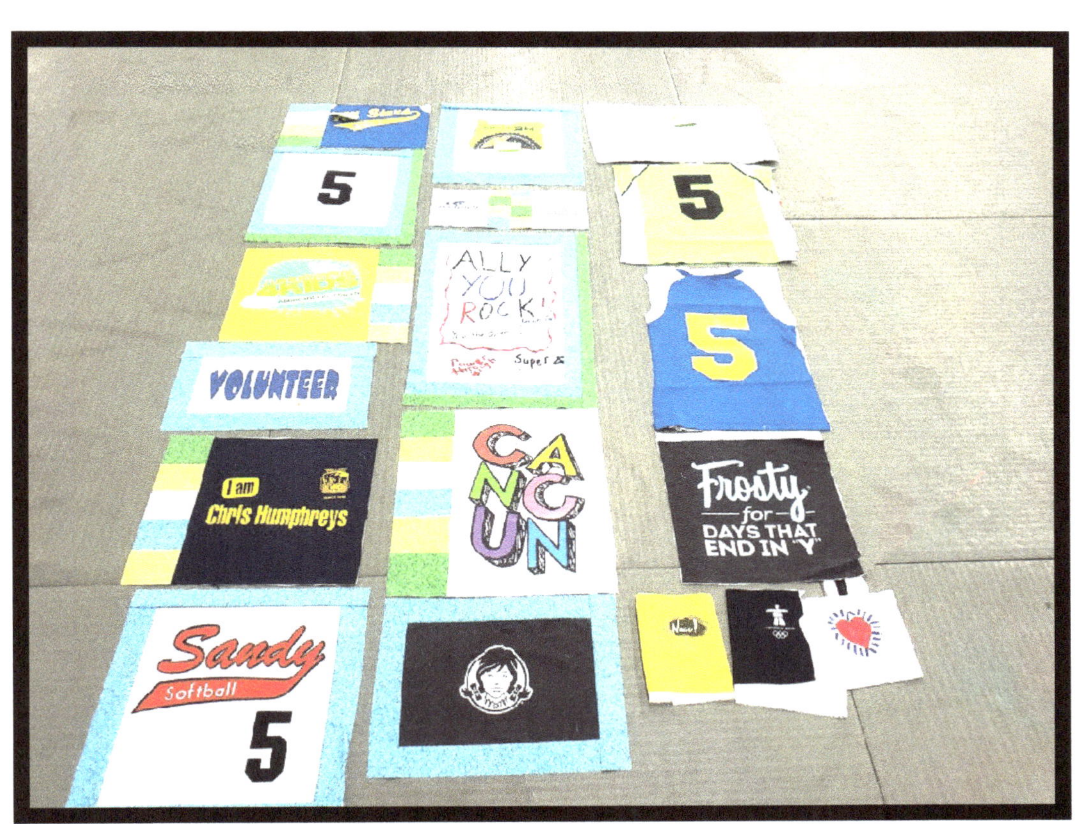

As you're doing the second column, alternate types of blocks from what you did in the first column. Example: If you started with a striped block on the first (All Stars), start with a bordered block on the second ("5" - below left).

If you have an extra long block, use a short block. Change it up to add variety and interest. Keep your colors the same to keep a continuity to your quilt. Note that the 3rd block in column two (Ally You Rock!) is a bordered block with the extra green border. I repeated the "mistake" from column 1 on purpose. I placed the "mistake" at an angle to the first mistake (below right).

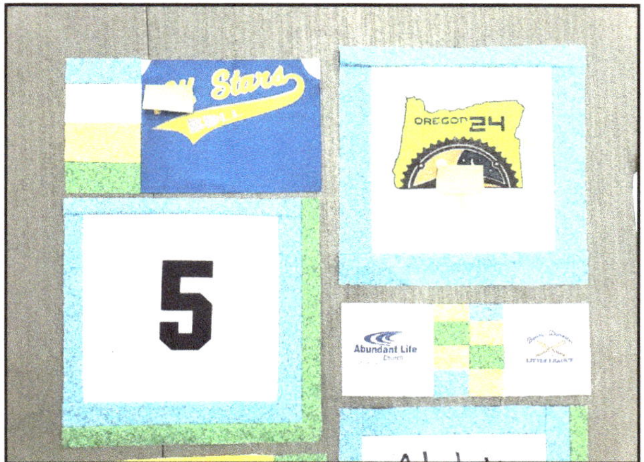

Striped border on All Stars and block border on "5".

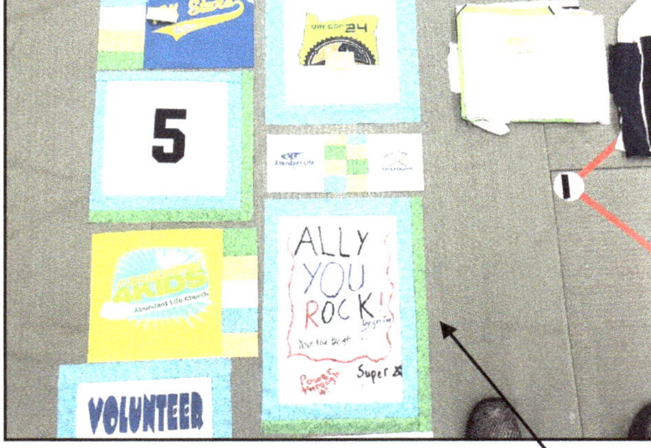

Extra green border on Ally You Rock!

Proceed in this manner for the rest of column two. Make column two as close to the size of the first column as you can (below left). Lay out column three (below right).

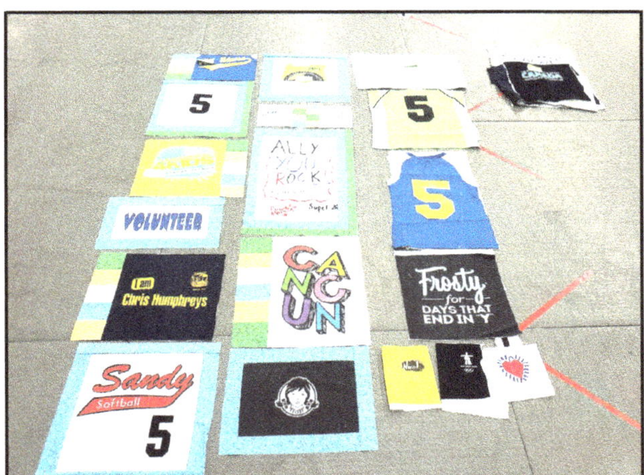

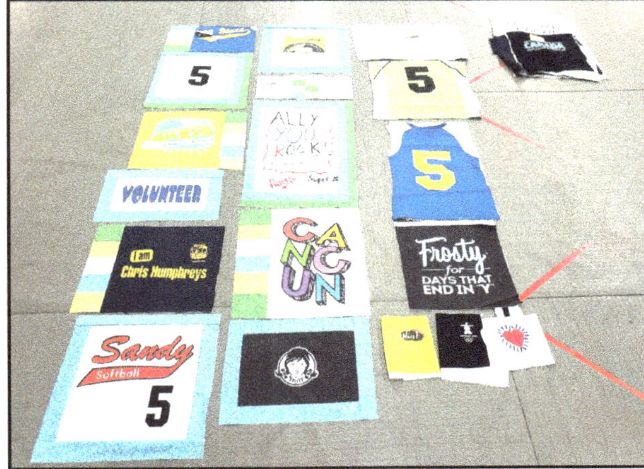

Now that your second column is done, you can begin to lay out column three.

I started with strips on both sides of the blocks, then borders, then strips on the right. The 4th block is a border block and it is diagonal to the column 2 "mistake". So this block gets the extra green border on the right and the bottom.   At this point I realize column 3 is too short. I decide to move some blocks around.

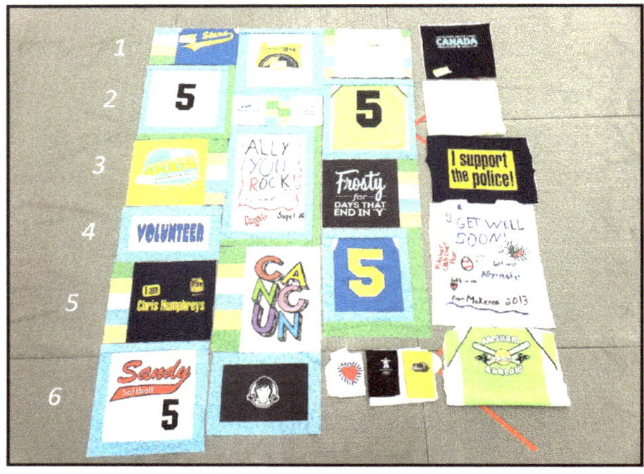

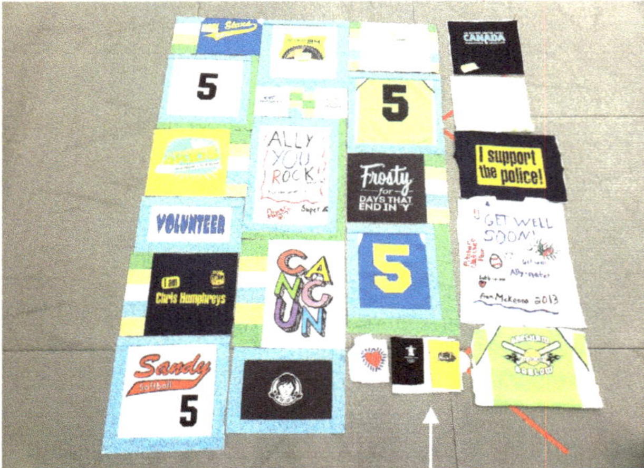

Blocks 1, 3 & 5 are stripes and blocks 2, 4 & 6 are borders.

Too short

I can add strips to the top of "Cancun" in column two (a) and move the three small logos under "Cancun" (b).   Canada can be moved to the bottom of column three and we can put strips on it (c). "Wendy" which already   has blue borders can be moved to the top of column four (d).

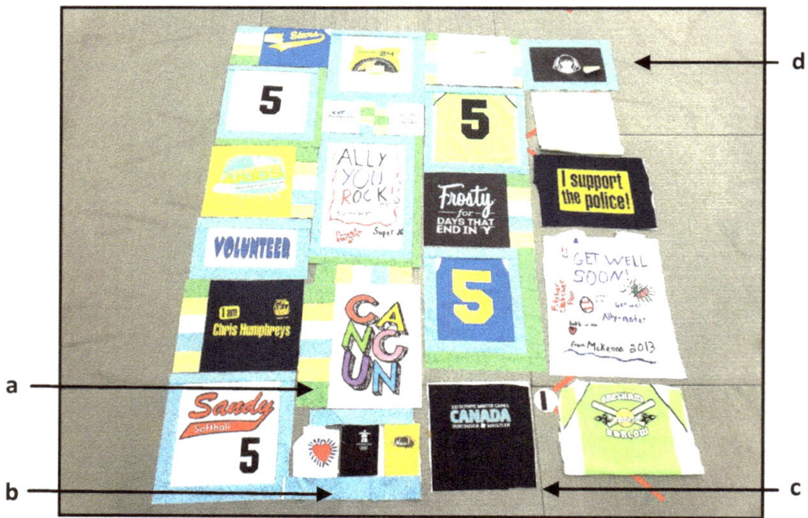

Switching around the blocks evens up the length of the quilt.

The heart logo needs to be patched. I am going to use yellow left over t-shirt fabric to patch it.

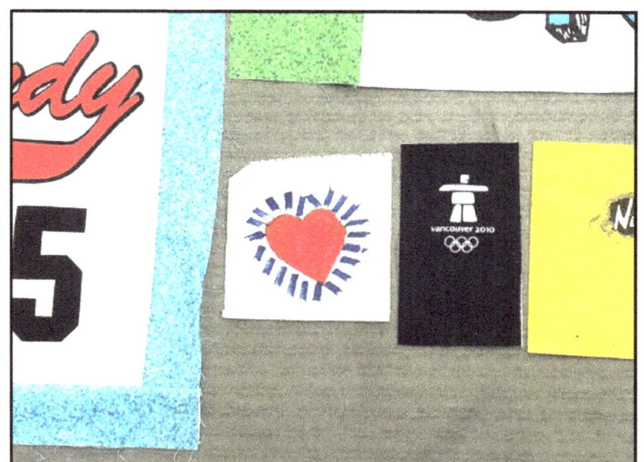 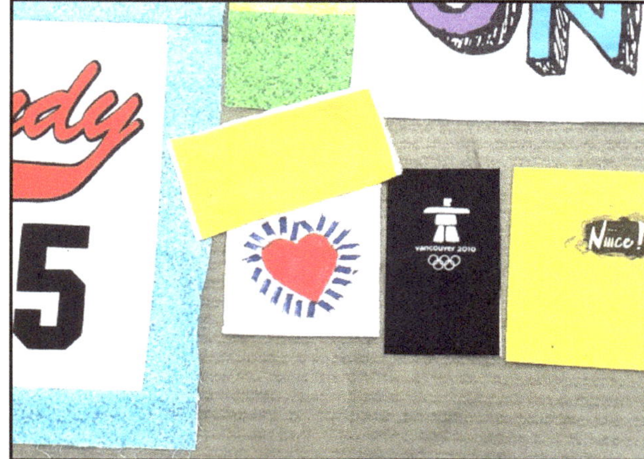

With right sides together sew the yellow patch onto the heart.

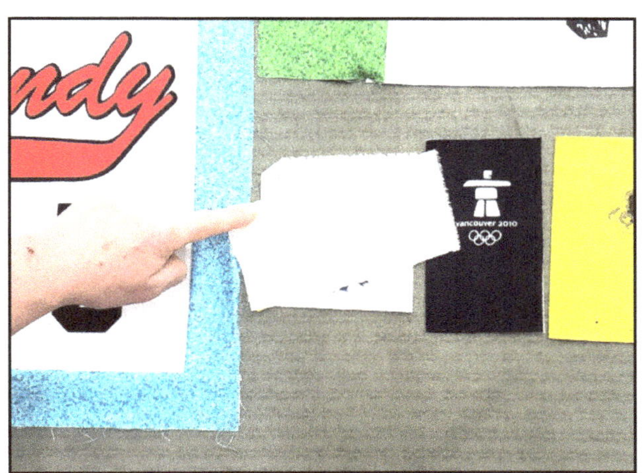 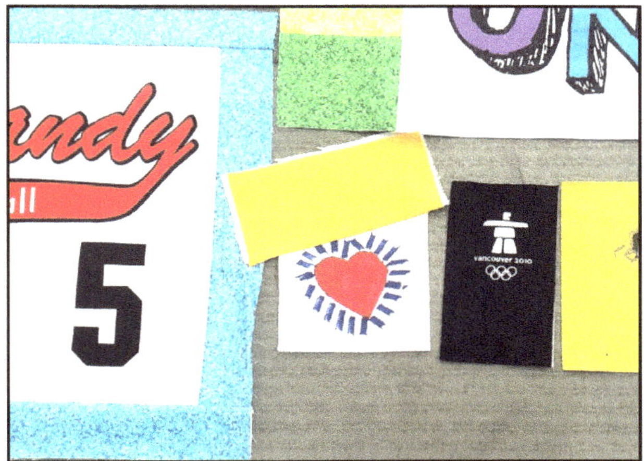

Cut the heart block to size (a). Sew the logo blocks together with 1 ½ inch strips between the blocks (b).

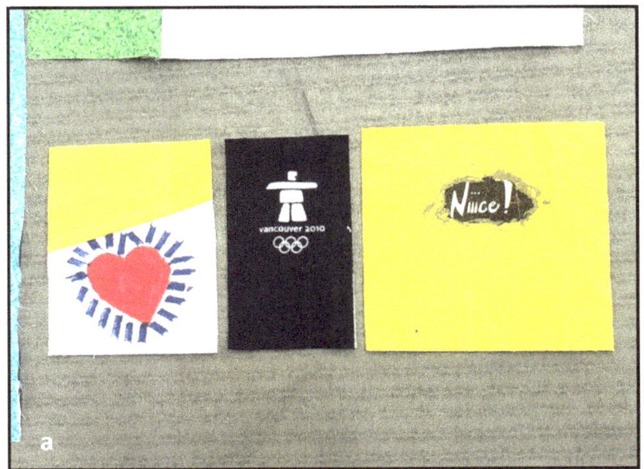 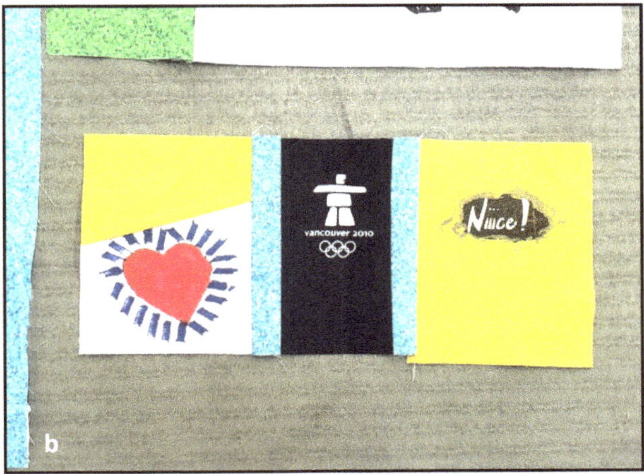

Add a border to the outside of the 3 logos. In this case I also added the extra green borders to the side and the bottom because the 3 finished logos were not wide enough (a).

Complete the 4th row alternating borders and strips and adding the extra border to carry through the "mistake." Note that the columns are a few inches different in length. Start with the shortest row, row 3 and sew the blocks together in a column (b).

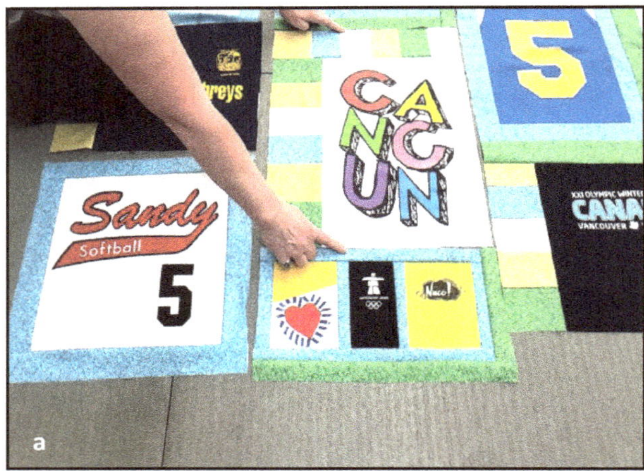
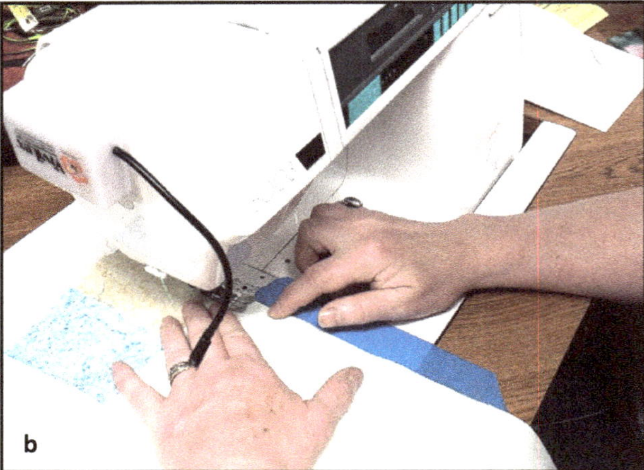

In the following pictures I point out where we can cut length off of the t-shirts to shorten the rows that are too long.

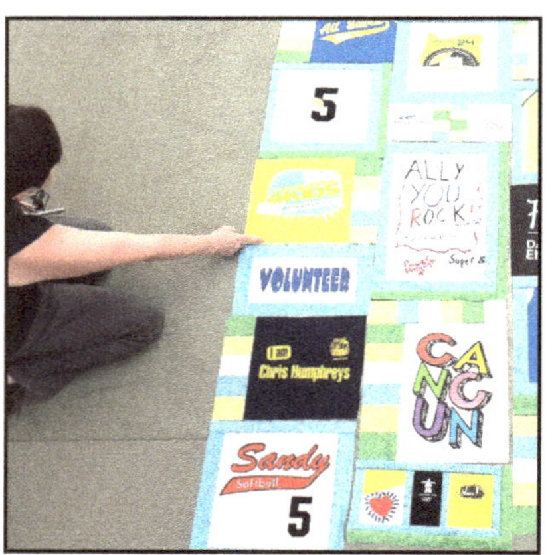
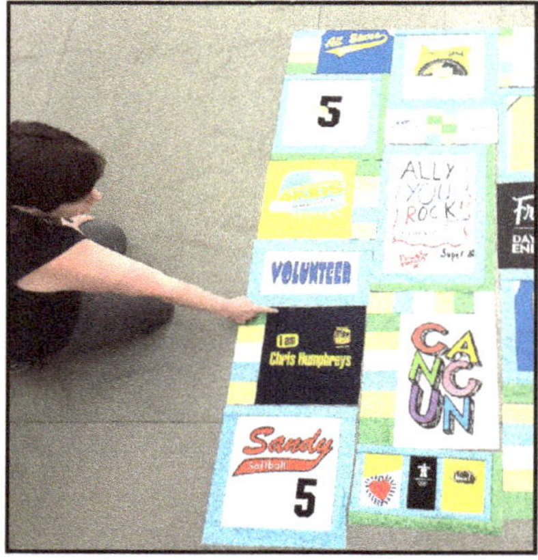
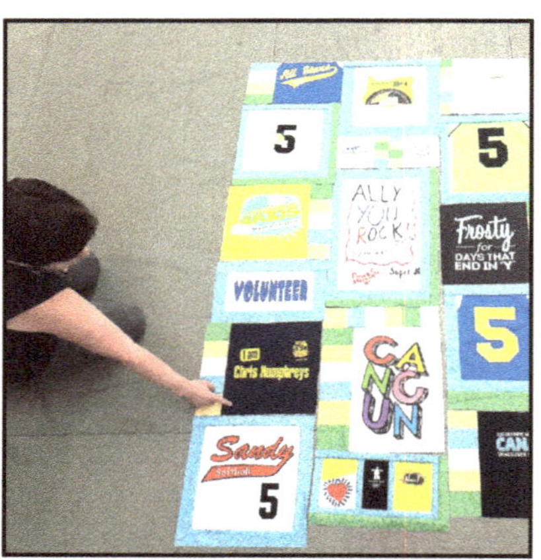

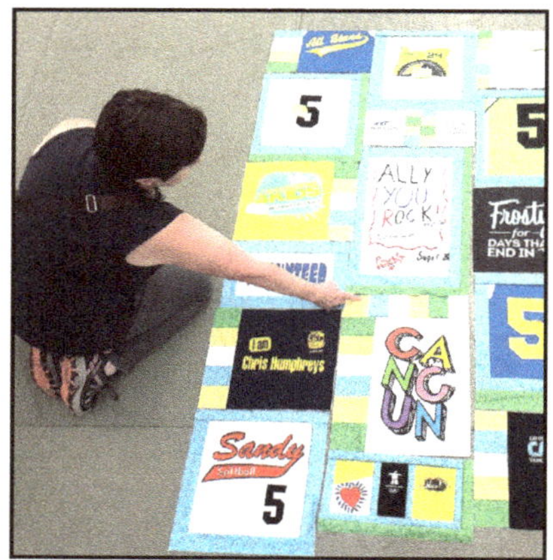
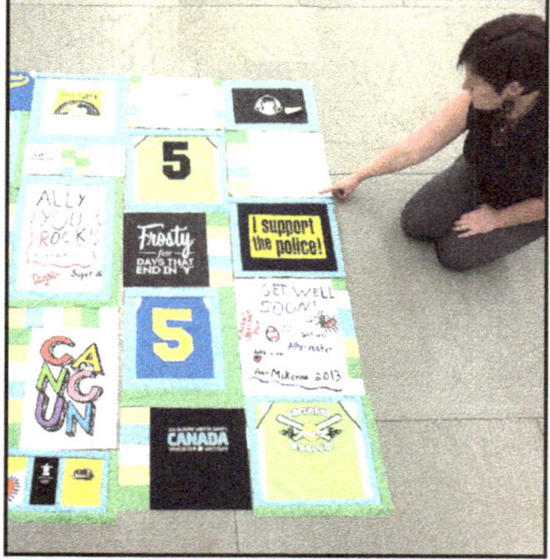

Take the next shortest column (column four) and sew the blocks together in a column <u>except</u> for the one block that can be shortened. Column four is 1 inch longer than column three.

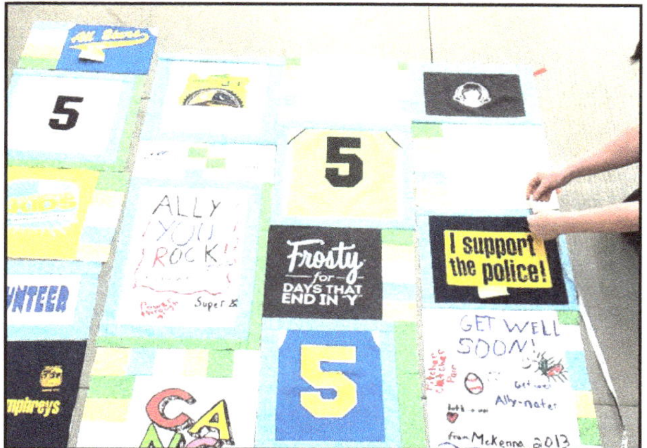

The tie-dye block (2nd down from the top can be shortened.

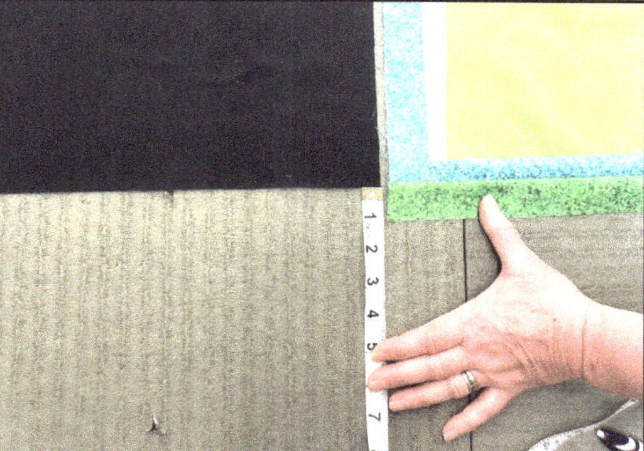

Column four is one inch too long.

Column four has one seam left to sew that will take up ½ inch making column four a ½ inch shorter. So   overall, after the seam is sewn, we need column four to be ½ inch shorter. We could cut it off the top or the bottom but that would cut off borders or blocks that would then be too small. So we take ½ inch off the green tie-die where there is plenty of extra fabric to remove.

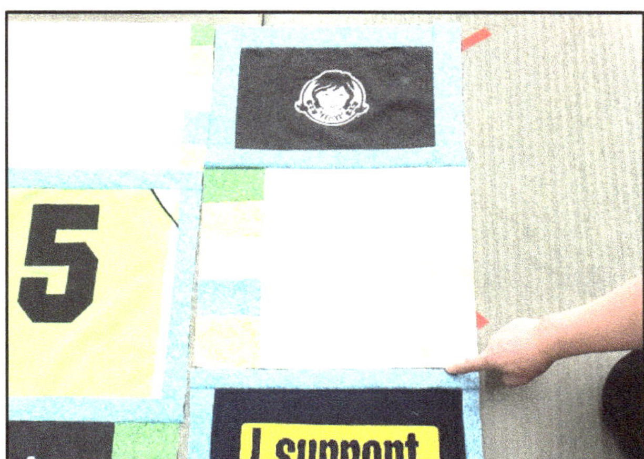

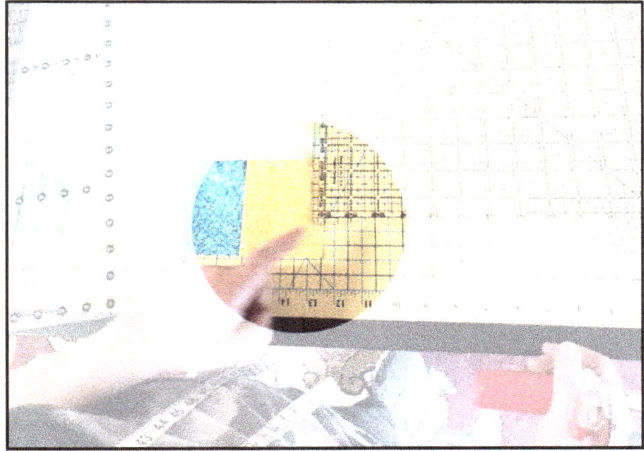

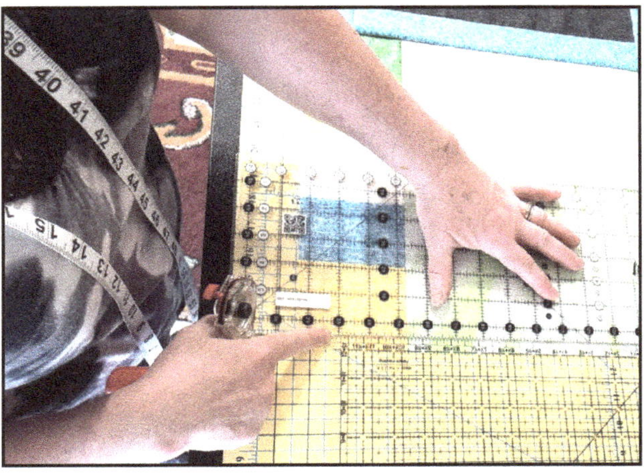

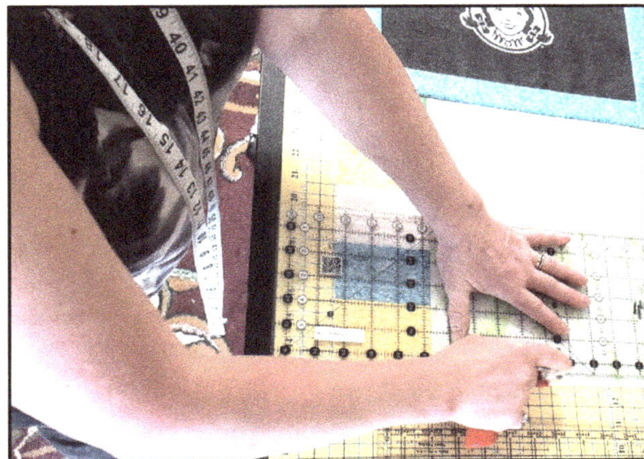

Sew the final seam of column four (a). As always, set the seams. Iron seams toward the lighter fabric (b&c).

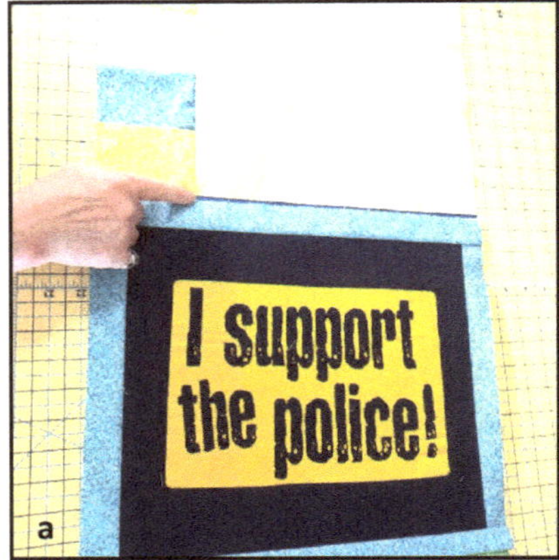

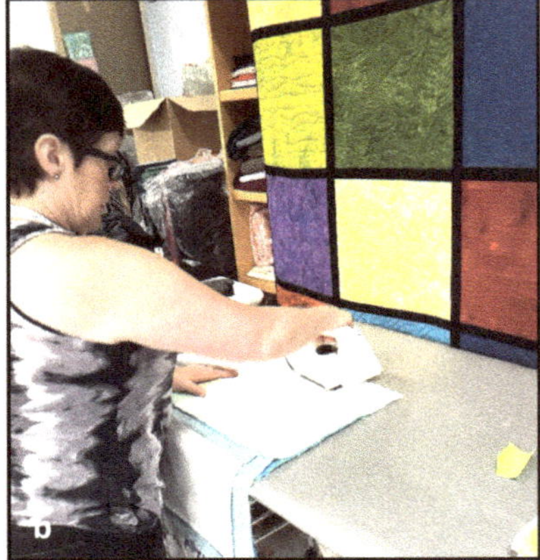

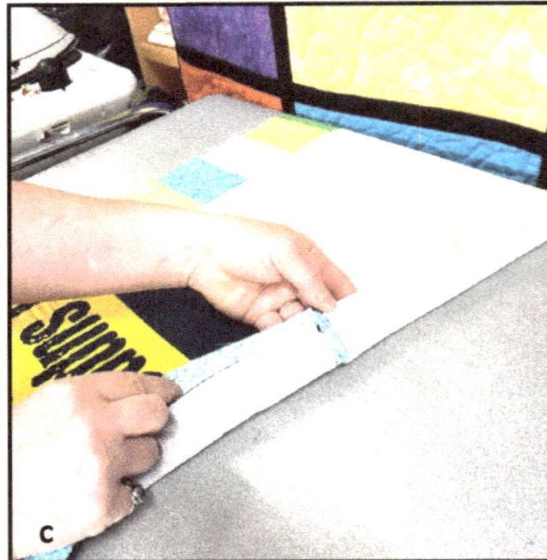

Note that column 3 and 4 are now the same length.

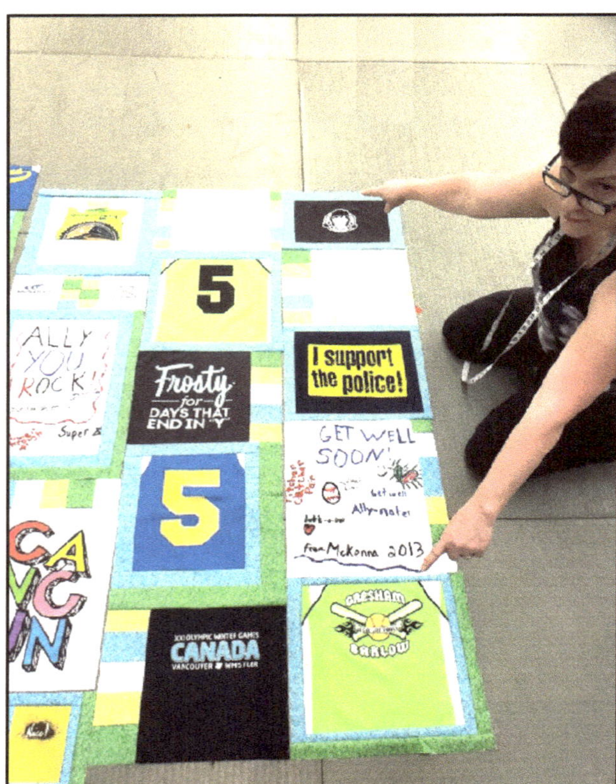

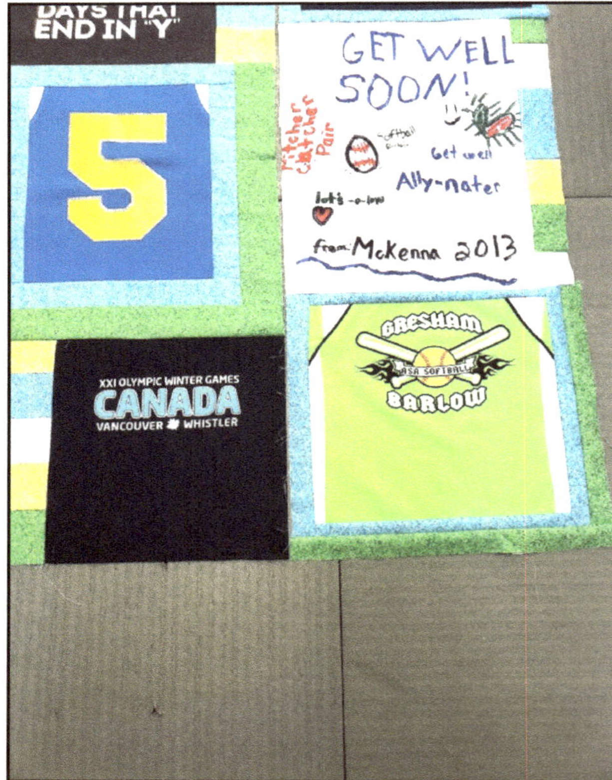

Now let's go to Column 2. It is even with column 3 at the top (a) There are four seams to sew – with ¼ inch seams – each seam takes up ½ inch. ½ inch 4 times is 2 inches (½ + ½ + ½ + ½ = 2). The "Cancun" block can have a ½ inch taken off the top or bottom or both (b). Column two is three inches too long (c).

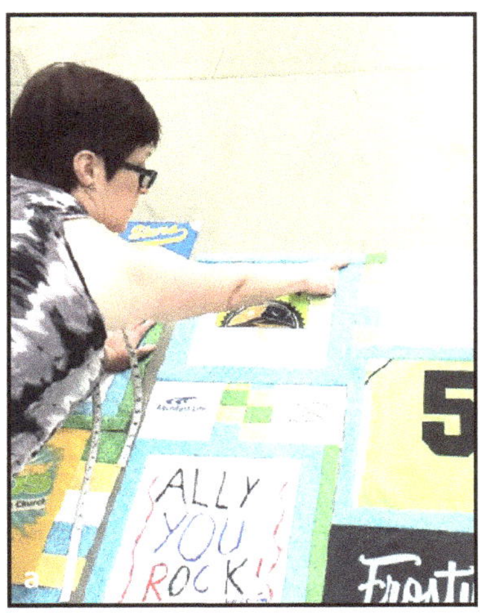 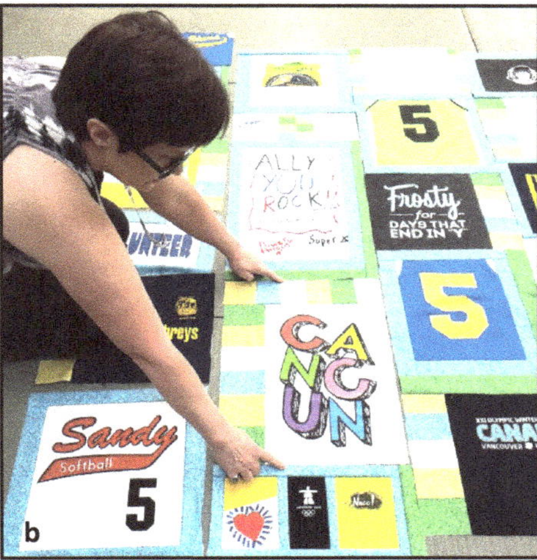 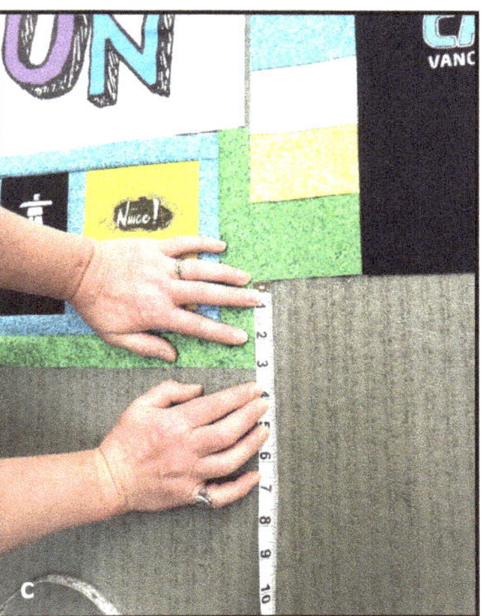

Sew all the seams together except for the "Cancun" block. Cut a ½ inch off the top and the bottom of the "Cancun" block and sew the remaining seams (a). Set the seams and press seams toward the lighter fabric. Place next to column three (b). Column one has five seams (b). Sew the first three blocks together. Cut one inch off the bottom of the yellow block (c).

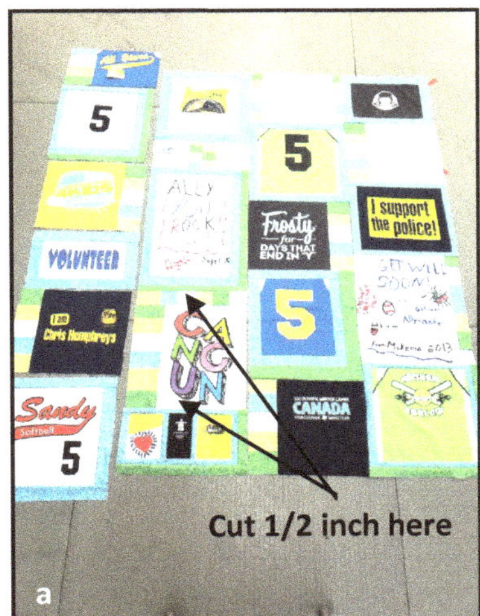

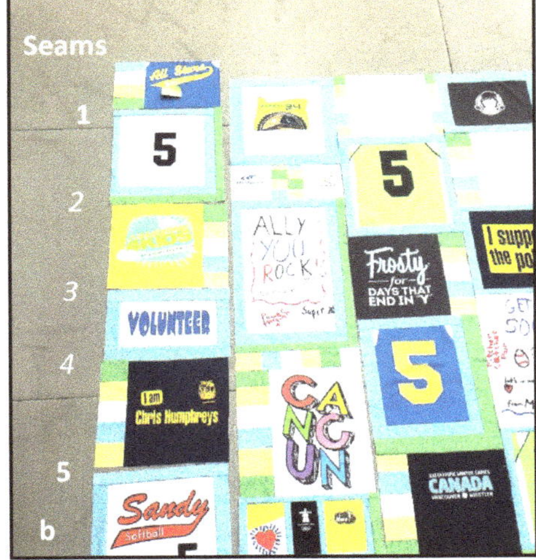

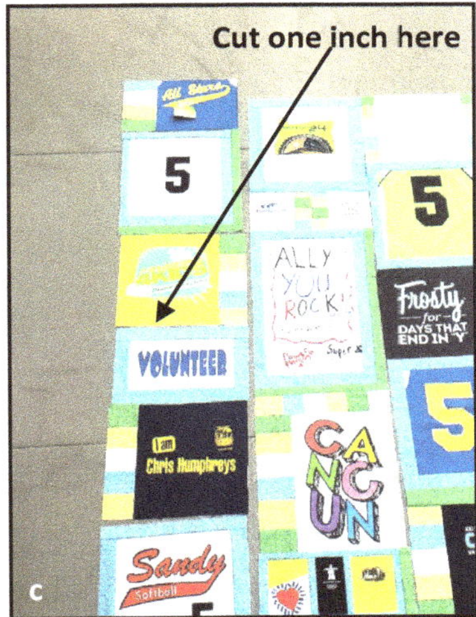

Column two is the same length as column three.

Cut one inch off the yellow block.

Sew on the fourth block (a). Column one now has two seams left to sew and the "Chris" block can be cut on the top and the bottom (b). Column one is three inches too long (c).

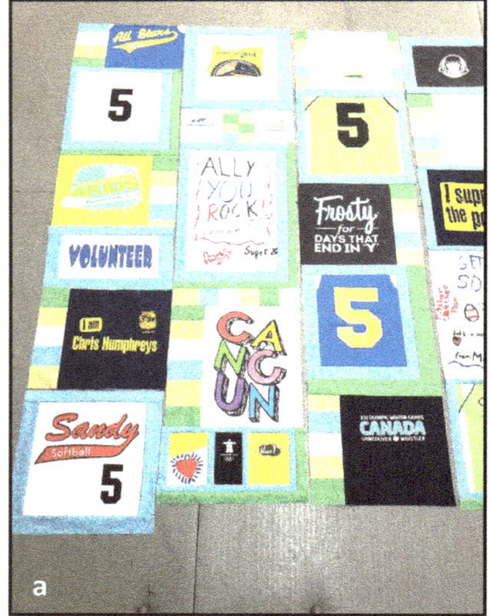

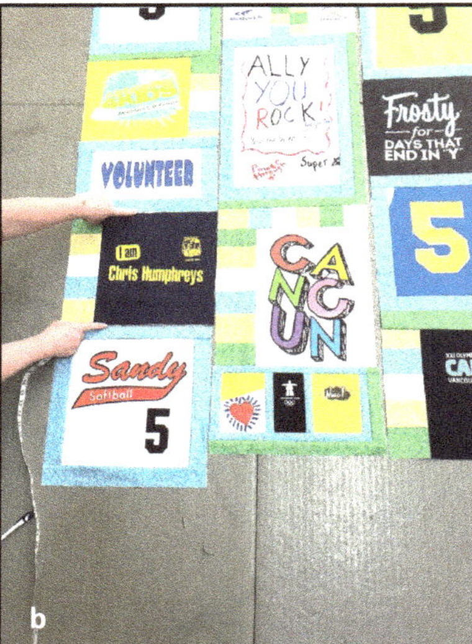

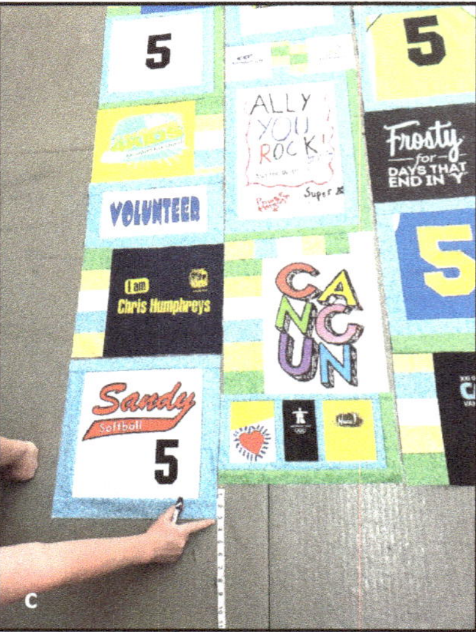

Cut 1 ½ inches off the bottom and ½ inch off the top of the "Chris" block (d & e). Sew the "Chris" block to the "Volunteer" block and the "Sandy Softball" block to complete the column (1/2 inch per seam). Column 1 is now the same length as columns 2, 3 and 4 (f).

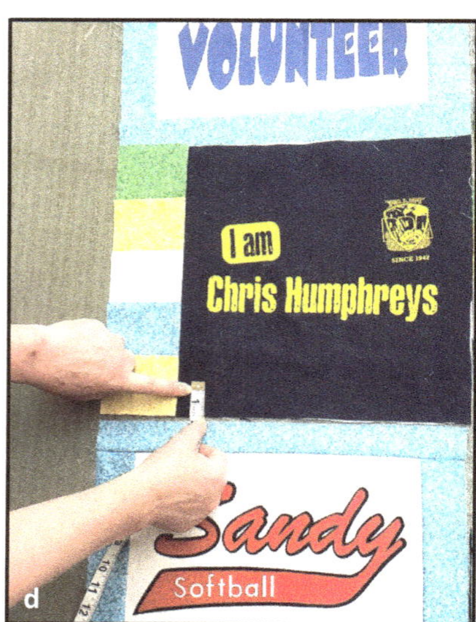

Cut off 1 1/2 inches here.

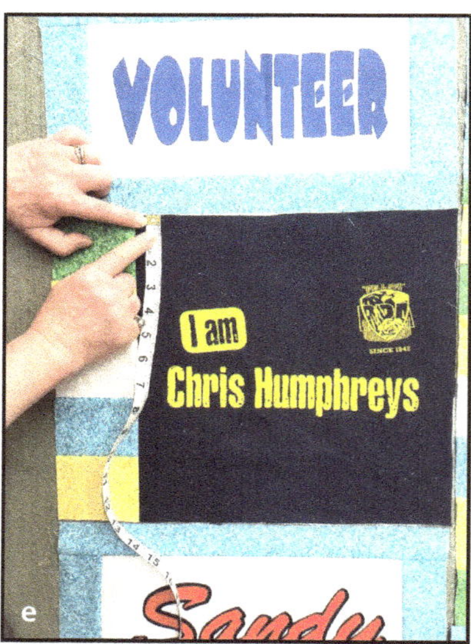

Cut off 1/2 inch here.

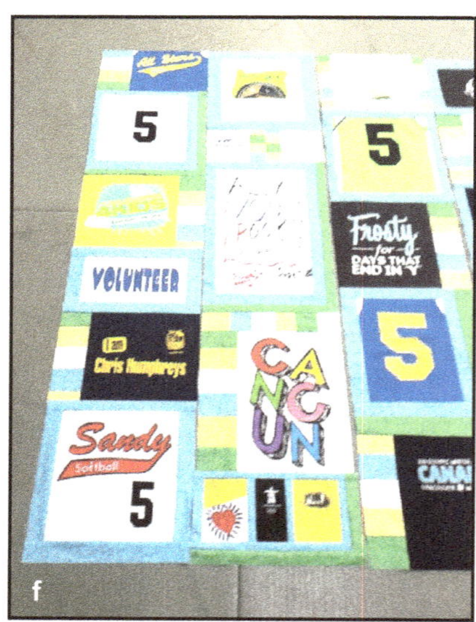

Columns one and two are now even.

Place column one on column two, right sizes together, and pin them before you move them (a, b, c & d).

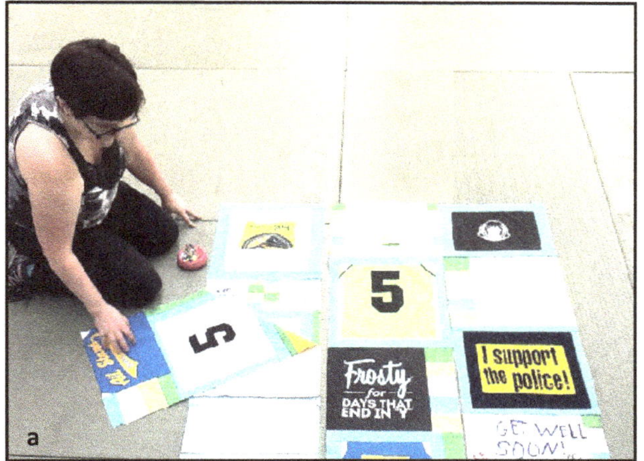

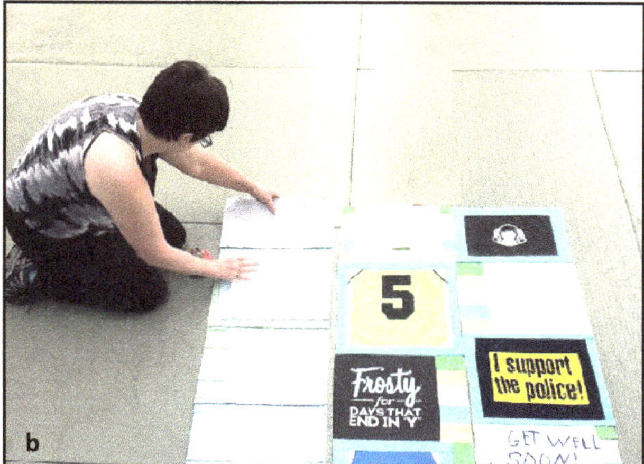

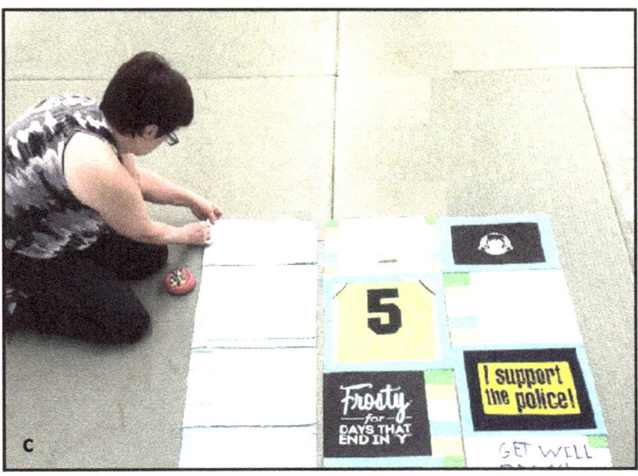

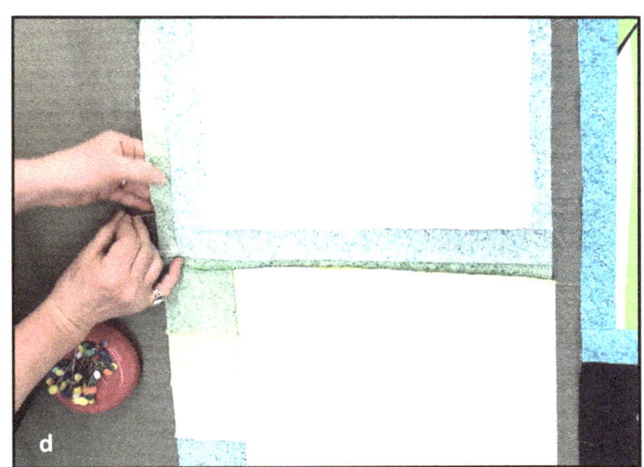

Place column three on column four and pin (e). Sew column one to column two and column three to column four (f).

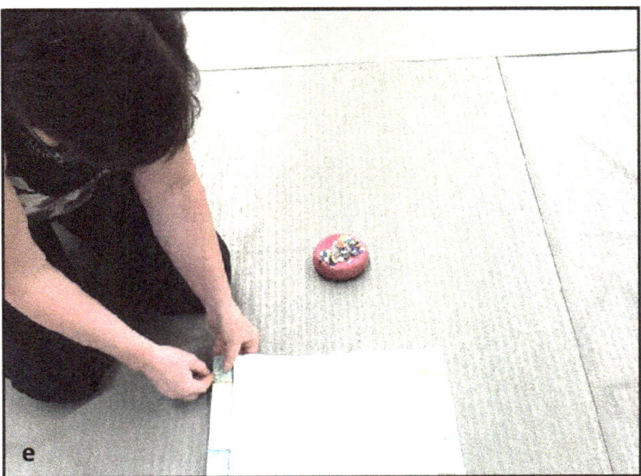

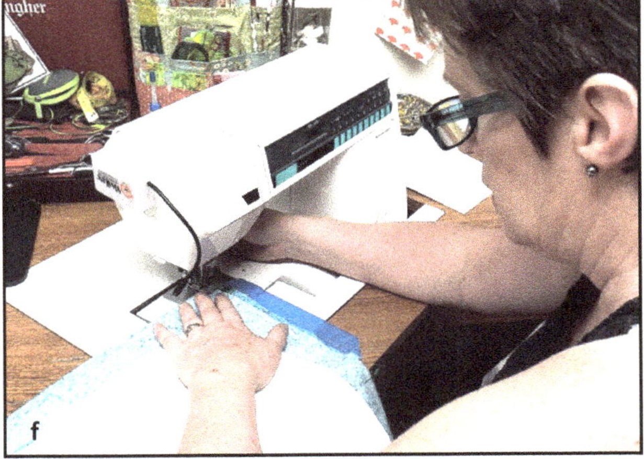

Set seams and press (a & b). Columns one and two, and columns three and four now are set side by side   and placed so they can be sewn together (c). Place one and two on three and four, pin and sew like you did before with the other columns (d & e). Set the seams and press. Your quilt center is now done (f)!

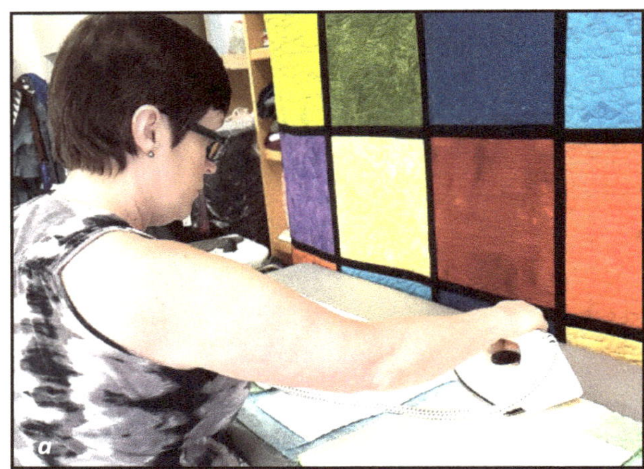

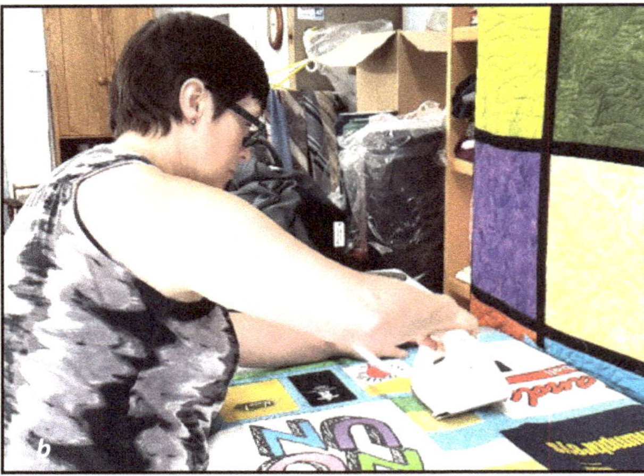

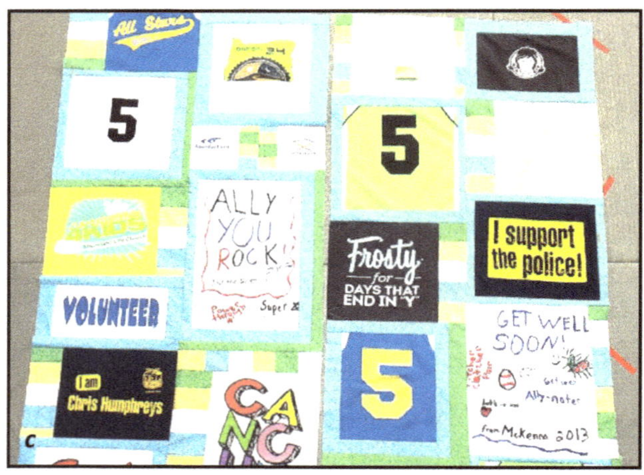

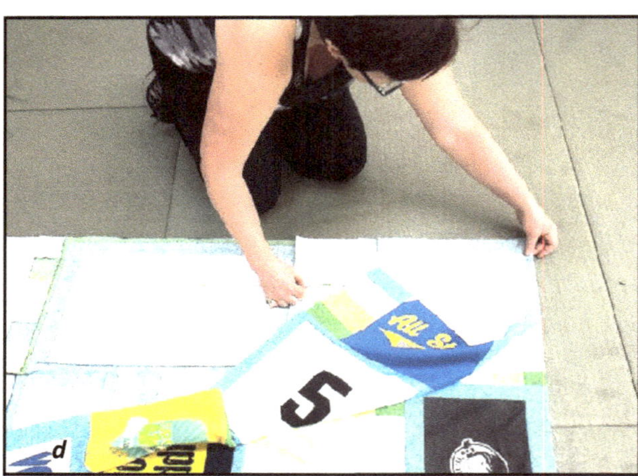

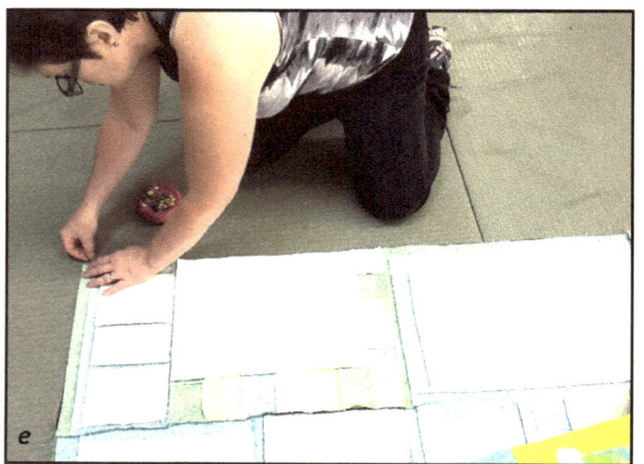

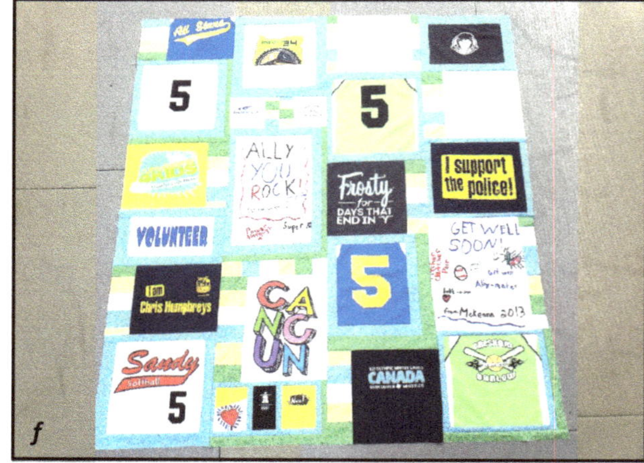

Chapter 7
Borders

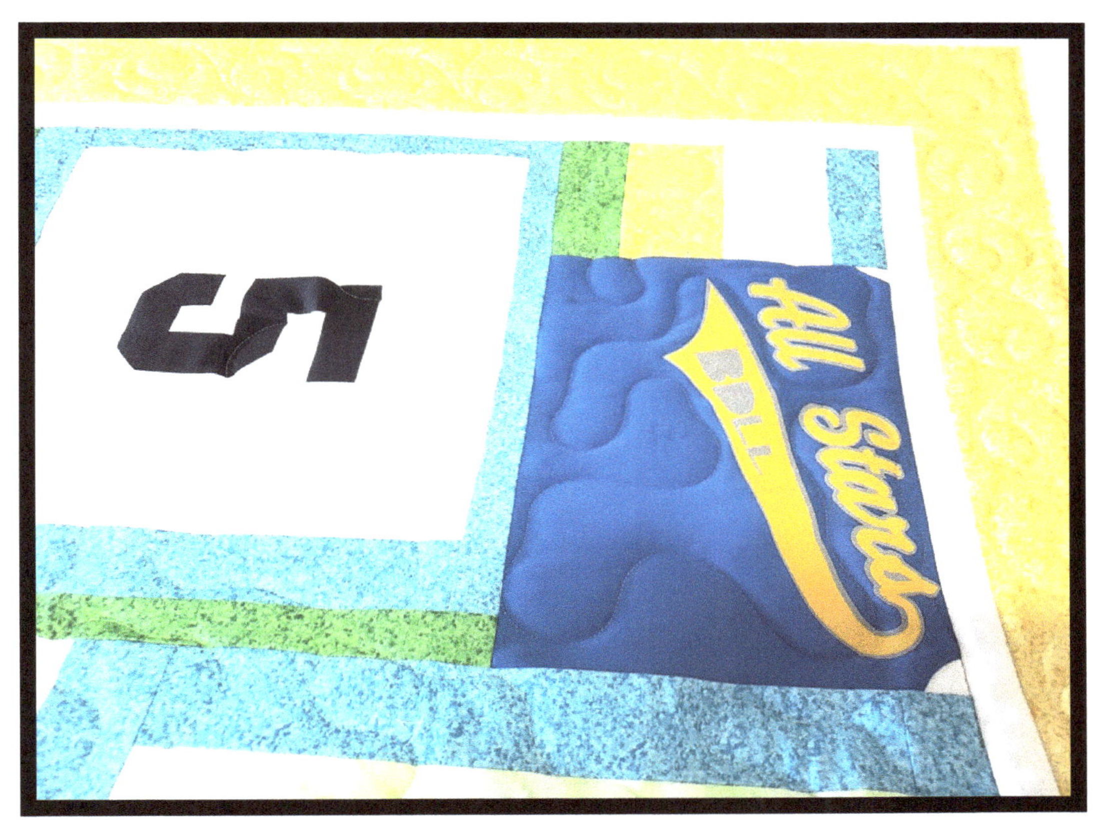

CHAPTER 7 - BORDERS

Borders frame your quilt center. They can bring out specific colors in the quilt. They can also be used to make your quilt bigger if you need it to be bigger. The way borders are added can mean the difference between making the quilt square or not and making the sides straight or wavy. I want my first border to be one inch wide so I cut several 1 ½ inch wide strips and sew them end to end.

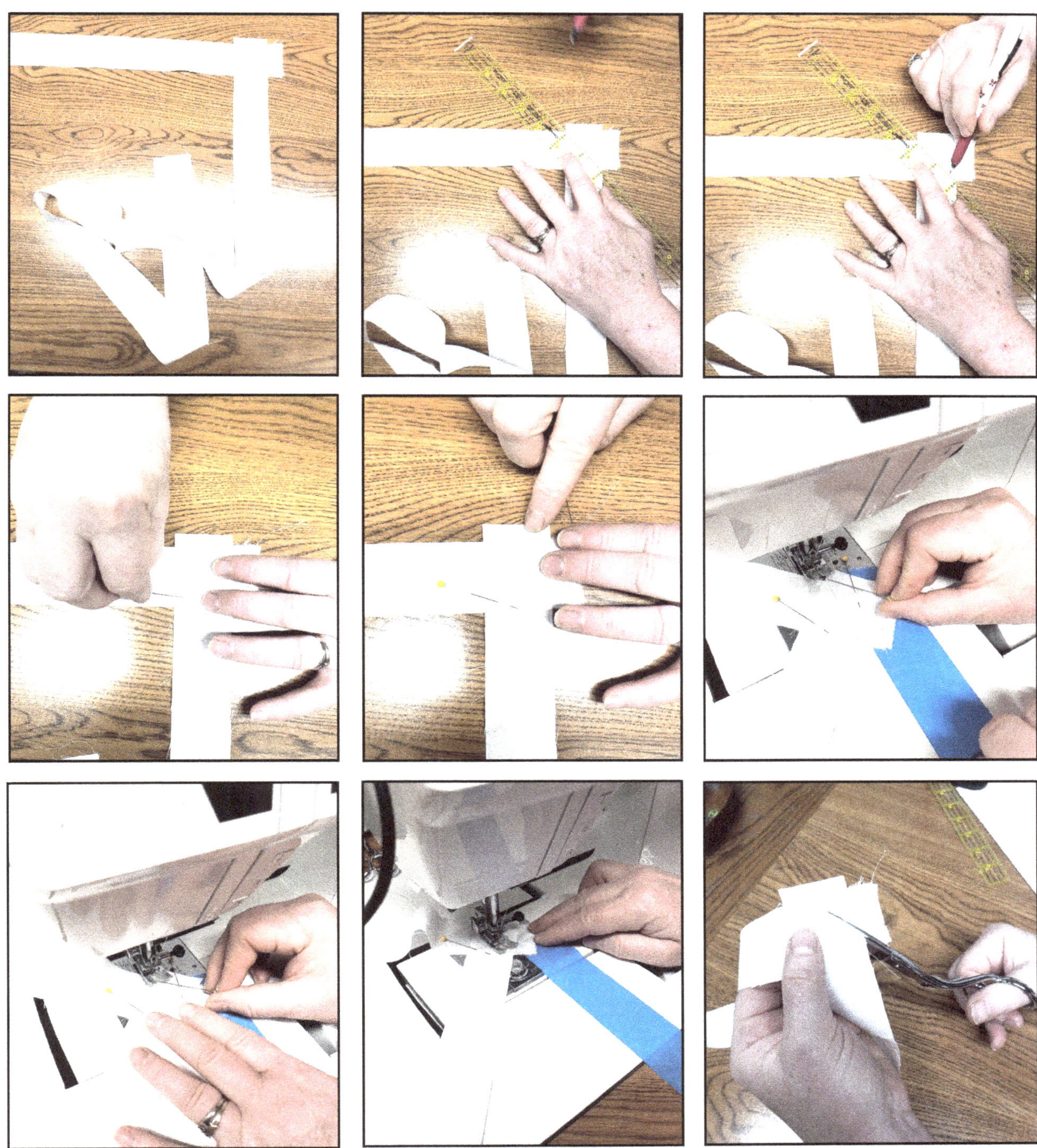

Set seams and press.

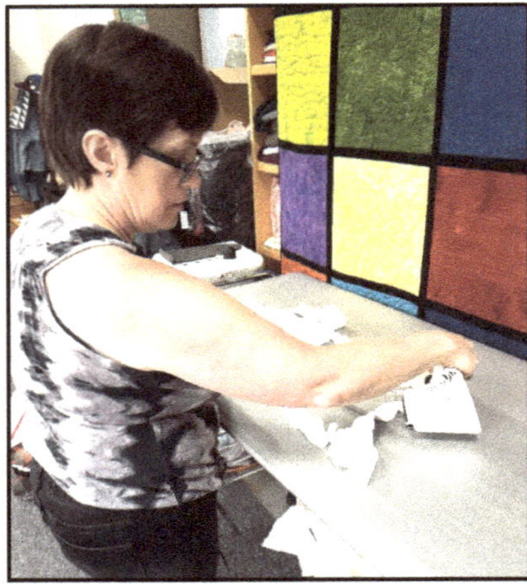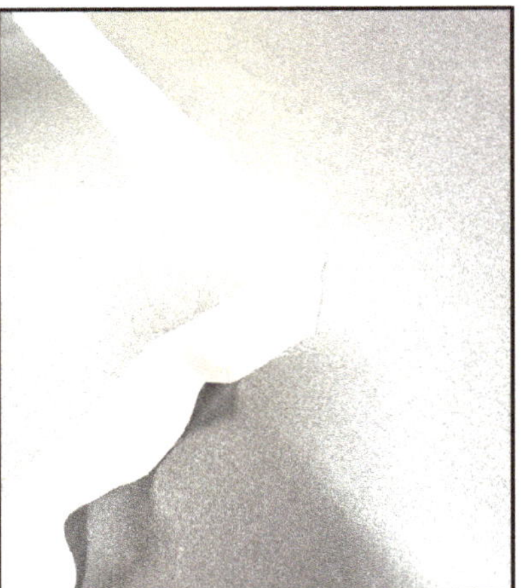

To square up the quilt and add the first border, measure your quilt center across the width in 3 different areas. Left to right are the top block, middle block and bottom block of the quilt.

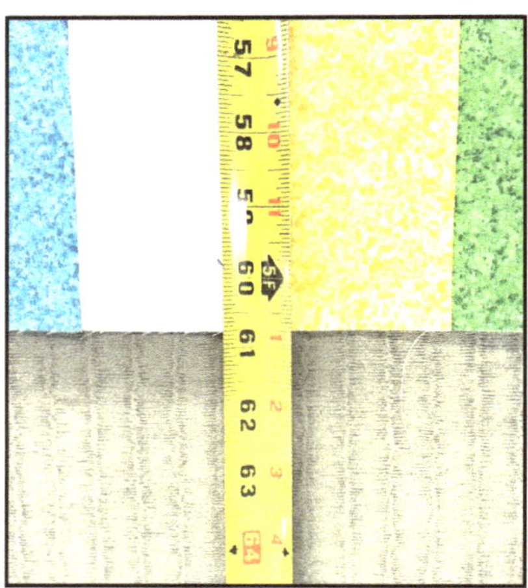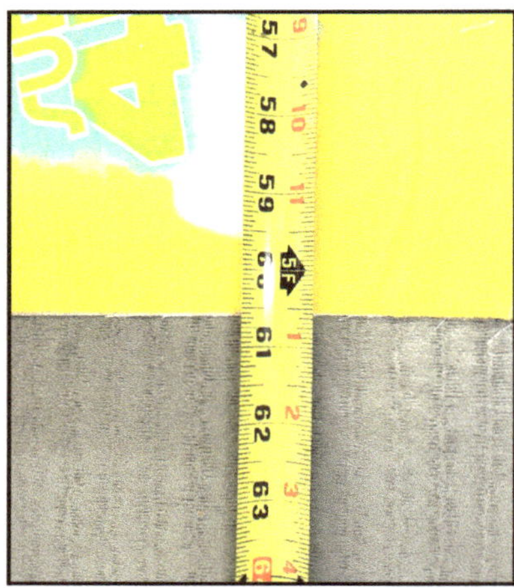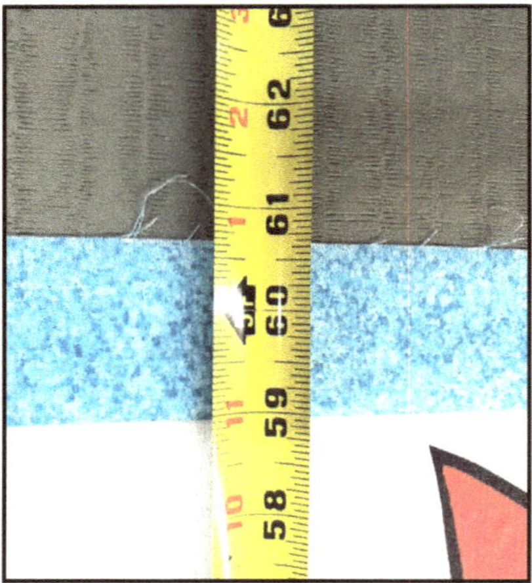

Add the 3 numbers together and divide by 3 to get the average.

Example:

The top horizontal measurement is 60 12/16".

The center horizontal measurement is 60 9/16".

The bottom horizontal measurement is 60 11/16".

The 3 numbers added together and divided by 3 equals a little over 60 10.6/16th.

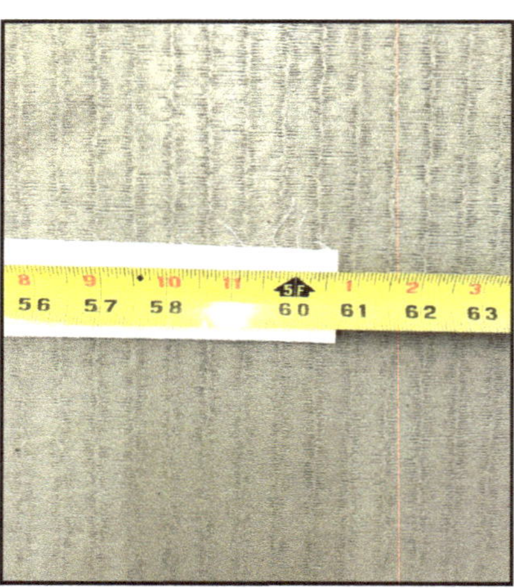

This is the length of the strips you will cut for the horizontal strips at the top and the bottom.

Fold the strip in half and in half again (4 equal parts). Do the same with the top and bottom of the quilt. Match the middle of the quilt and the middle of the strip. Match the quarter marks. Pin at these points.

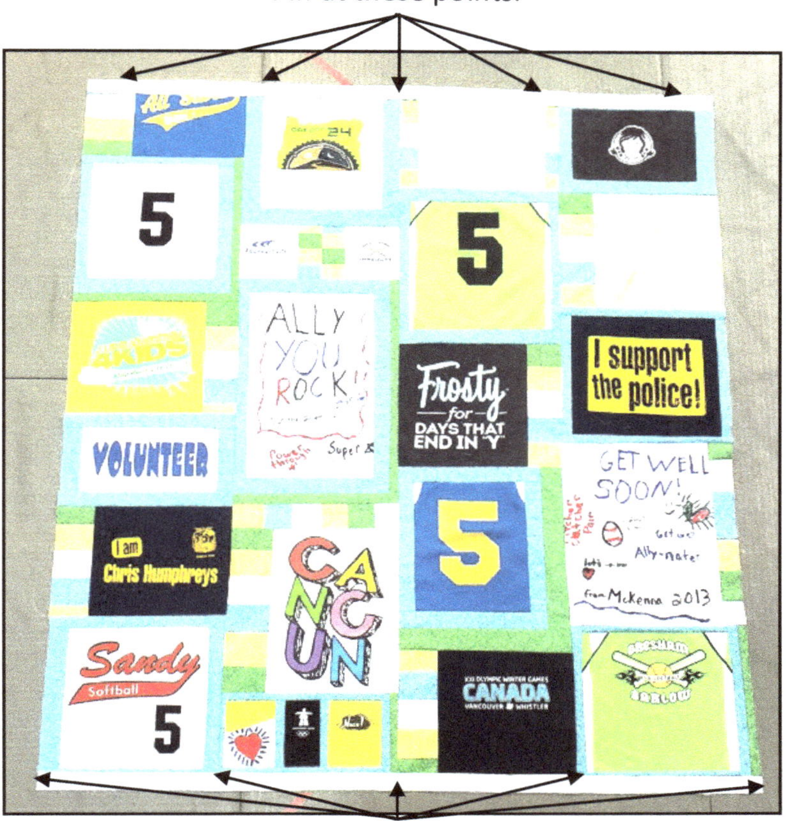

Pin points

Sew the border strips to the top and bottom of the quilt, easing in the excess fullness of the quilt top or the border depending on which is a bit bigger than the other.

If you have divided and pinned this isn't too hard to do. It helps, however, to place the longer piece on the bottom (near the feed dogs) and the shorter piece on the top (just under the presser foot.)

The feed dogs take up the excess on the bottom piece and you can GENTLY pull the top to make it fit the bottom as you sew.

Sets seams and press them toward the outside edge of the quilt.

Proceed in the same way to add the sides: measure in three places, add the three numbers. Divide the total by three. Cut the strips. (see photos on next page).

Example of measuring the strips, adding the three numbers, dividing by three and then cutting the strips by the resultant number.

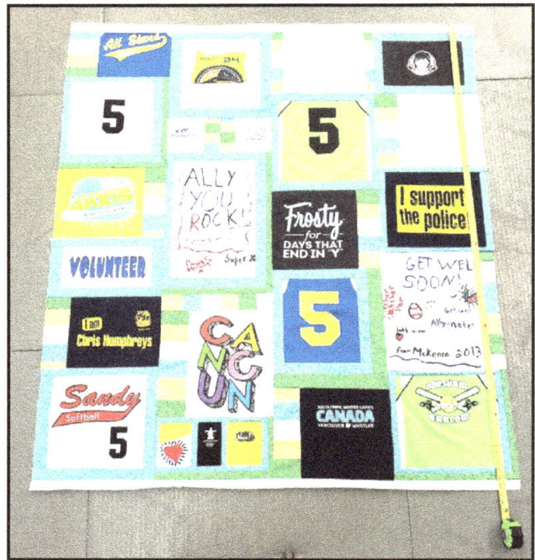

Measure from top to bottom

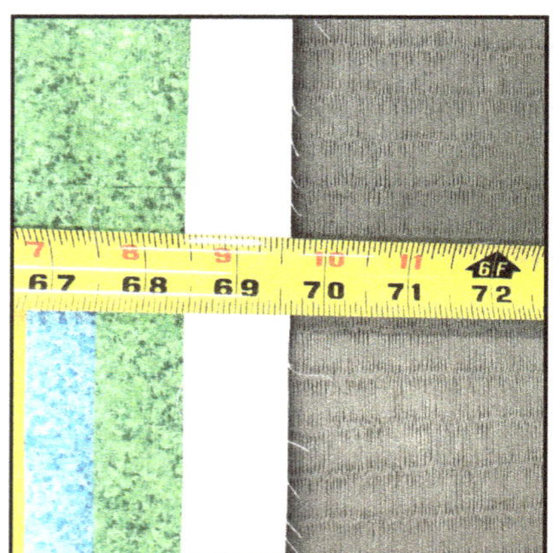

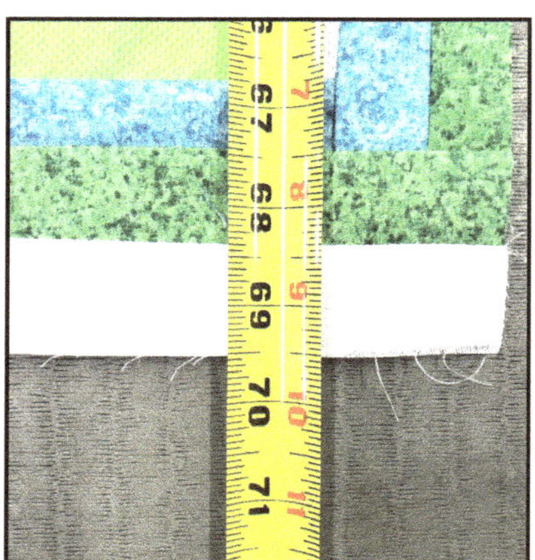

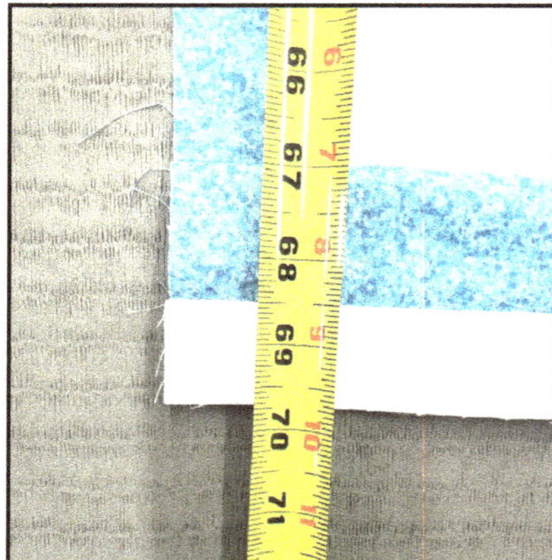

Cut the strips.

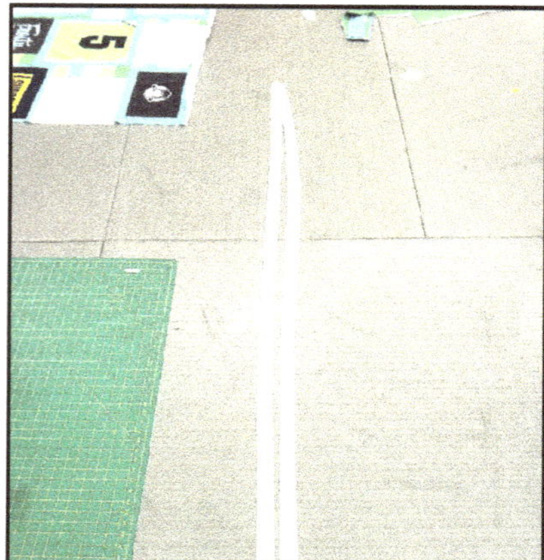

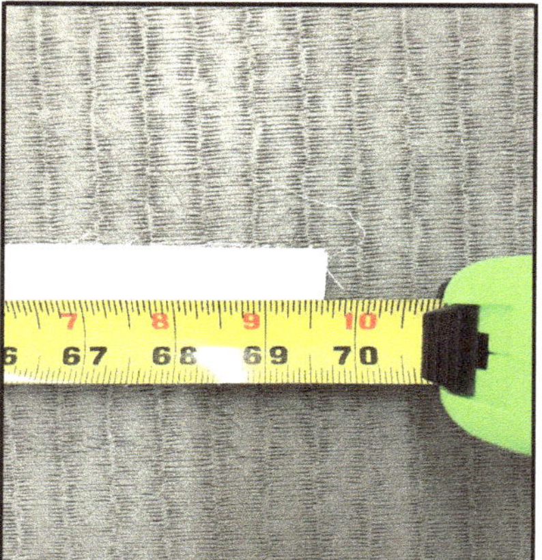

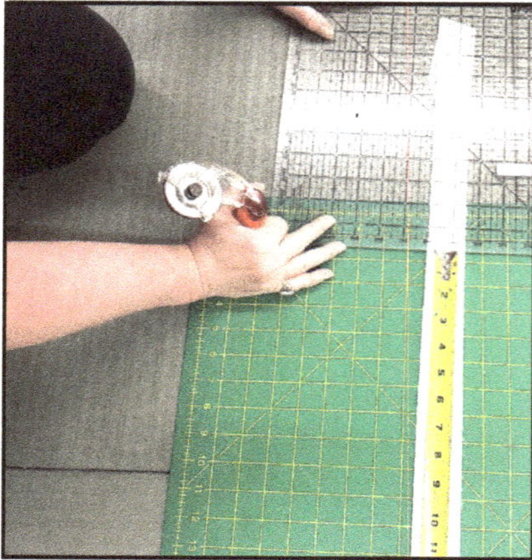

69 5/8 is the average between the three measurements so that is the length I cut my strips to.

Place the side strips on the quilt (a). Note it is 1/4" short on the left (b) and a 1/4" long on the right (c).

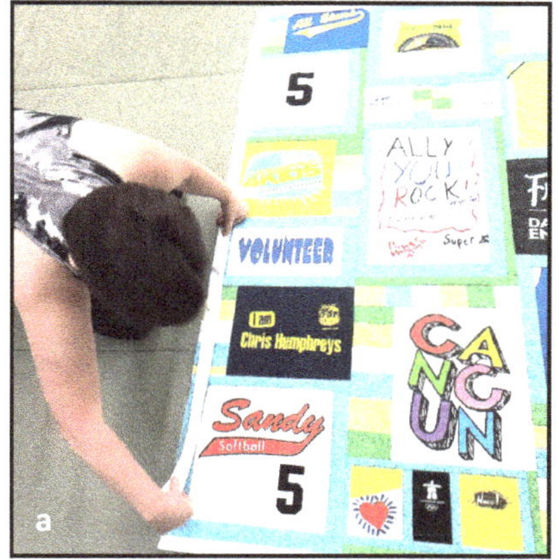
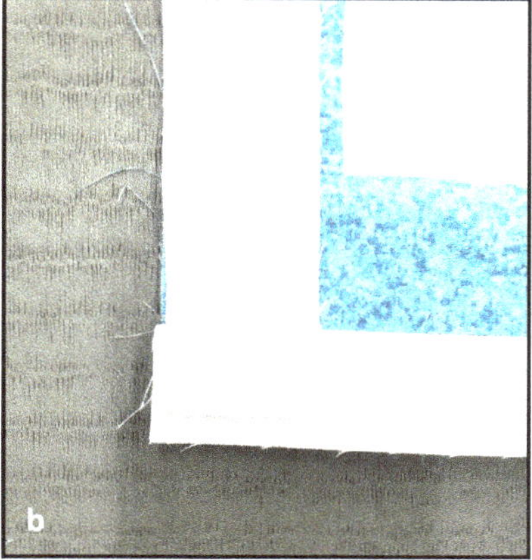
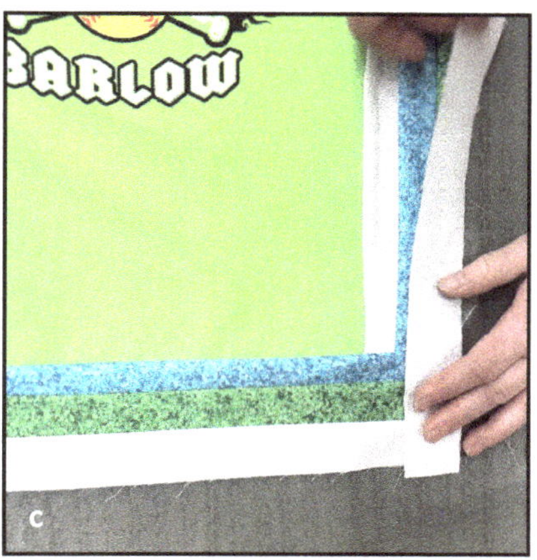

Find the center and quarter marks on the quilt center and strips. Pin. Ease to fit and sew. Continue adding the borders in this way until your quilt is as big as you want it. Cut 3 1/2 " strips of your next border color (or whatever width you want). Sew them end to end.

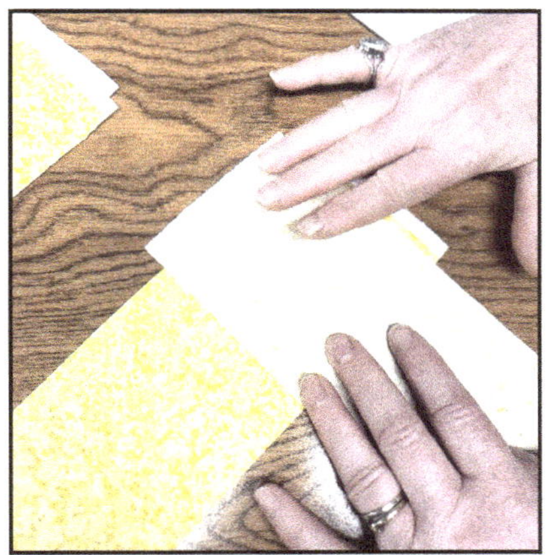

Yellow border strip placement

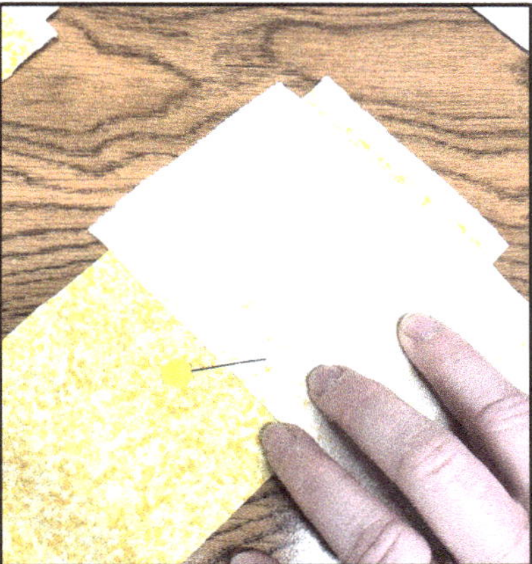

Yellow border pin

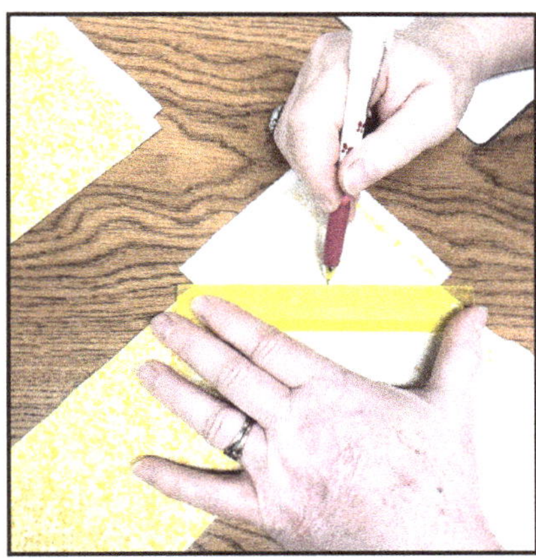

Yellow border draw line

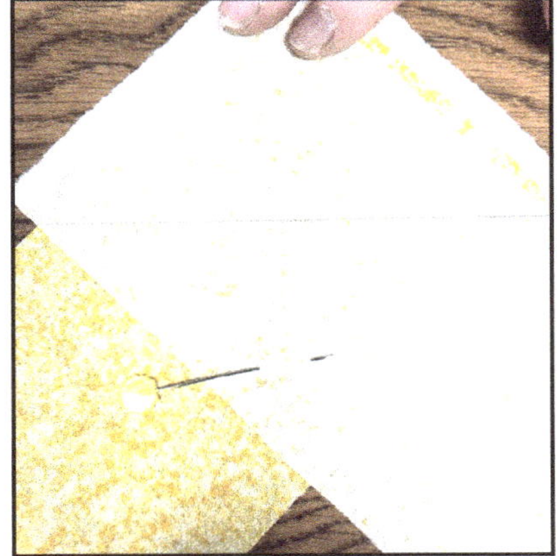

Yellow border line drawn

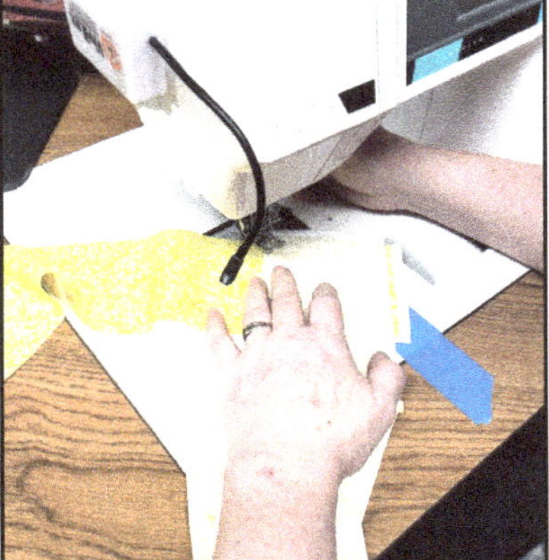

Sew

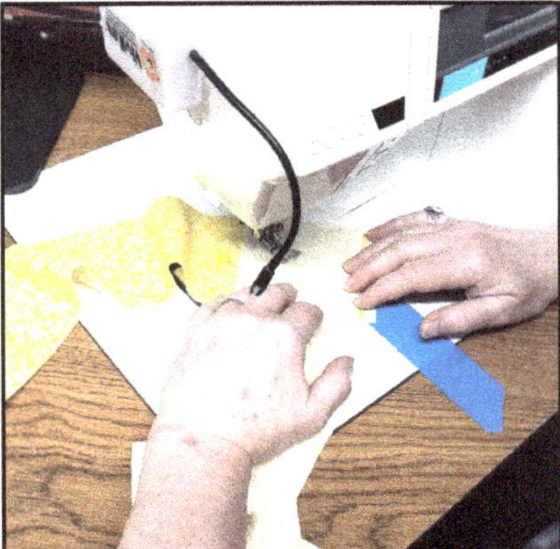

Measure the quilt top in 3 places and find the average width.

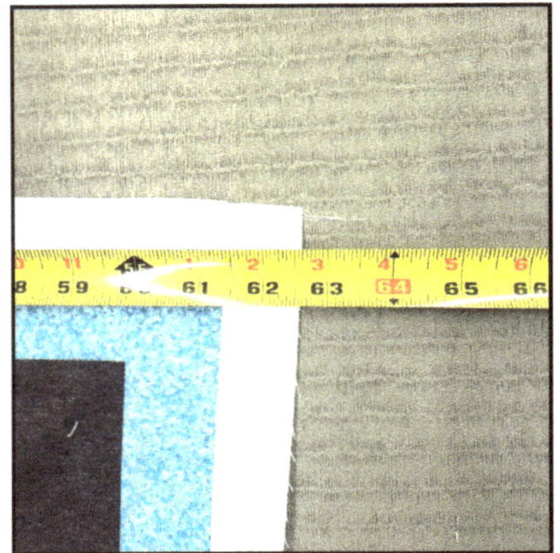 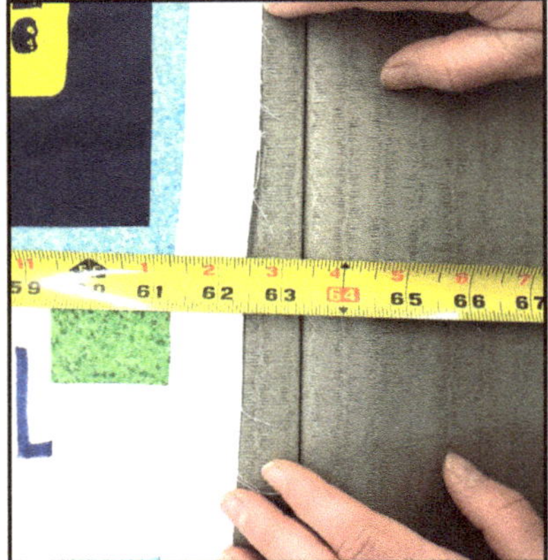 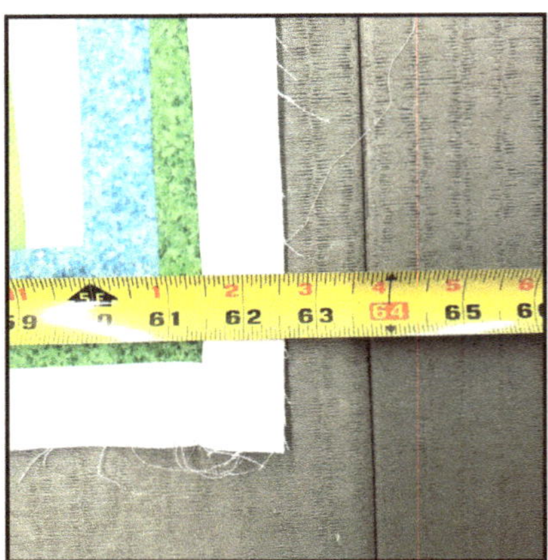

Measure the border strip and cut it the length of the average (a & b). Place on the quilt and pin to fit (c).

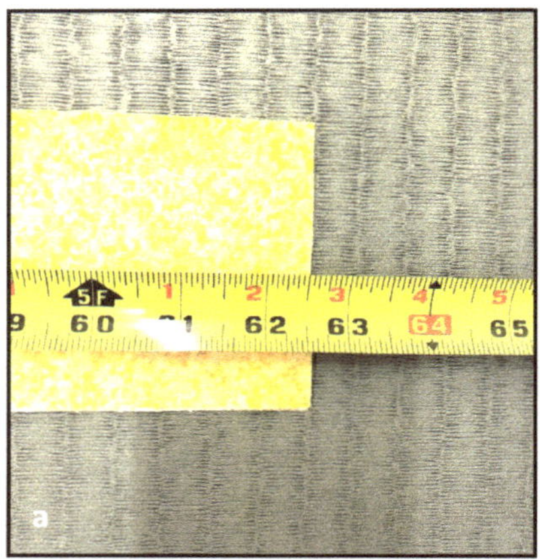 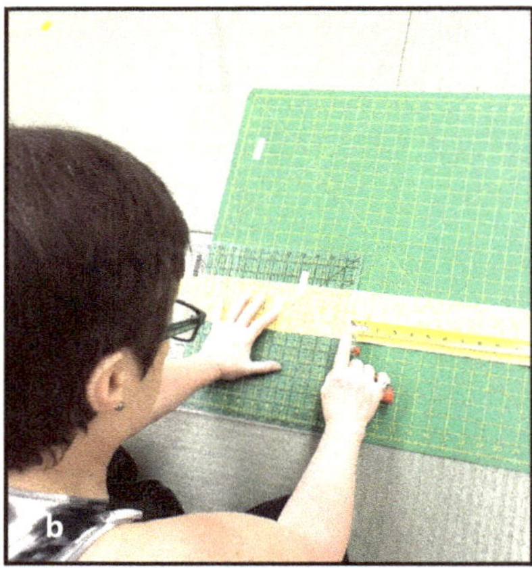 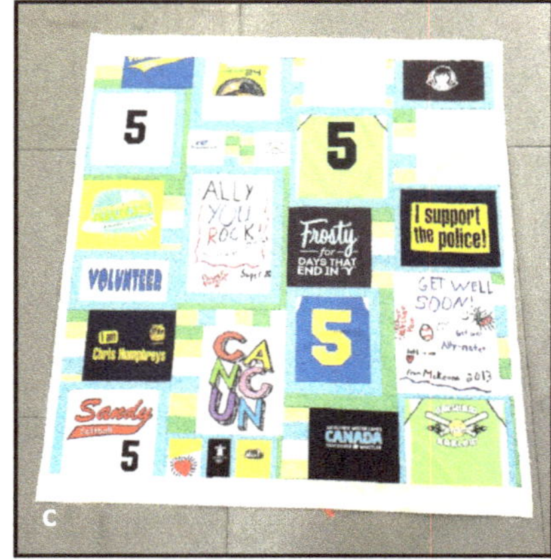

After you set the seams and press, measure the length in 3 places, divide by 3 to find the length of the strip.

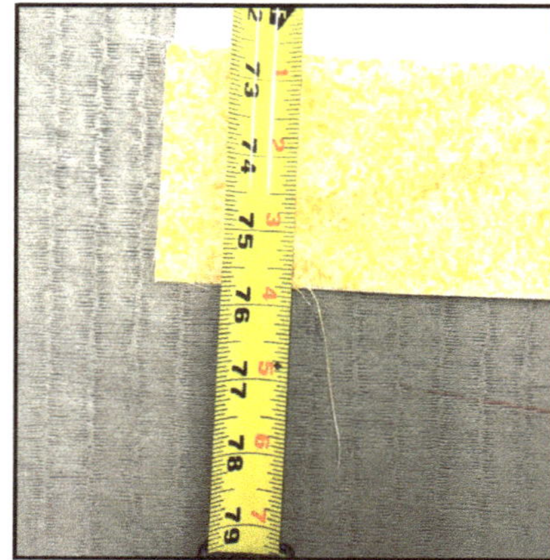 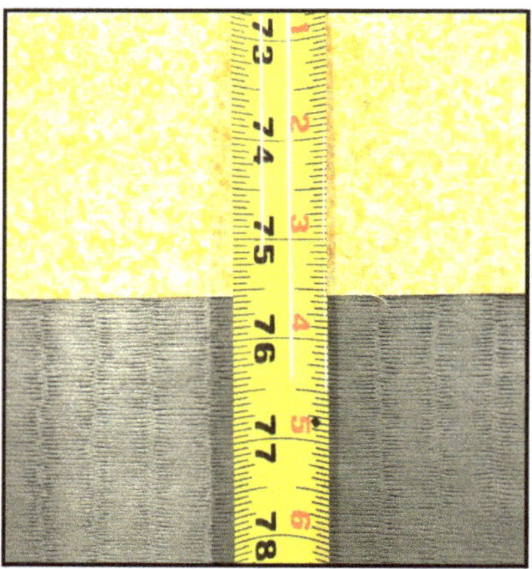 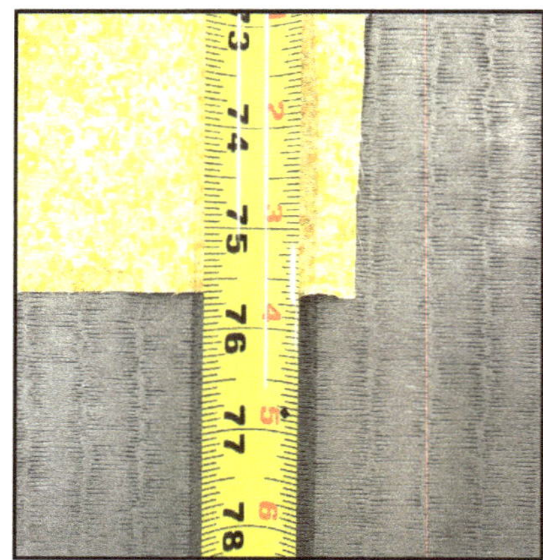

Left edge measurement *Center measurement* *Right edge measurement*

Here is a full length view of measuring your quilt in three places.

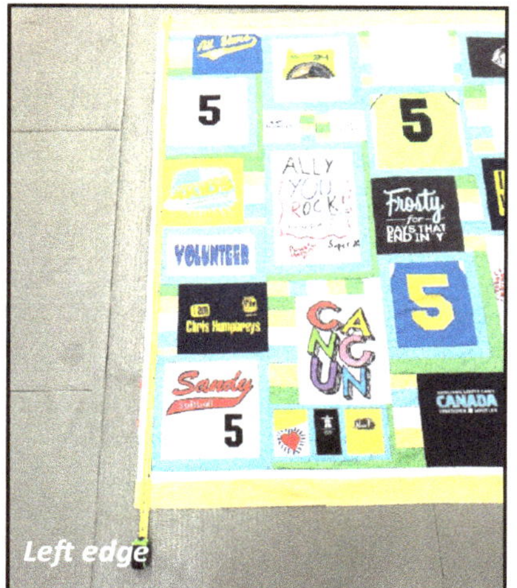

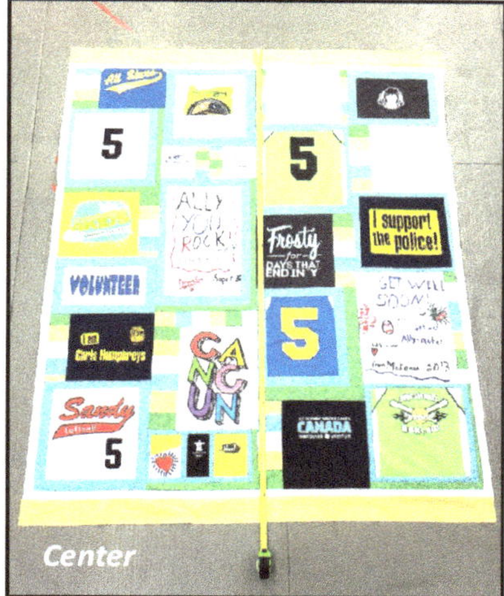

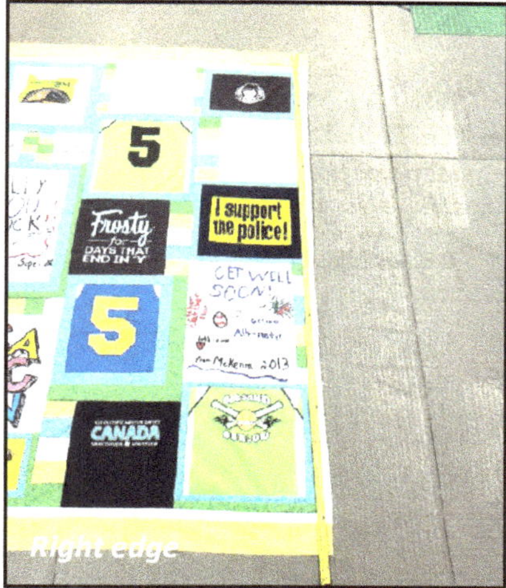

Measure the strip and cut.

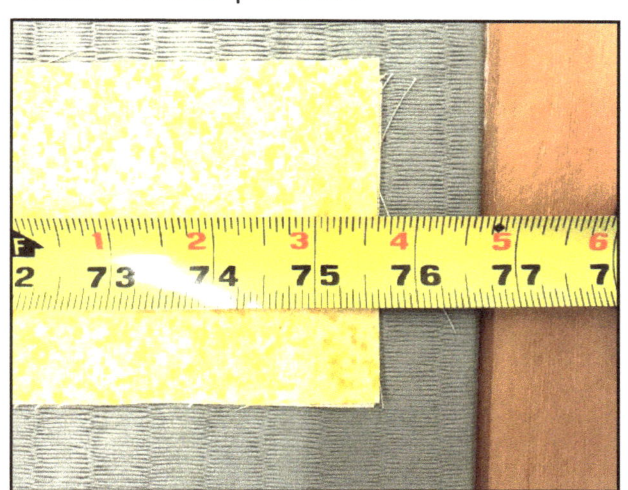

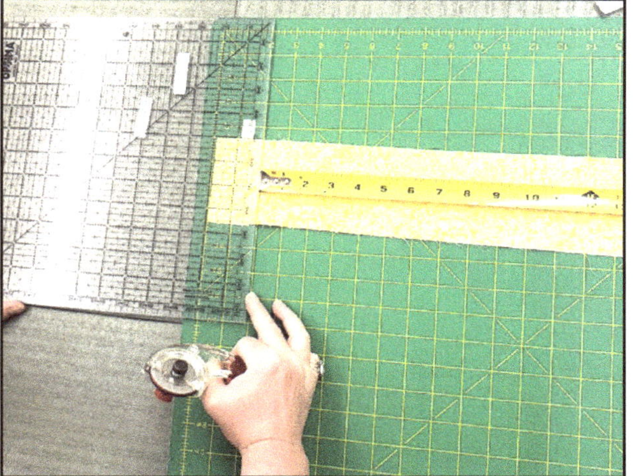

Place the strip on the quilt top on both sides. Pin to fit, sew, set seams and press.

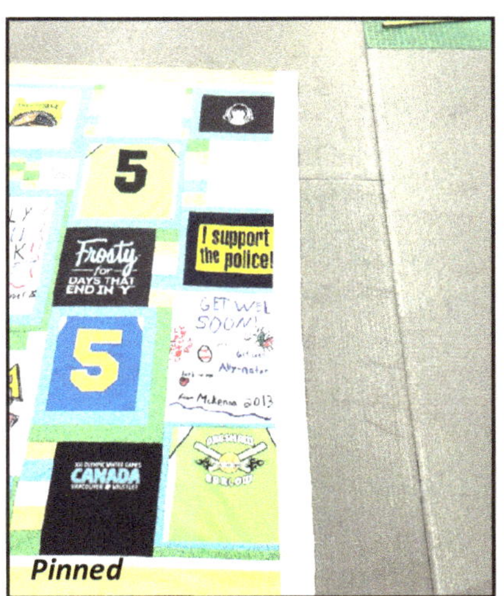

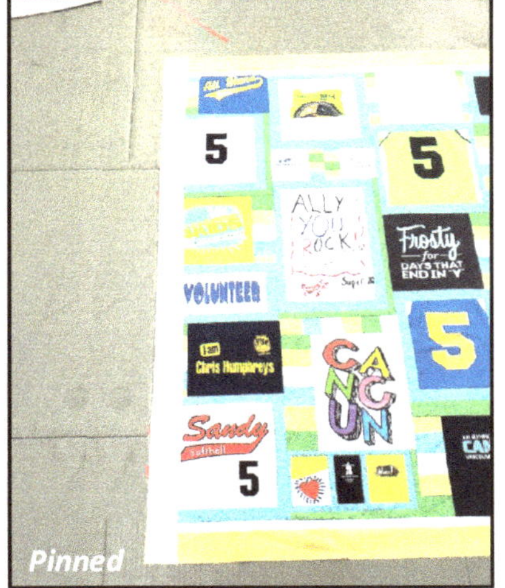

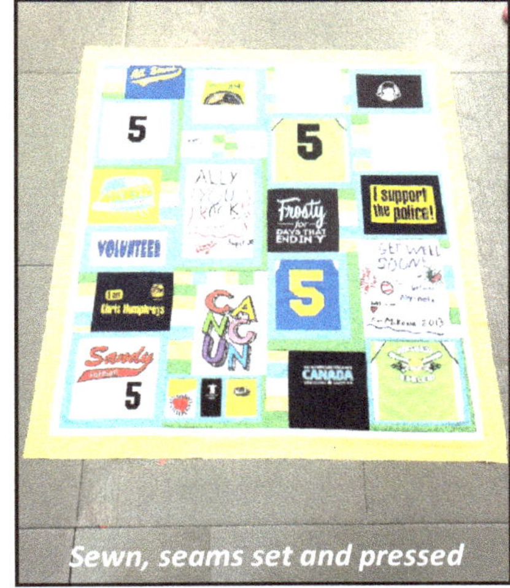

Find random threads and carefully trim. Make sure you use curved small scissors. Carefully put the blades next to the threads and apply pressure with the threads. Don't use the scissor function – use it like a knife. The last thing you want to do is to cut a hole in your quilt top just as it is completed!

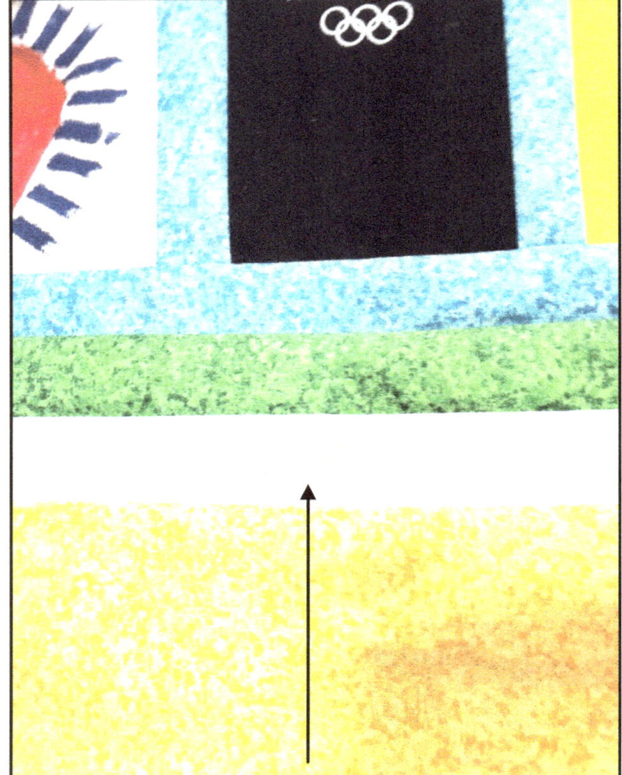

Finding the random threads.

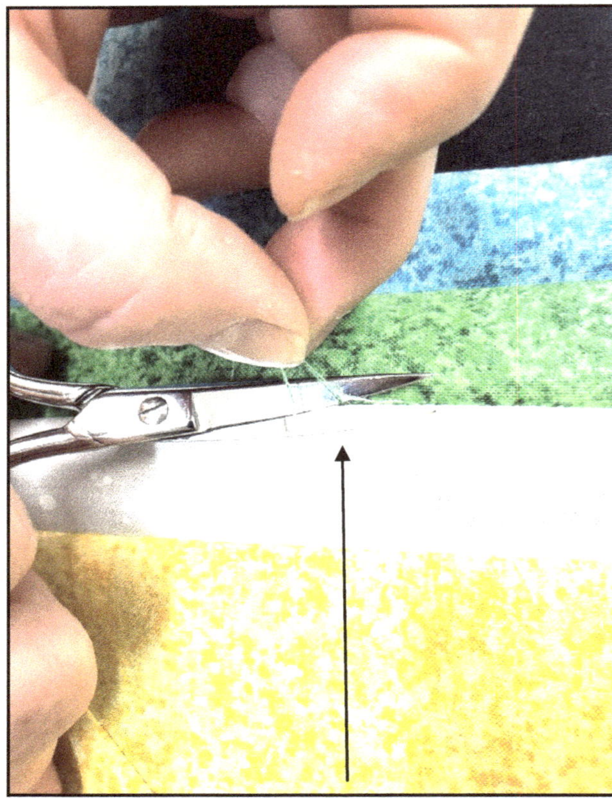

Using the scissors like a knife.

Chapter 8
The Back & Batting

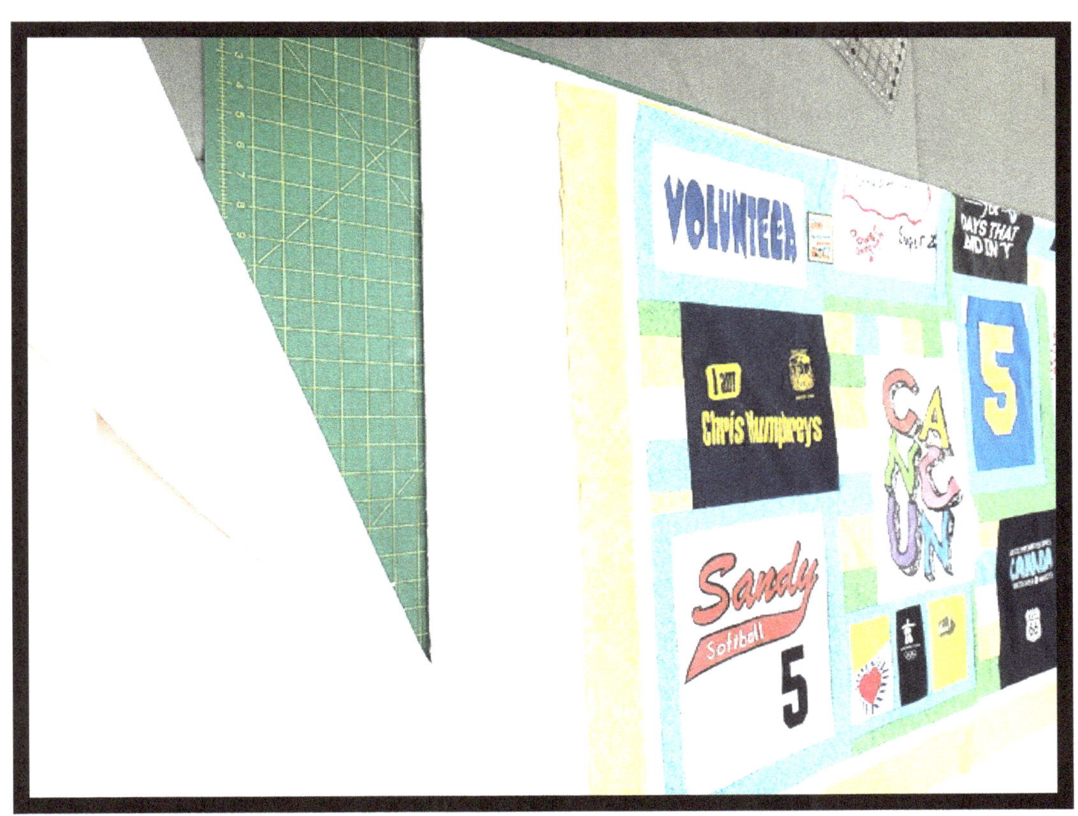

Choose a back: I like to take my completed quilt top to the fabric store at this time to pick my back. The reason I wait until this time is I might have a lot of fabric left over from my borders and accents. So I might not need much more fabric. (I can use the leftovers from the top fabrics.) Or might have a different look/color from what my initial vision was and so I may want my back to be a different color.   Choose the fabric you want for the back.

In this particular case I chose to use a cream colored Cuddle fabric. It has a soft velvety feel to it and looks beautiful quilted. (a)

Inspect the fabric for marks, snags, cuts, etc. In my case I had already purchased the full bolt of fabric. I saw the mark when I was cutting the fabric and I could tell it would be positioned outside of the quilt. I marked it to ensure I would not position my quilt over the top of this (b).

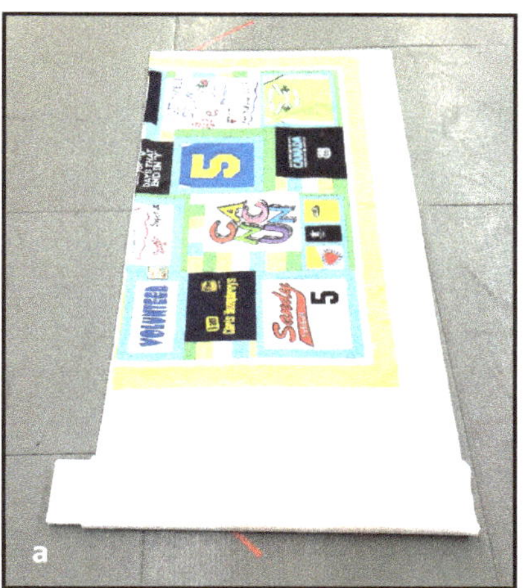
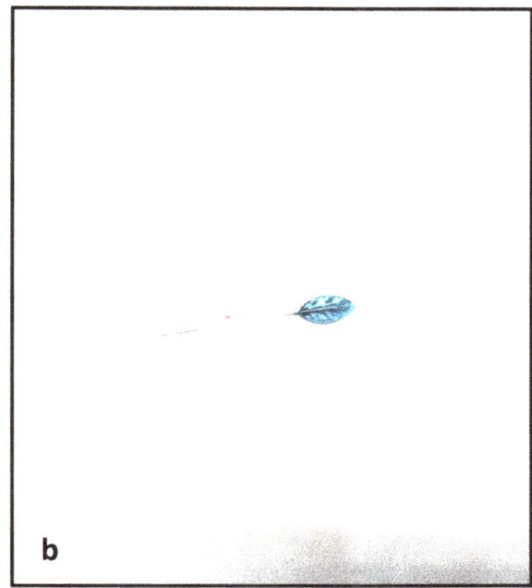

I quilt my quilts on a longarm. So I need the back to be about 4-5 inches bigger than the top fabric all around the quilt top. You can measure your top and then cut the back – but I like to just lay the quilt top on the back and cut the piece bigger. Cut the back with the extra length and width in mind (c & d).

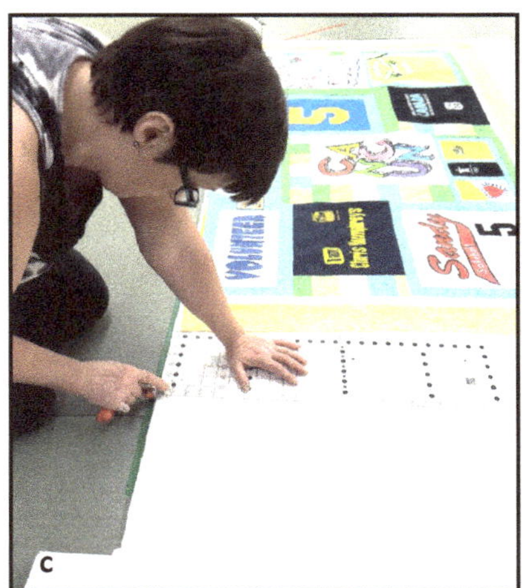
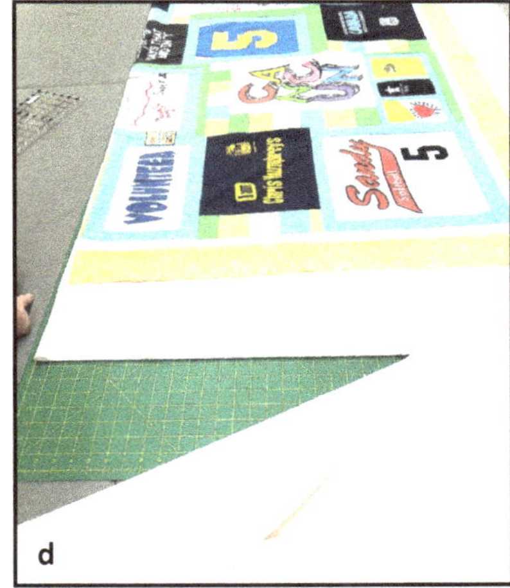

When I cut the Cuddle, the soft fuzzies go all over the room if you aren't careful. I use a garment cleaner (sticky roll thing-I forget what it's called) to catch the little fuzzies before they go all over. You can also vacuum, just be careful not to stretch the edge of your fabric .

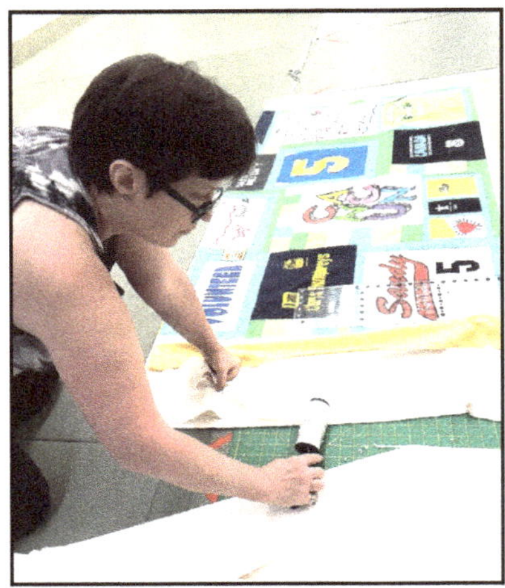

Measure the batting the same way. Roll out batting and place the quilt top on top of it. Measure and cut the batting to be at least 2 inches all around bigger then the quilt top.

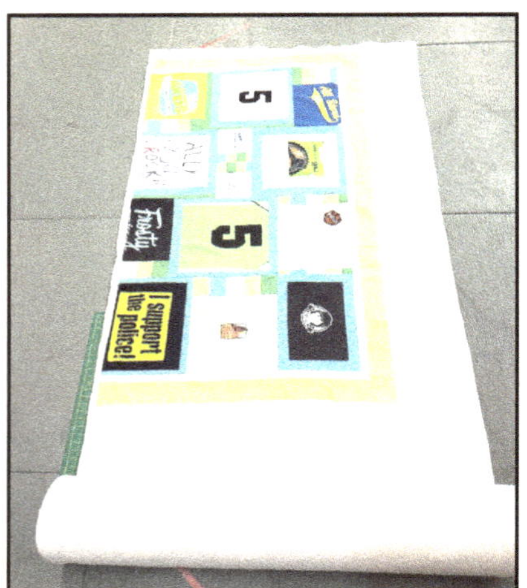

Lay out batting.

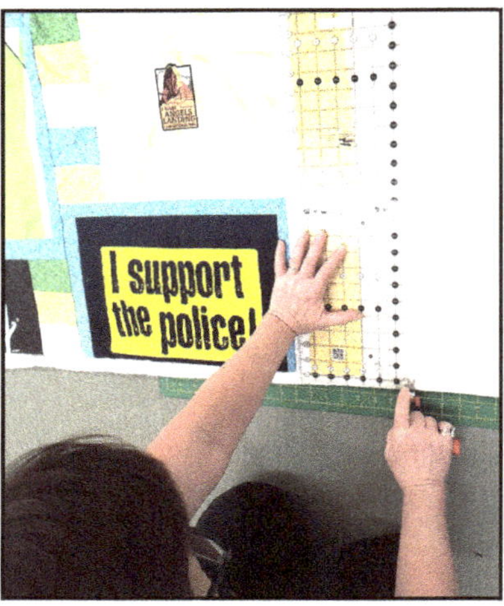

Cut batting.

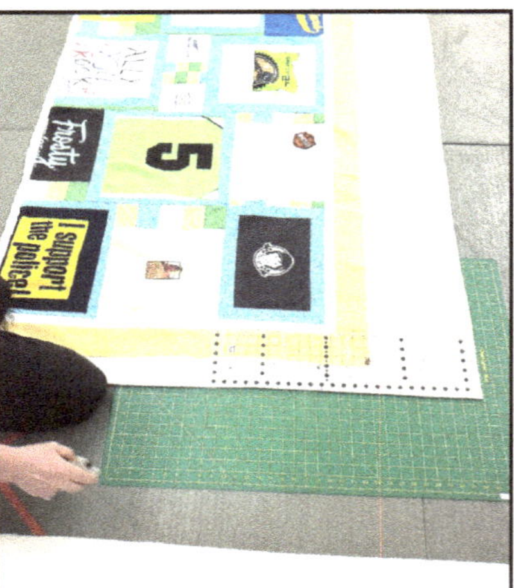

Batting is cut.

Types of batting: I love the loft and drape of 100% wool batting. This is my favorite when I am using a cotton material for the back of the quilt.

When I am using "cuddle" or a thicker back I will use a thinner batting such as 100% cotton or an 80/20 cotton/wool blend.

If your t-shirt is dark or your back is a dark color, you may want to use a black batting.

Chapter 9
The Quilting

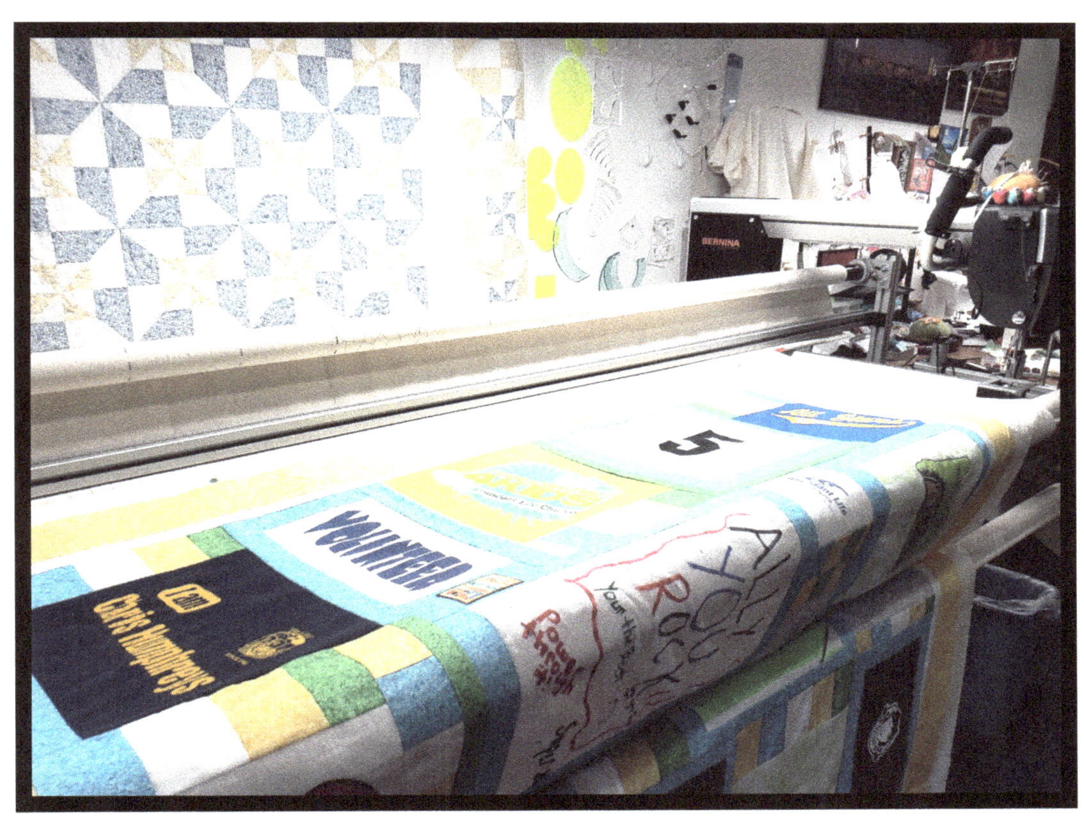

Quilt: for those of you who quilt with your domestic machine I applaud you! I have done simple straight line stitching that turned out beautifully. This type of quilting will let the piecing and material shine and be the focal points of the quilt.

For those of you who own your own longarm or who are sending your quilt to be longarmed, here are some ideas. Chose a thread that will complement the colors in the quilt. You can pick a color that will contrast if you want the thread to show one sentence a lot or you can pick a thread that will blend in with all the other colors (a).

Load the quilt on the long arm following the directions for your machine (b).

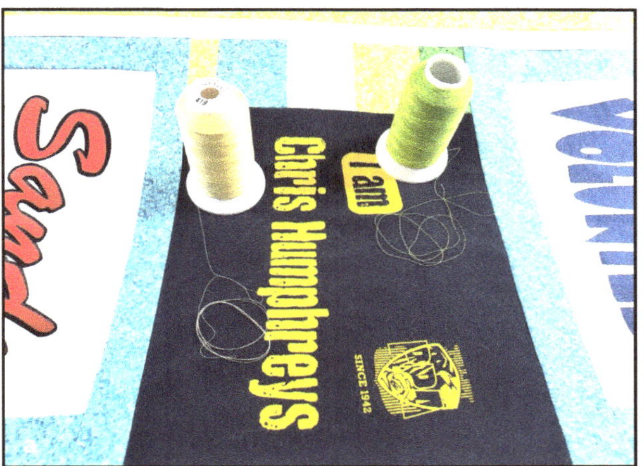
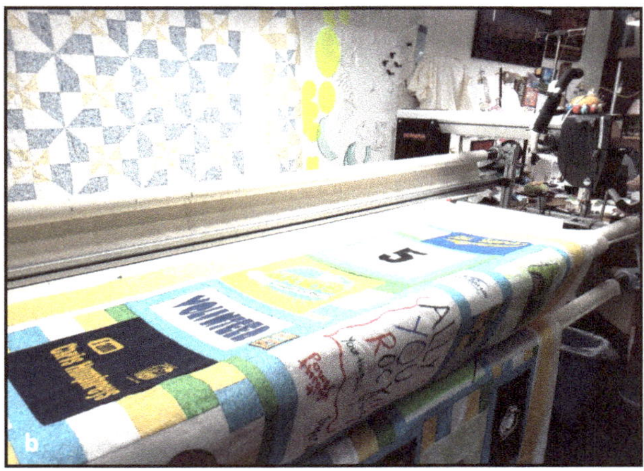

Start quilting. I like to do planned random designs in each square. By this, I mean that I plan to stay off heavily painted areas of a t-shirt logo, faces or important writing. On this quilt I am doing an all-over meander on the blocks and sashing.

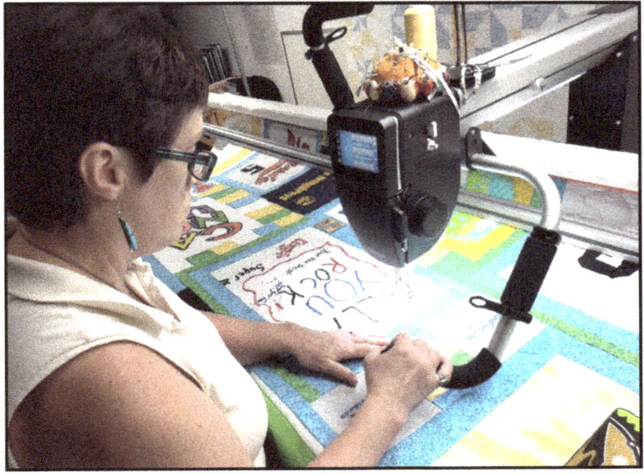
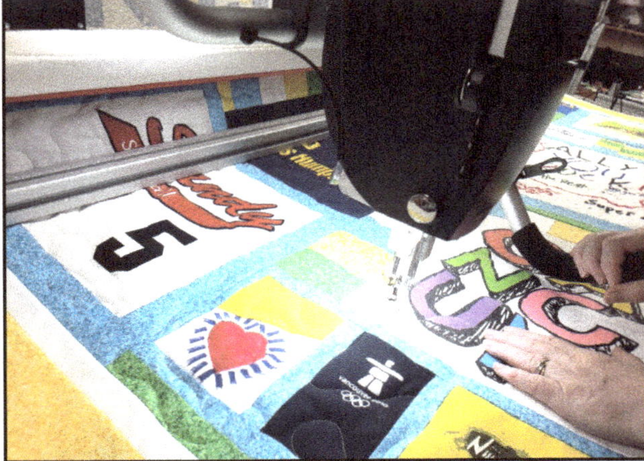

I tend to do the borders last. This is also where I add embellishments like patches.

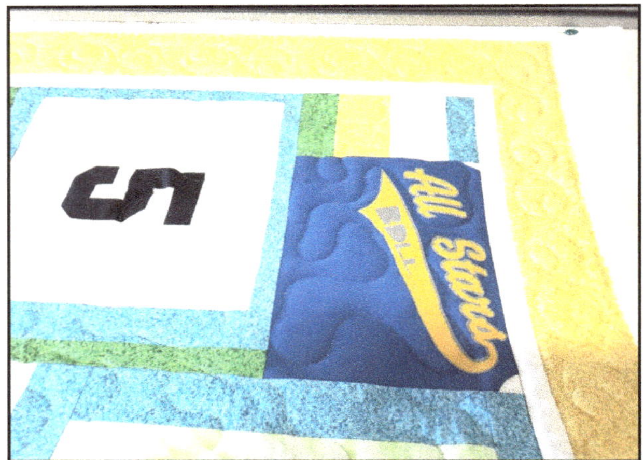

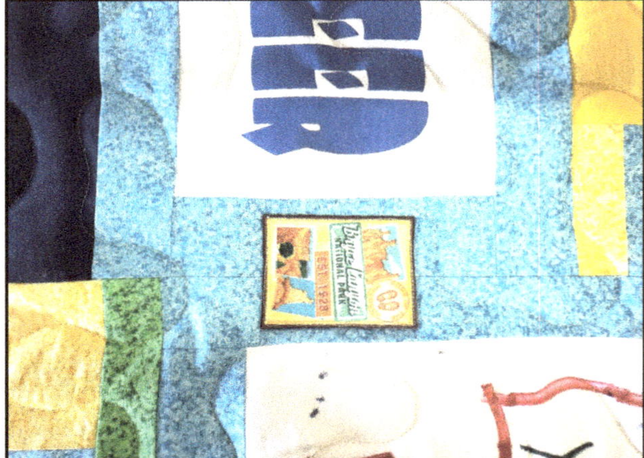

I will also quilt around pockets so that they are open and usable. I might change the quilting slightly to fit the way a particular t-shirt is. I also might add another patch to a plain shirt.

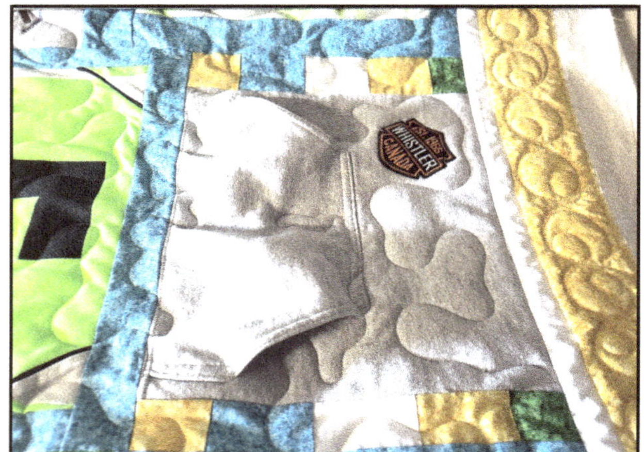

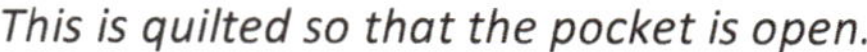

This is quilted so that the pocket is open.

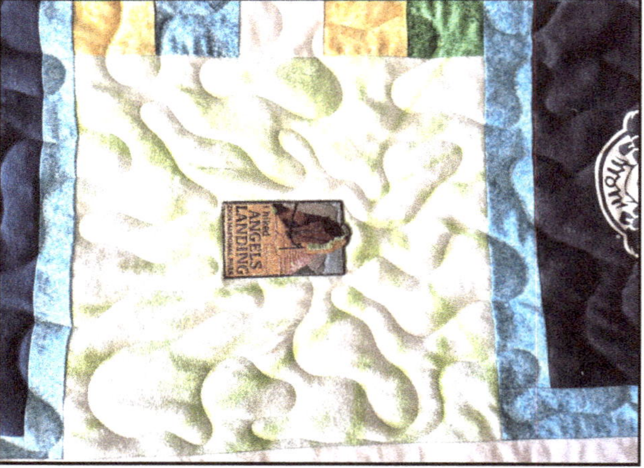

This is a plain T-shirt with embellishment.

I will meander around names and try to stay off the logos as much as possible.

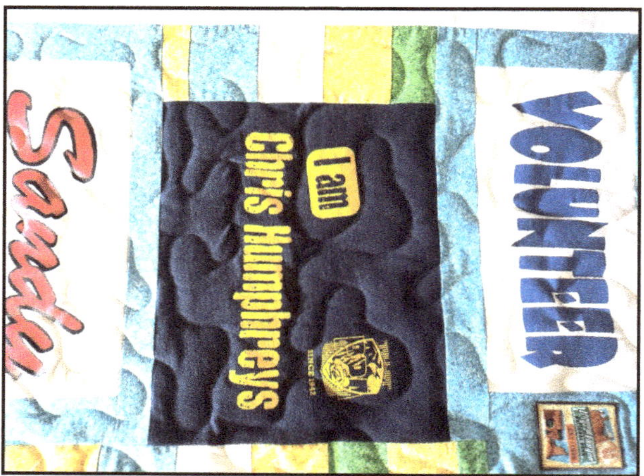

I might put another patch in the sashing to balance out where other patches have been placed.

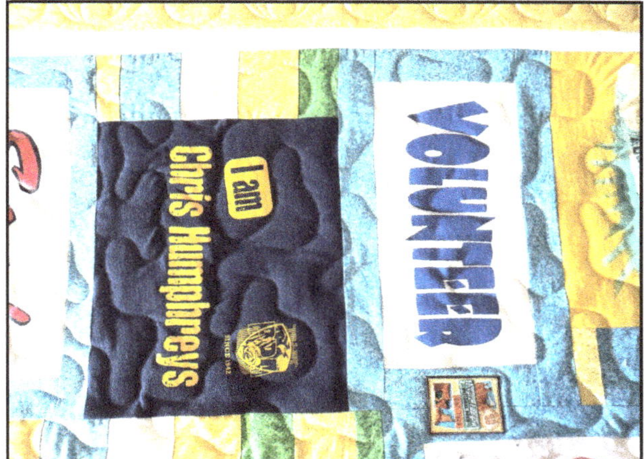

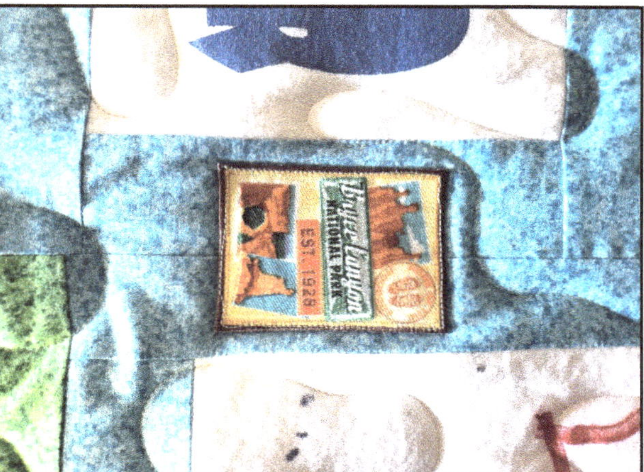

These patches had glue on the back and could be ironed on. I ironed them on to keep them in place and then I sewed them on using the longarm (a). I stitched in the ditch around the outer sashing. This really adds to the framing of the quilt and will make the center "Pop" (b).

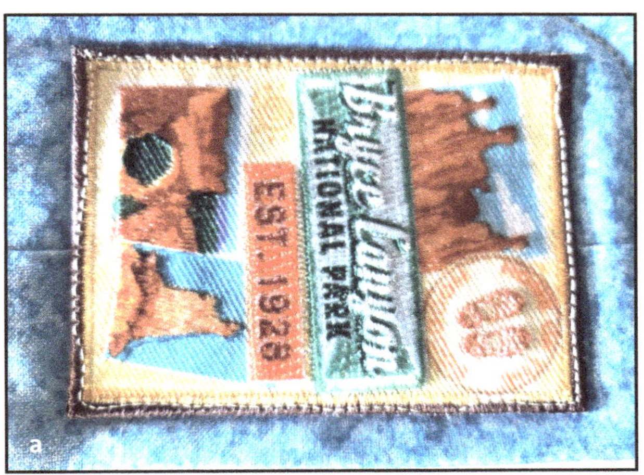

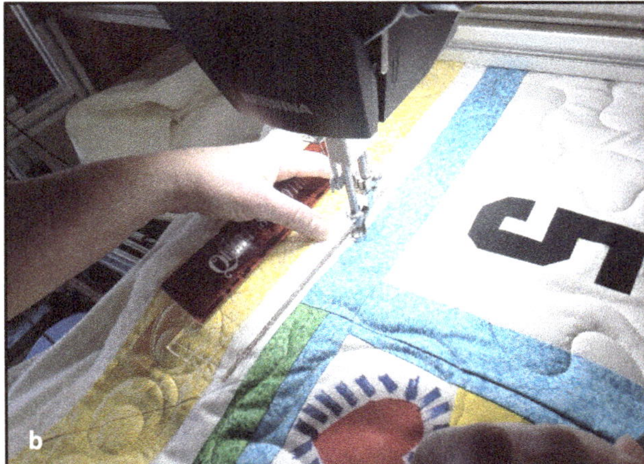

Chapter 10
Square It Up & Bind

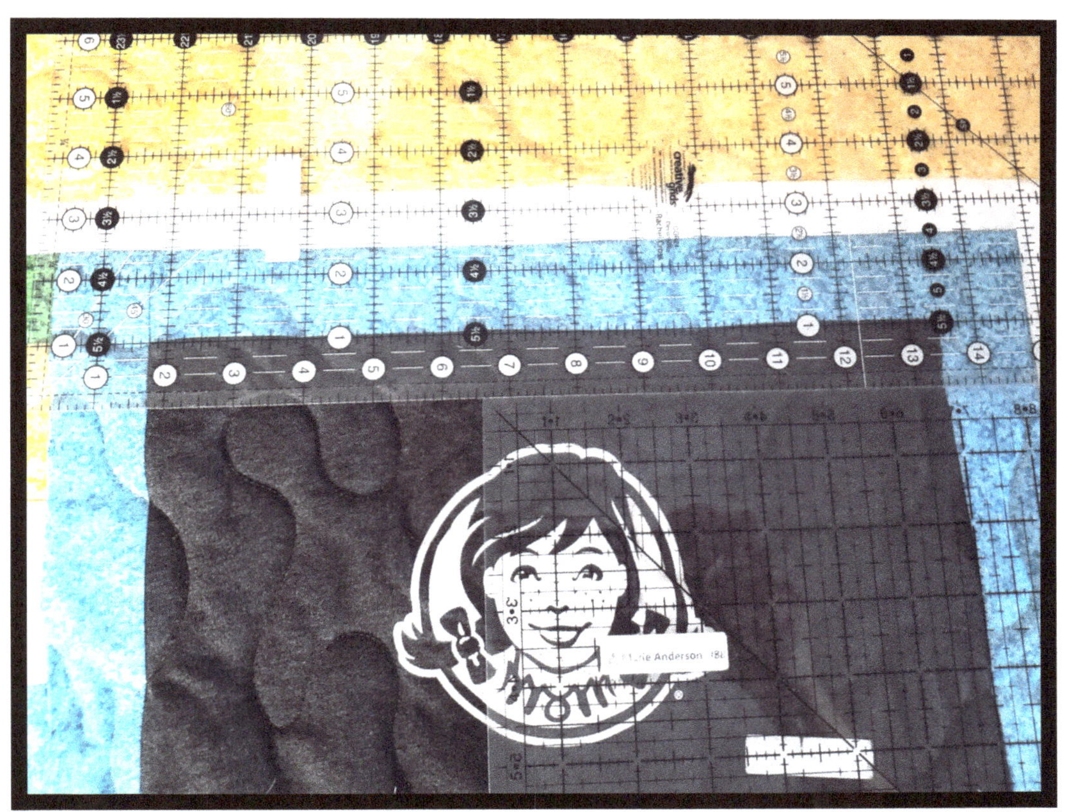

CHAPTER 10 - SQUARE IT UP AND BIND

Cutting off the excess edges. I like to use a table, cutting mat, rotary cutter and my 6 1/2 by 24 ½ inch ruler with my 12 ½ x12 ½ inch ruler (a). I usually cut a straight line just on the outside of my top fabric (b). Notice how I use my 12 ½ X 12 ½ ruler to the left of the 6 ½ x 24 ½ ruler (c). This keeps my long ruler at a 90 degree   angle and makes my corner square (d). If you have done a good job piecing, everything will line up (e). If you have not....cut as close to square as you can (f).

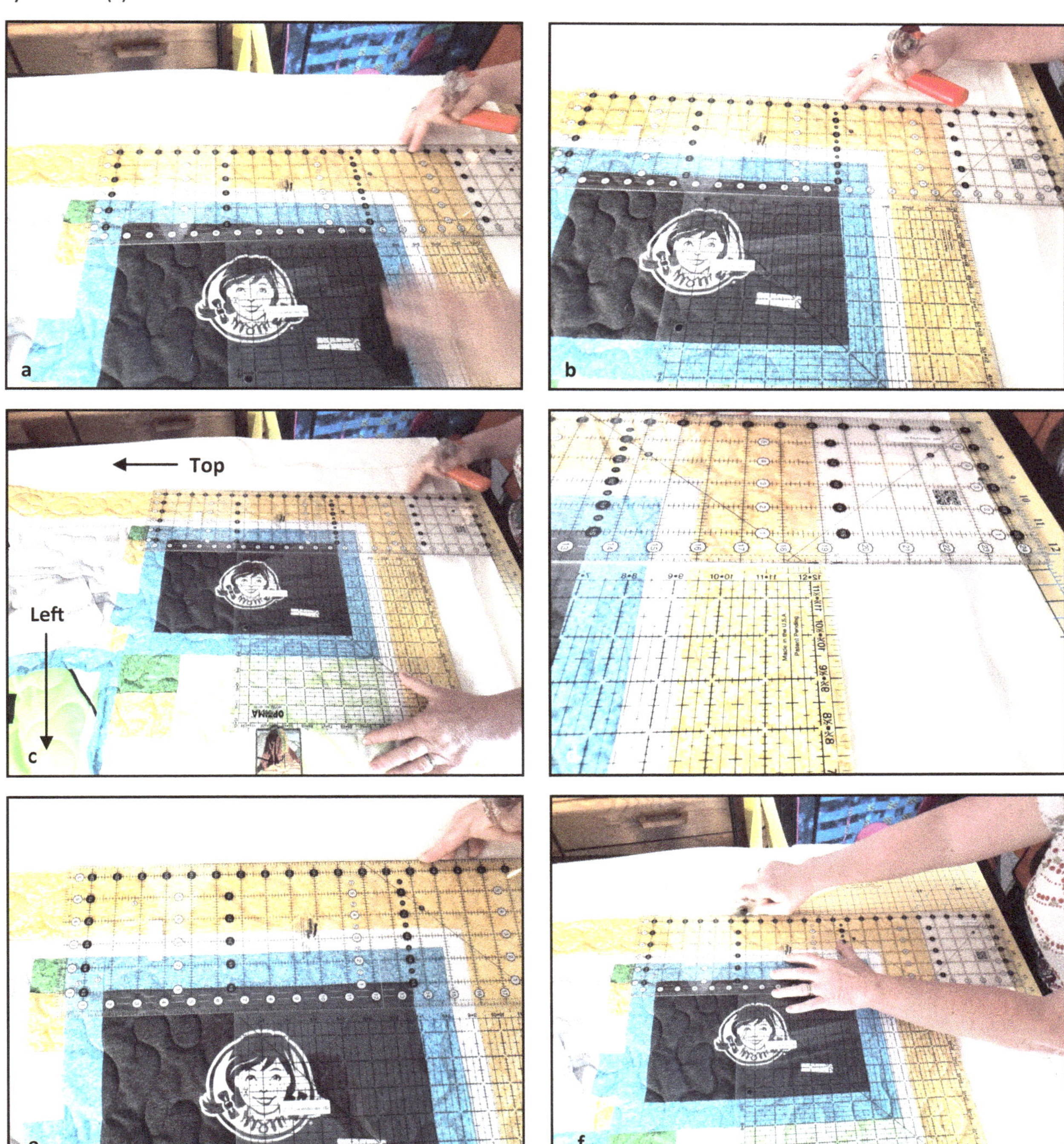

Continue up the edge of the quilt, lining up the ruler so that it is square. Cut all the way through to the next corner. Turn the quilt, square it up with 2 rulers and continue for the remaining 3 sides.

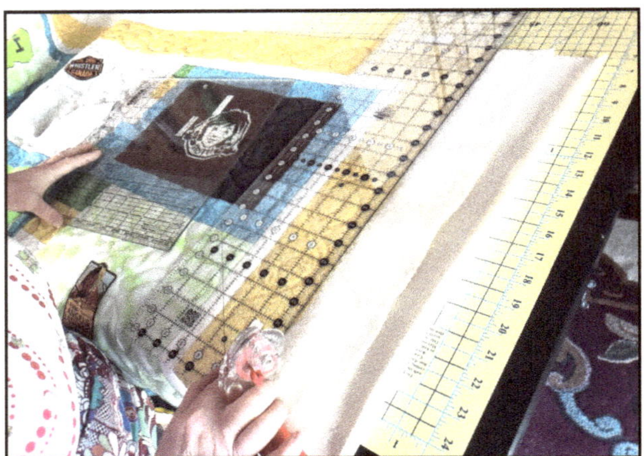 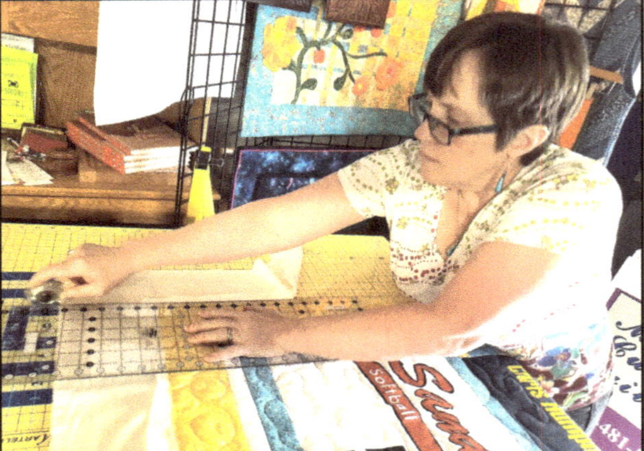

Binding: I make my binding 2 ½ inches wide. Some people like a thinner binding, some like it wider. As you make more quilts you will have your favorite. Measure 2 ½ inch using the two rulers.

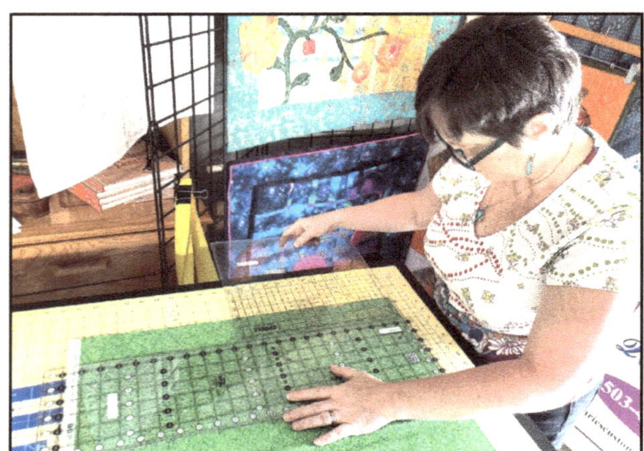 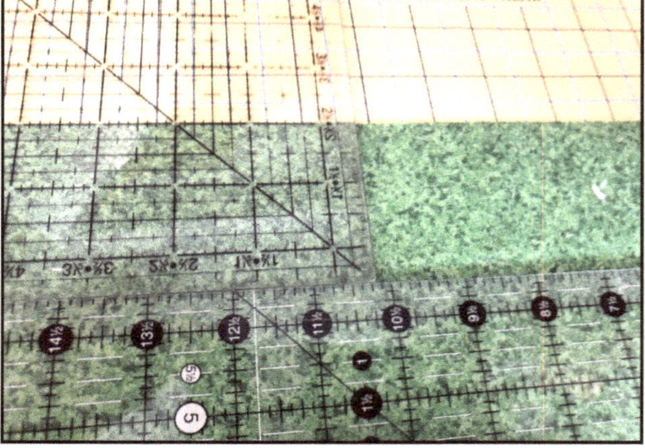

Cut several strips.

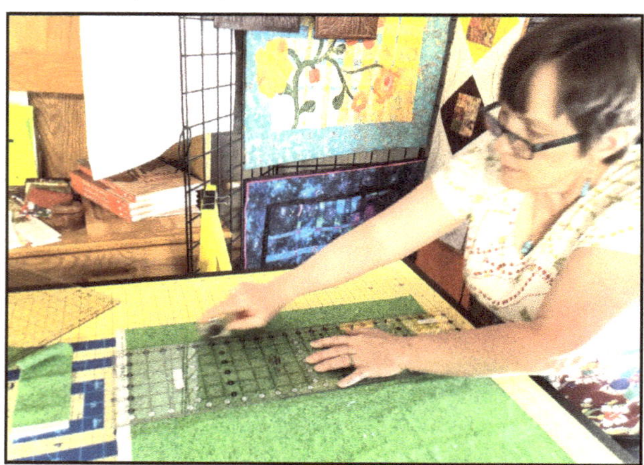 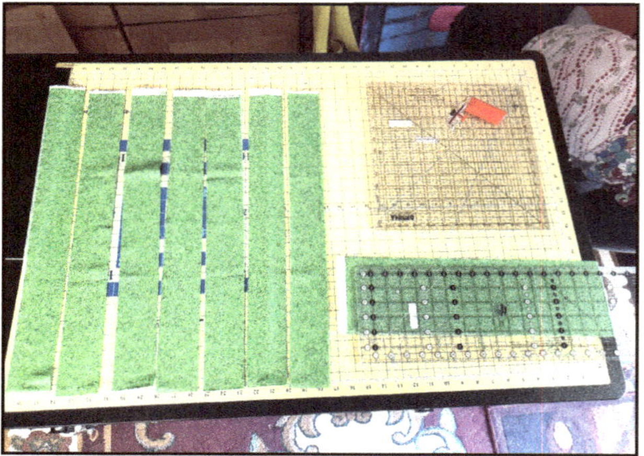

Place two strips end to end at 45 degree angles. The reason you sew at an angle is to reduce the bulk in the binding. It makes it easier when you are attaching the binding to the quilt (a). Use a ruler and pencil or chalk pen to draw a line at an angle (b, c & d).

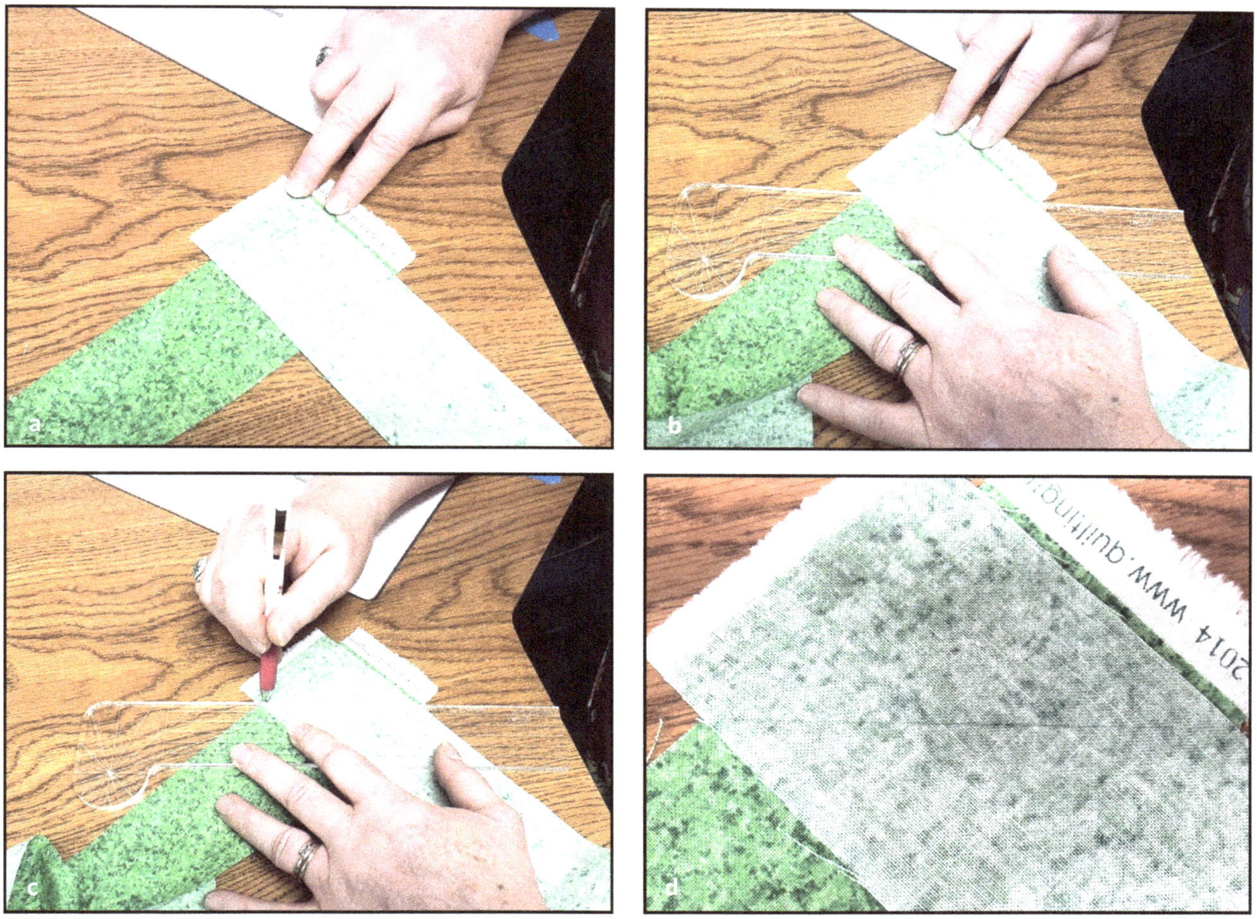

Pin the fabric to stabilize it (lower left). Position at the machine needle (lower right).

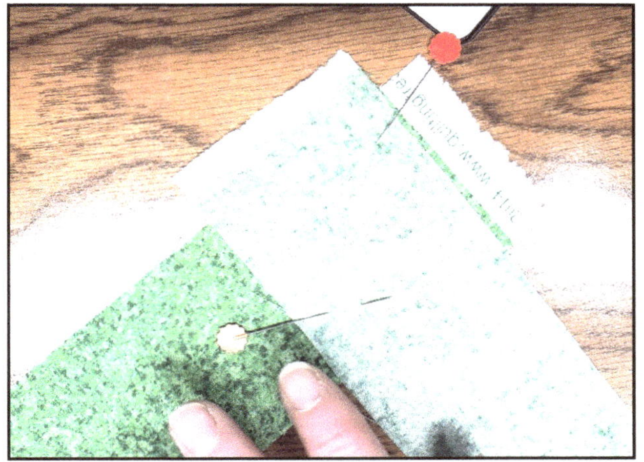
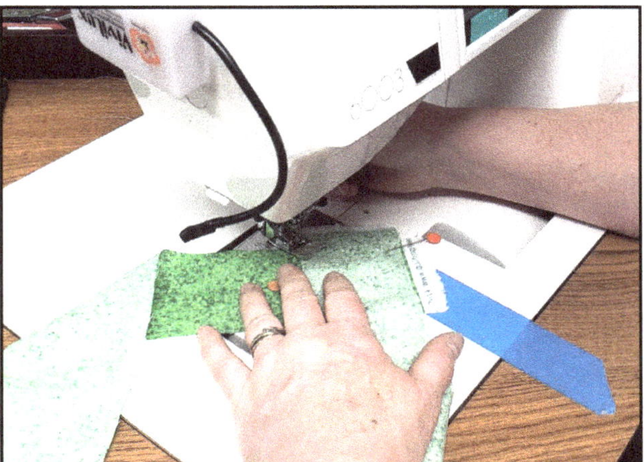

Sew down the line that you drew. Cut off the edges.

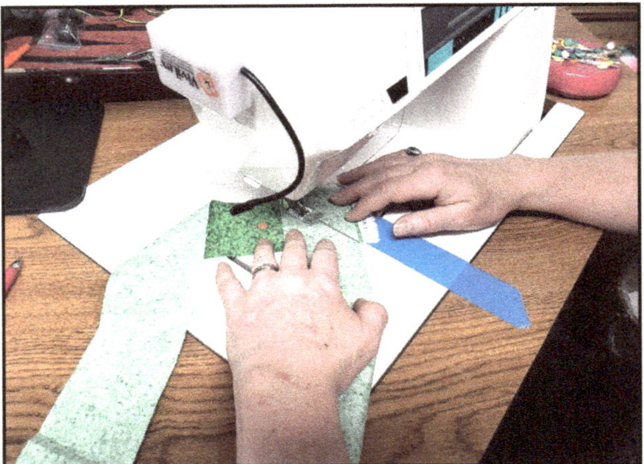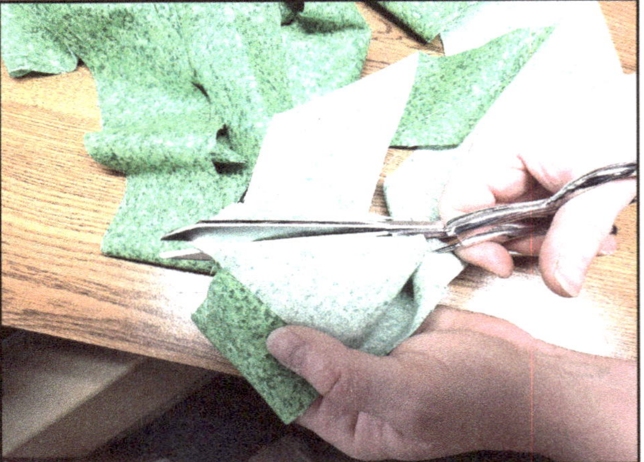

Just a funny note. As I was doing this I had a pile of binding pieces that I was sewing together – end to end. I wasn't paying attention and I grabbed a wrong end and had this as the result! Remember to laugh and have fun as you do this! I cut it apart and fixed my mistake.

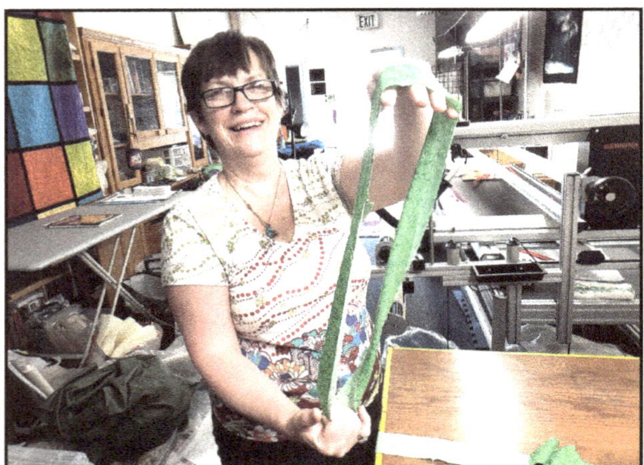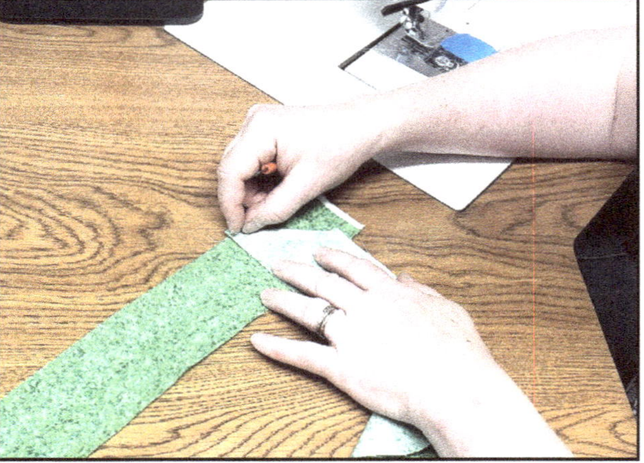

Fold your binding in half long ways and attach it to the quilt leaving an extra 2 inches at the top.

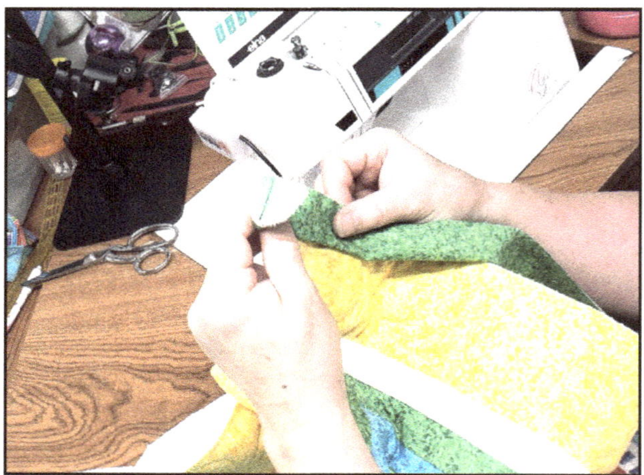

Measure ¼ inch in from the edge at the corner and mark with a pin.

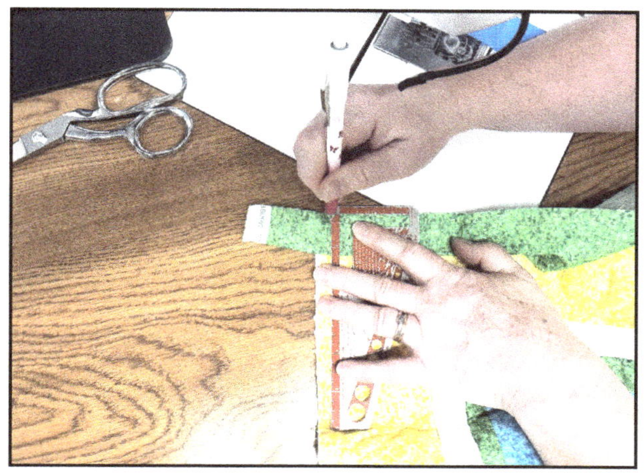
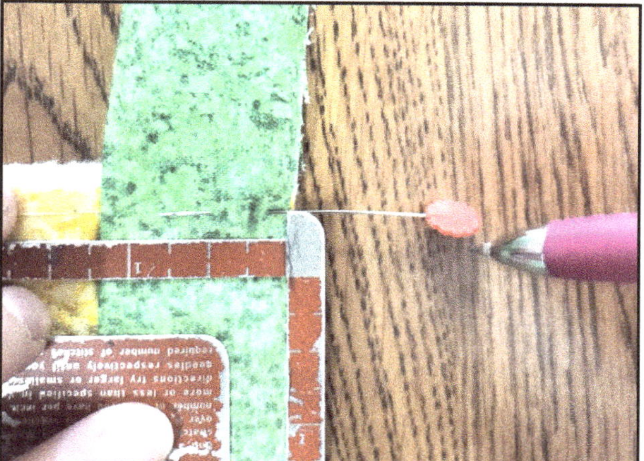

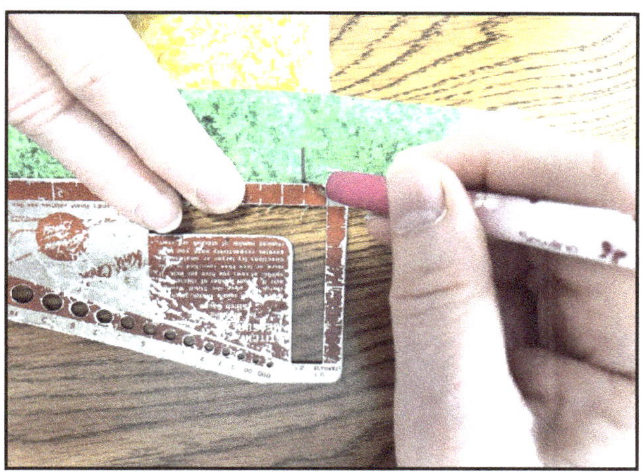
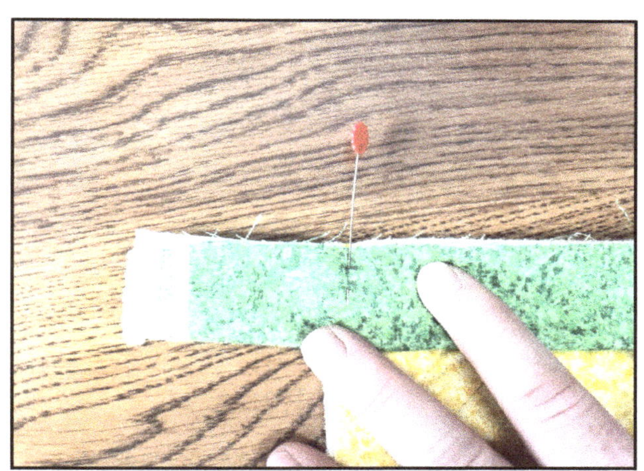

Start sewing at the mark that you made.

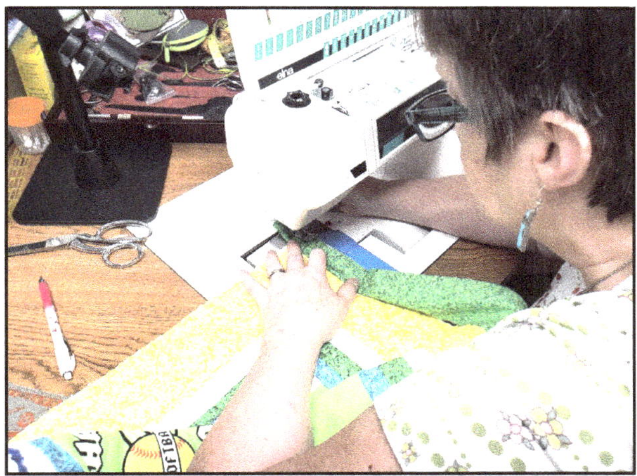
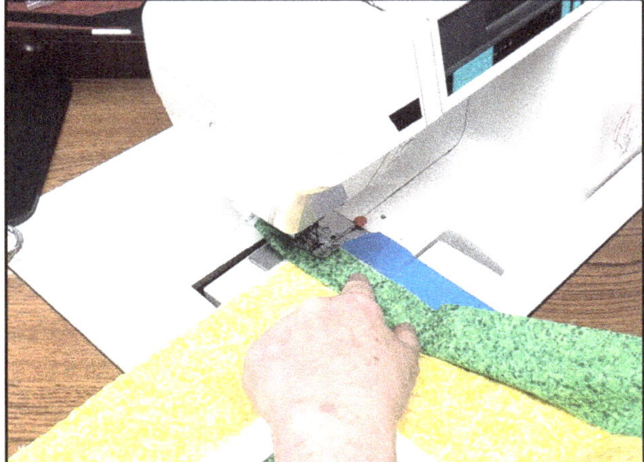

Continue sewing, lining up the binding with the quilt.

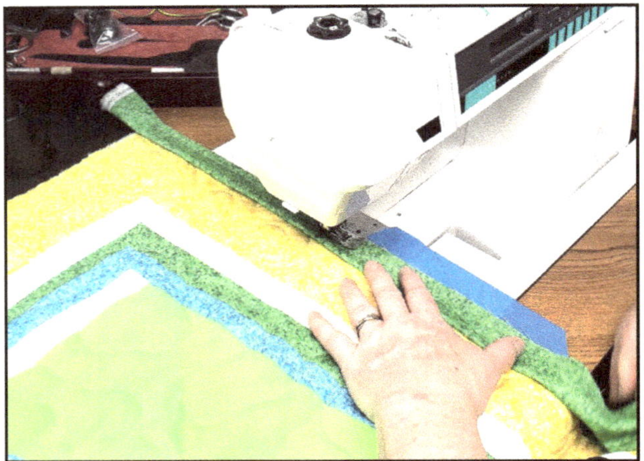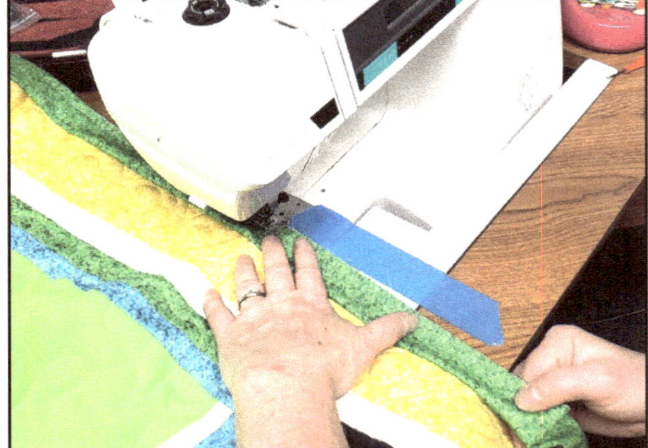

Sew to the next corner and mark ¼ inch inside.

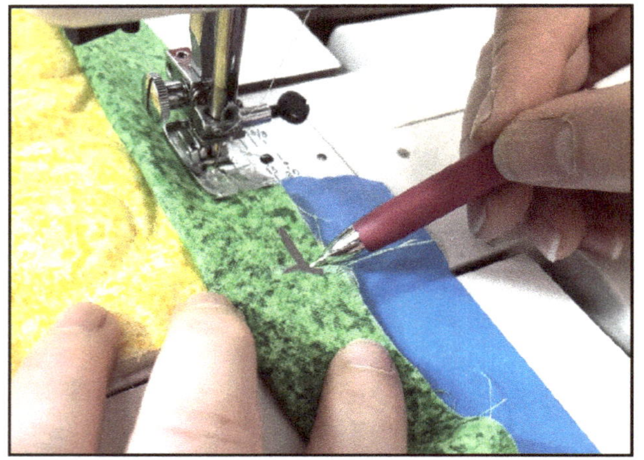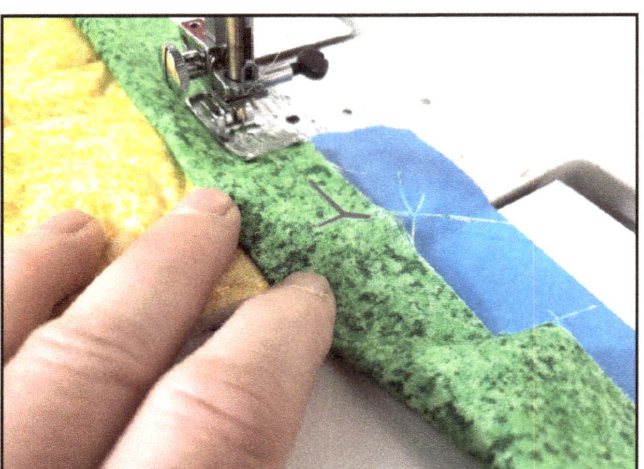

Sew backwards so the stitching doesn't unravel.

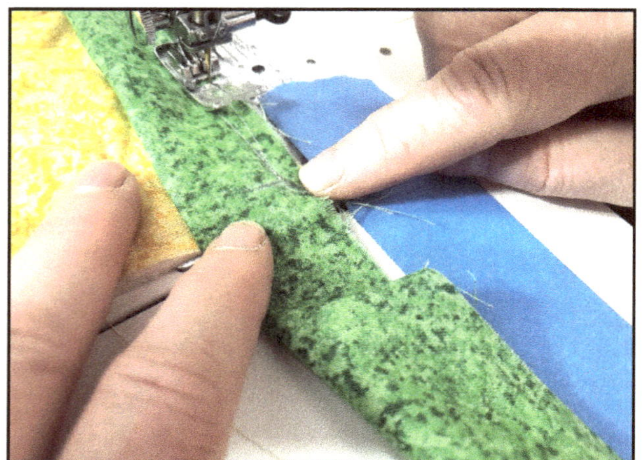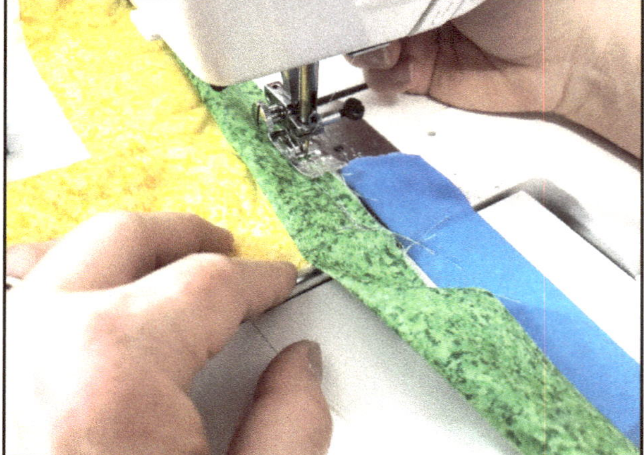

Remove from the machine, fold the binding like you are making hospital bed corners and then pin it.

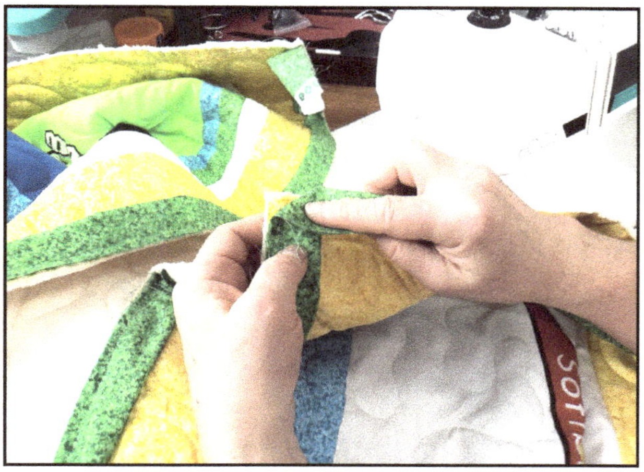

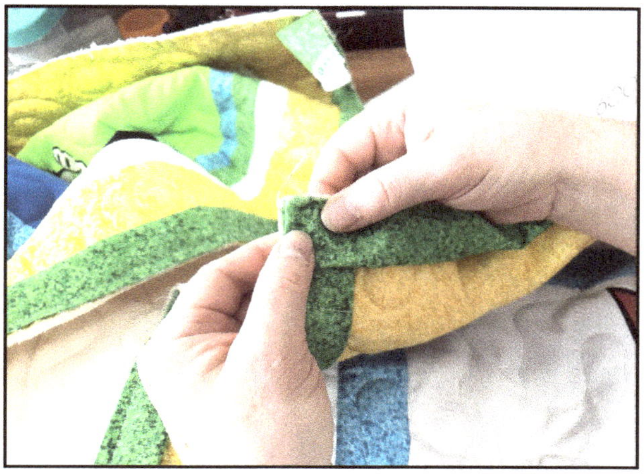

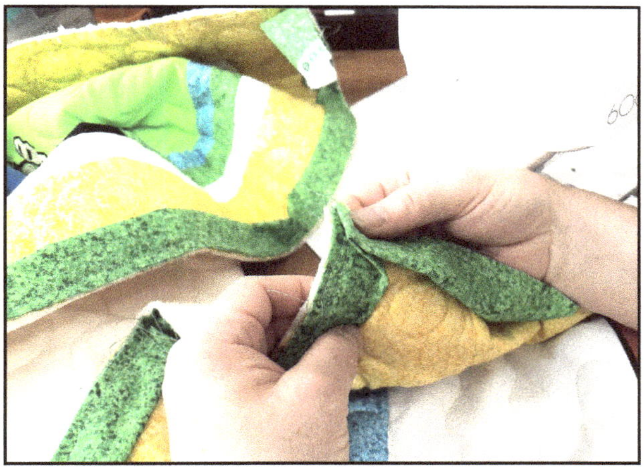

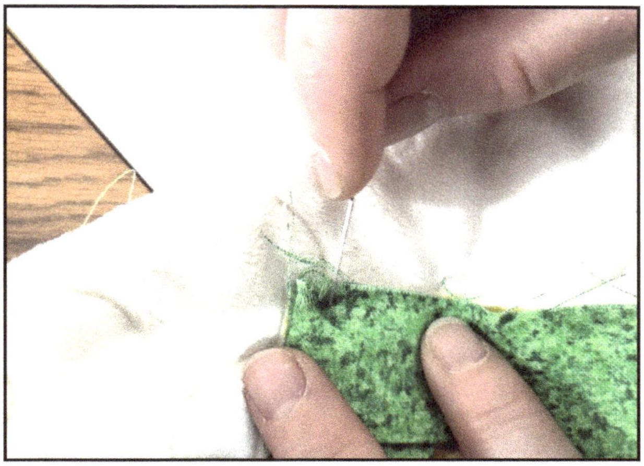

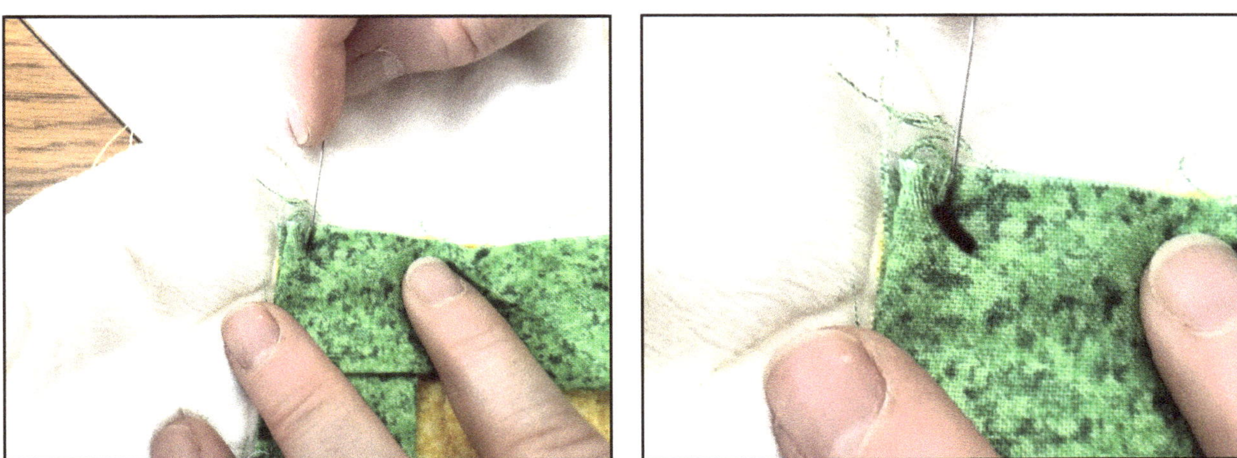

Mark a ¼ inch in at an angle.

Start sewing at the mark.

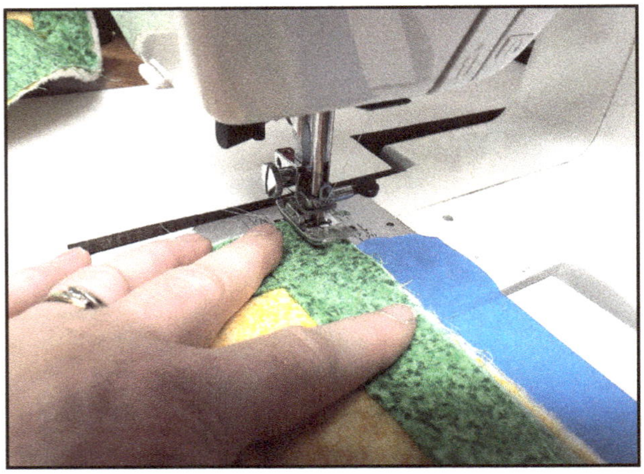

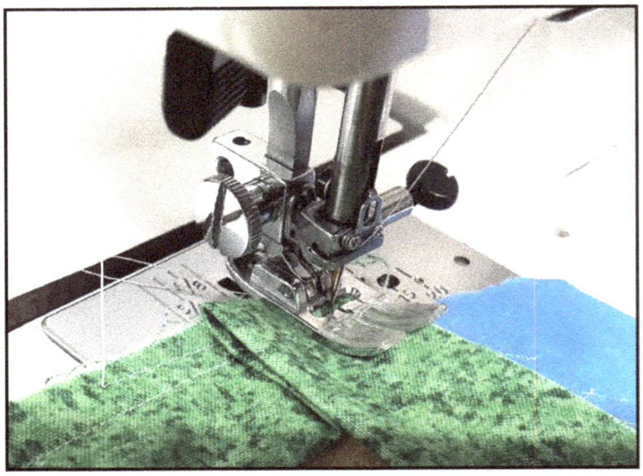

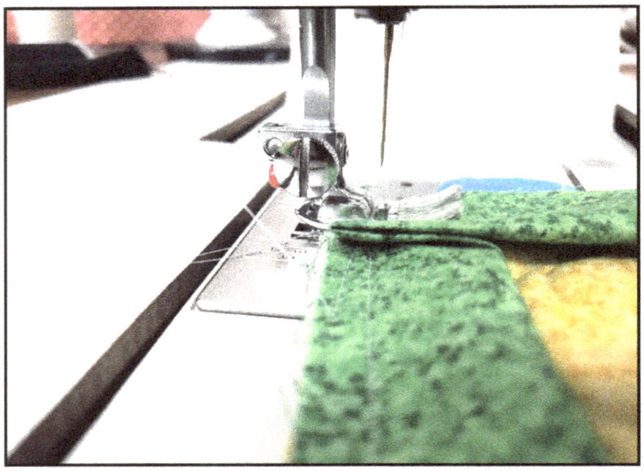

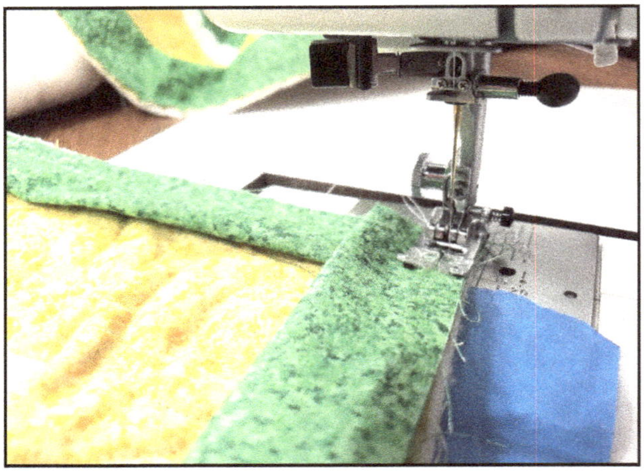

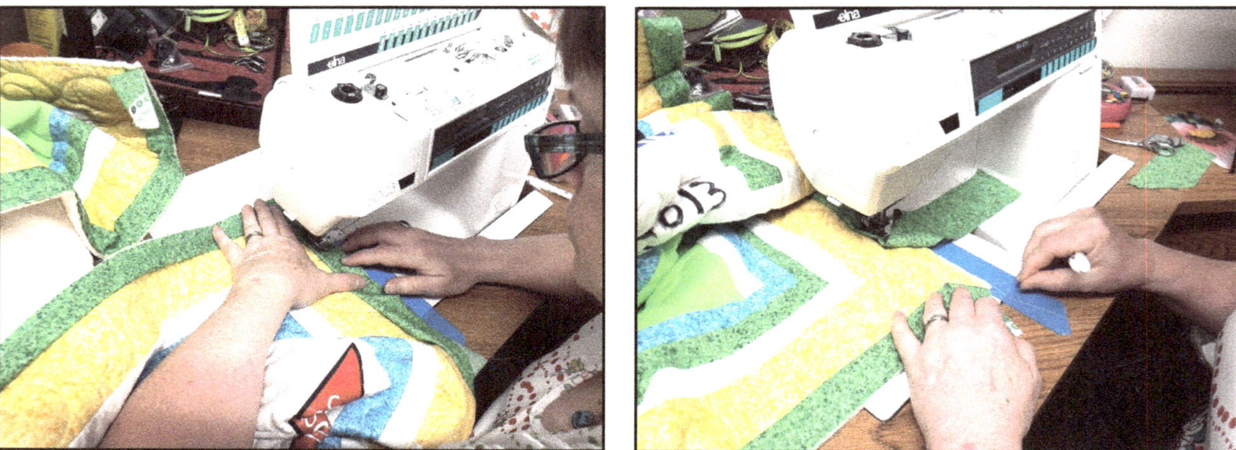

Continue sewing down the next side and subsequent corners until you get back to where you started.

Sew the binding all the way to the angle at the corner of where you started. Mark the fabric so you can tell how far to sew.

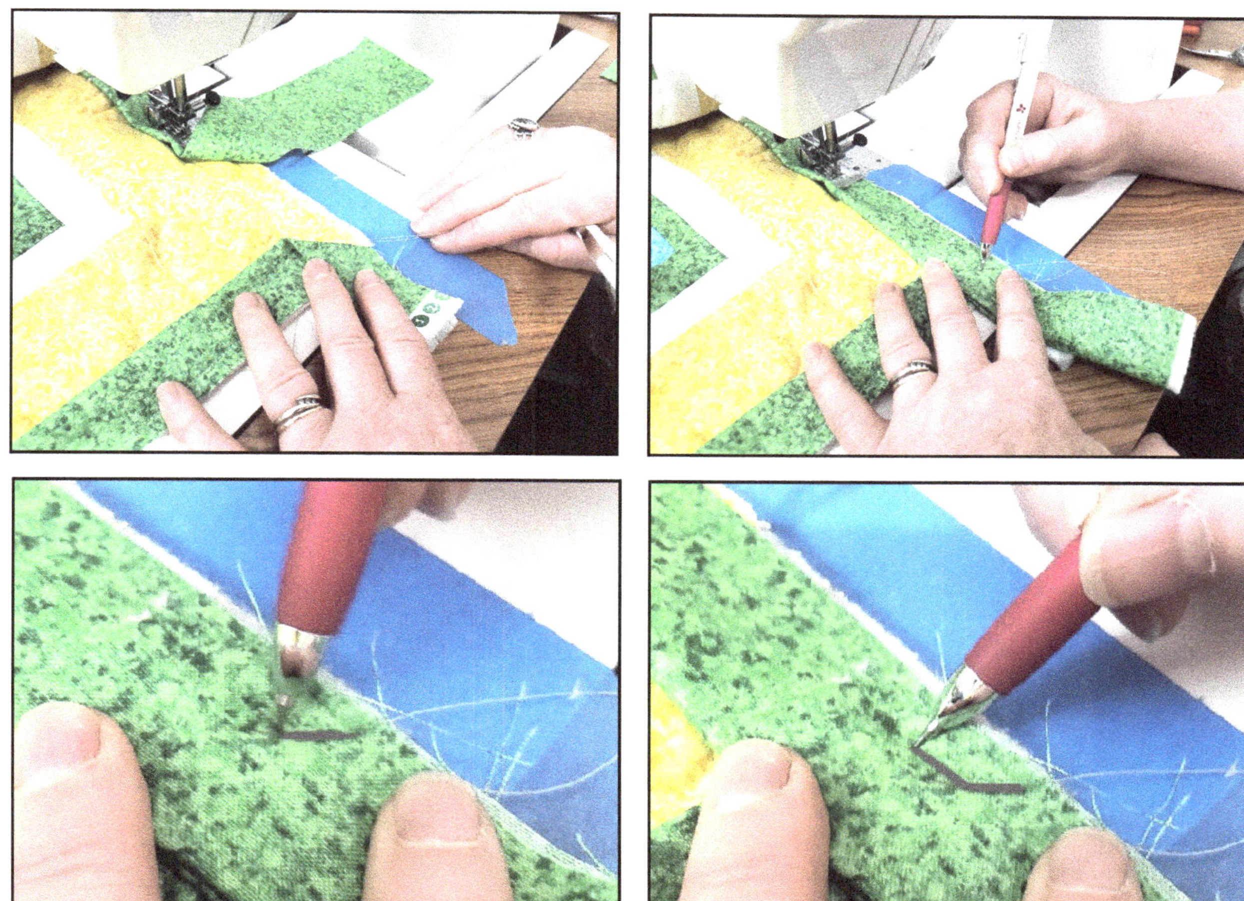

Sew to the end and back stitch.

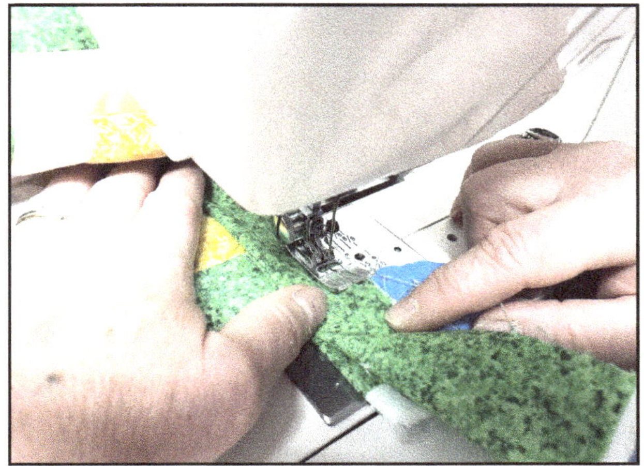

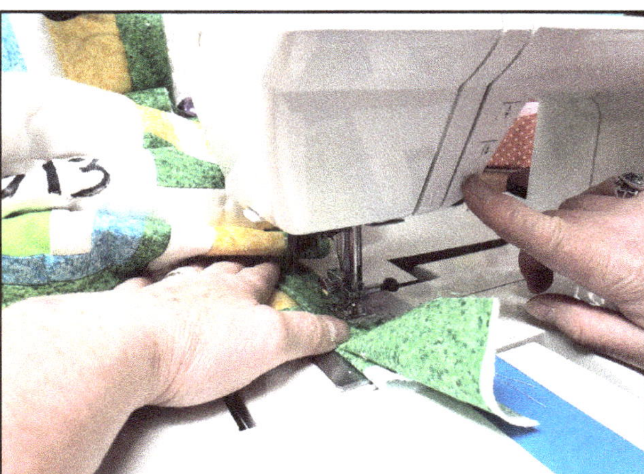

Now back stitch to keep the stitching from unraveling.

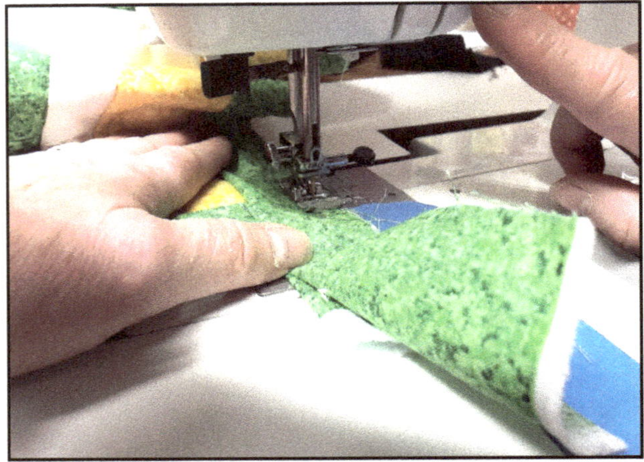 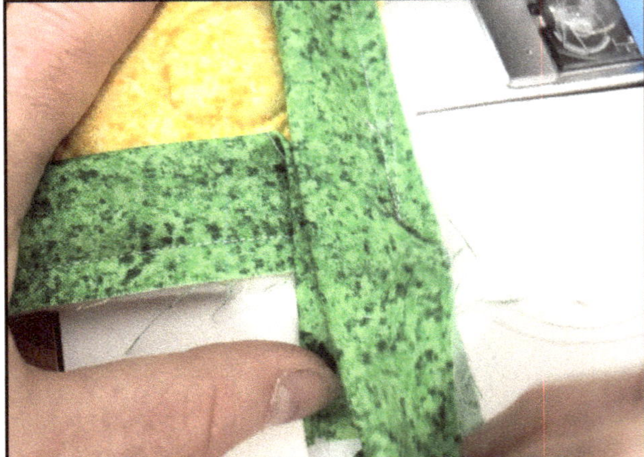

If you stitched it correctly it should look like this!

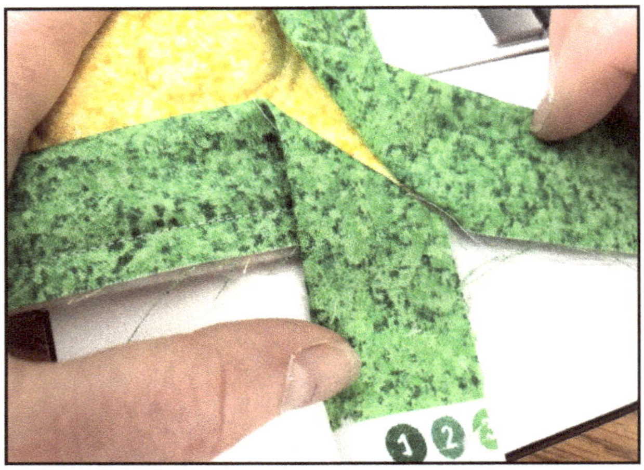

Miter this corner of the quilt: Pull the bindings flat with right sides together so that the corner of the quilt folds to a triangle and pin.

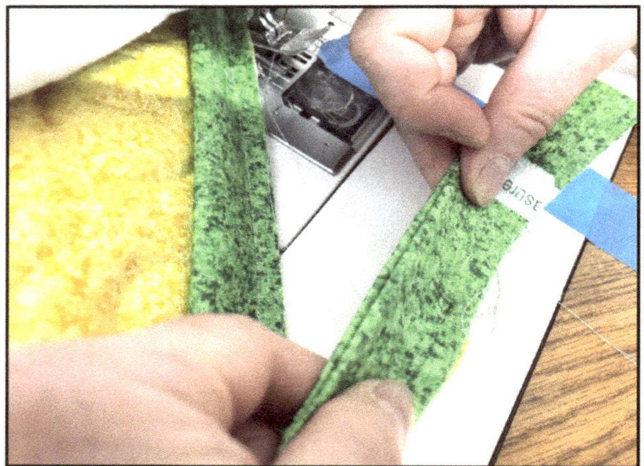 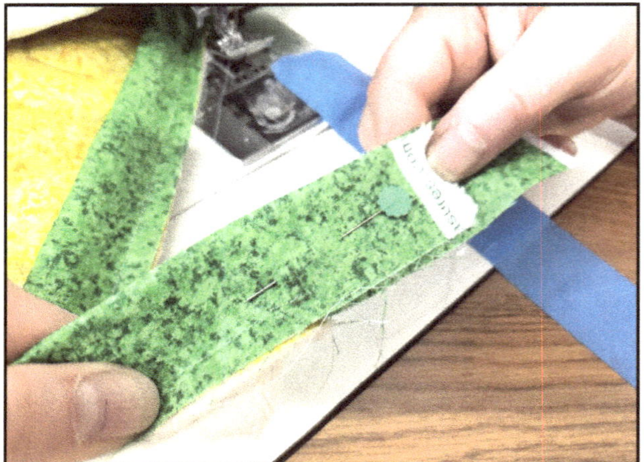

See how the bindings are flat and the quilt is folded in the corner. Draw a triangle that is wider than it is tall.

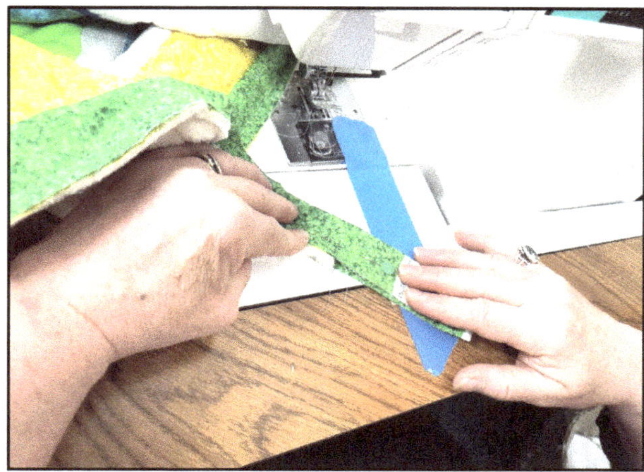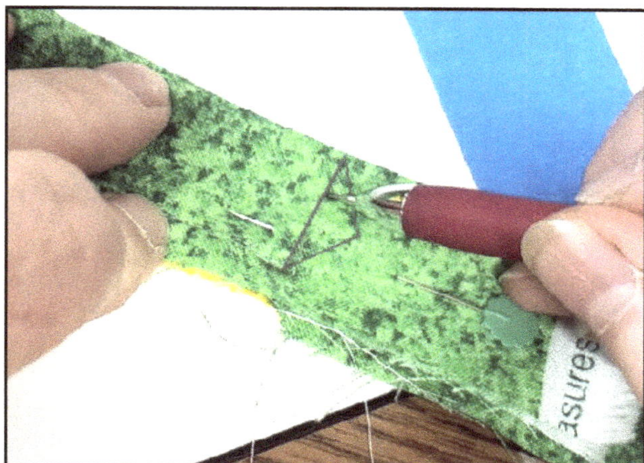

You can use a tool for this (below left) or just draw it freehand (below right).

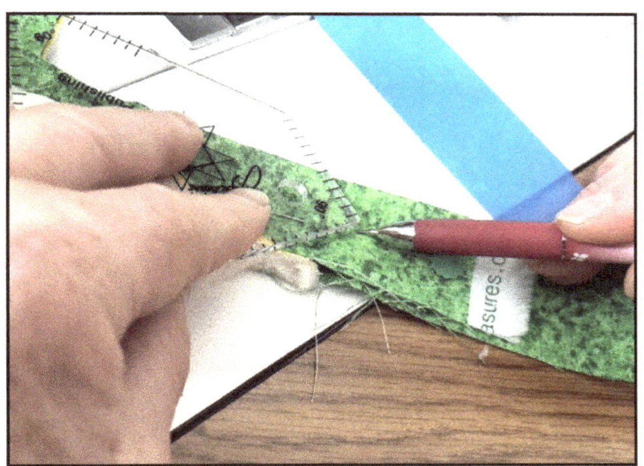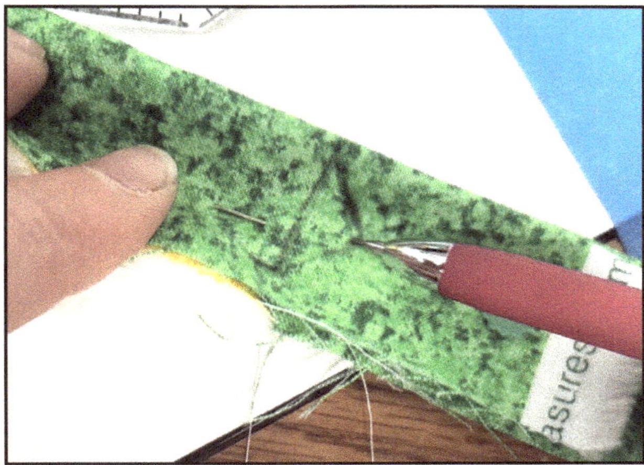

Sew the triangle top. The photo at far right shows the completed sewing.

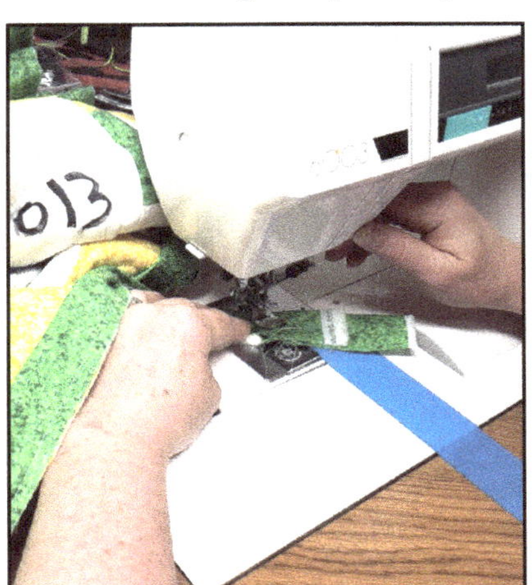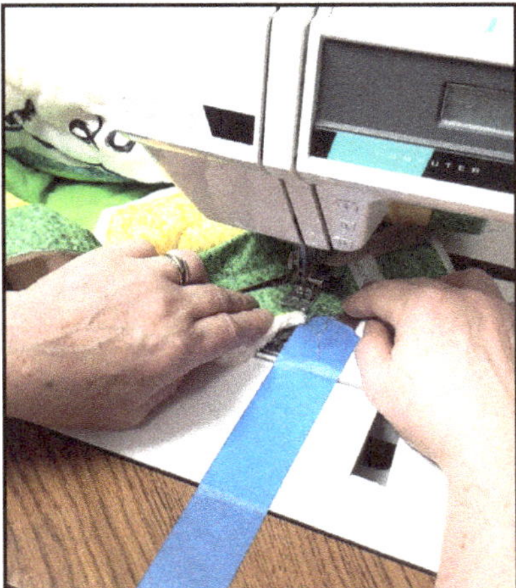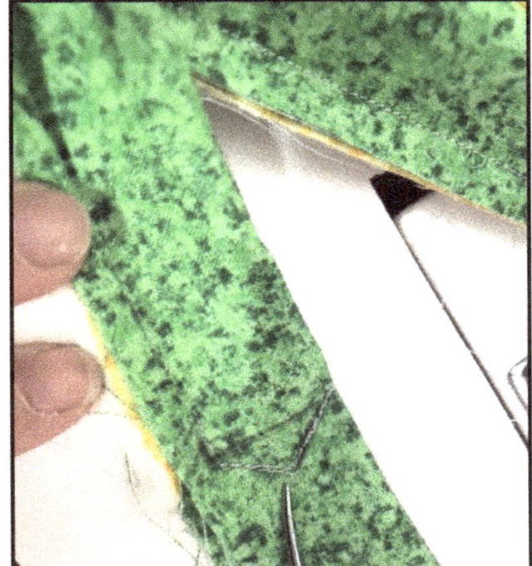

Trim the corner. Cut the batting in the corner to reduce bulk.

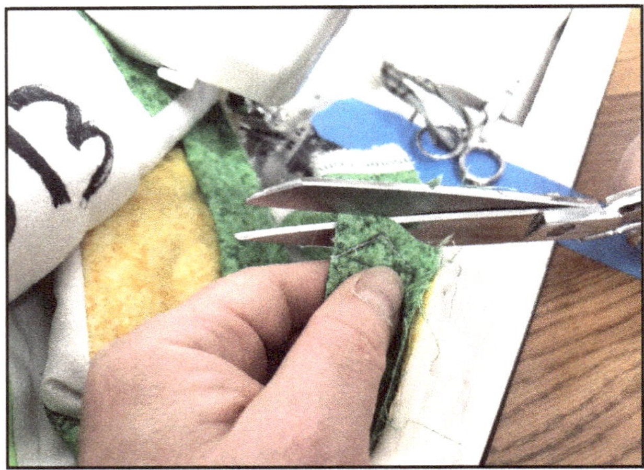

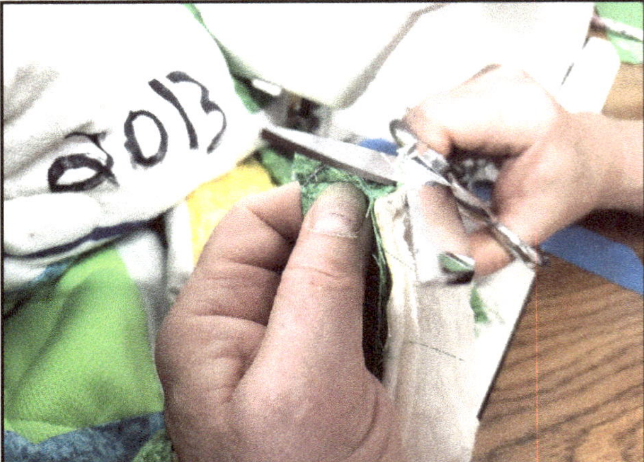

Turn the right side out.

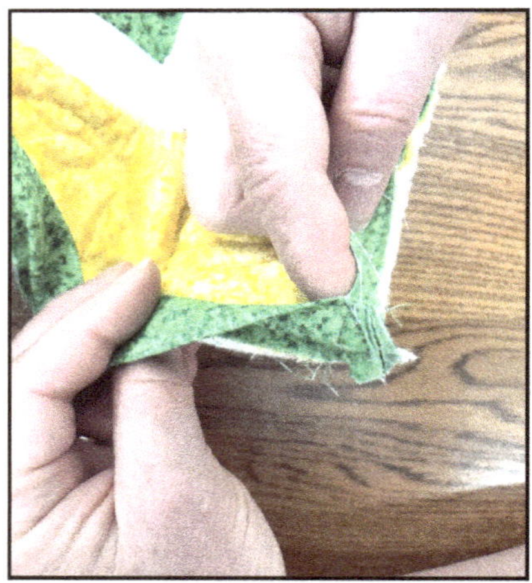

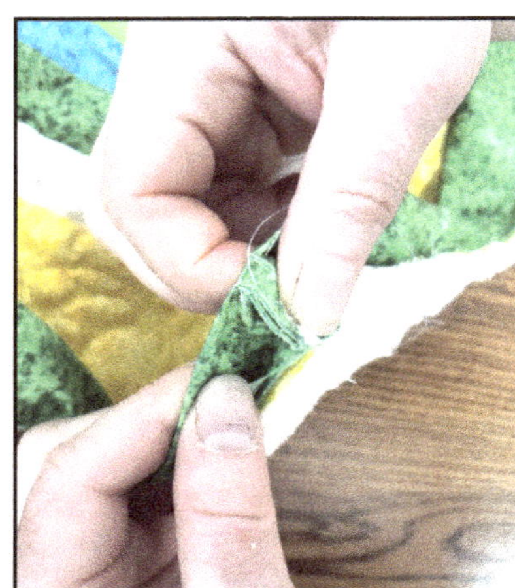

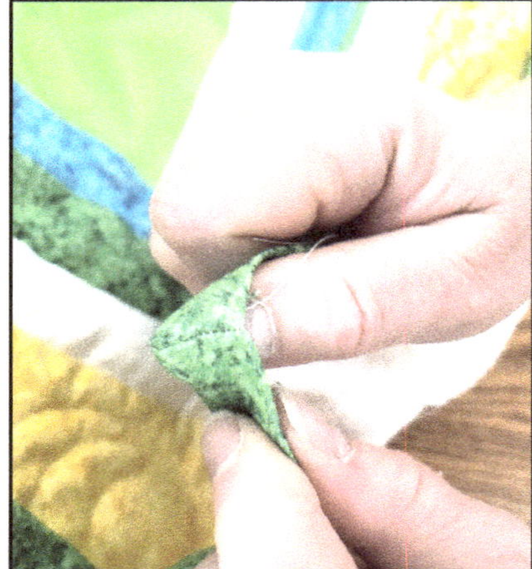

To make the corner nice and square you can use a chop stick or a pin.   Here is a finished corner.

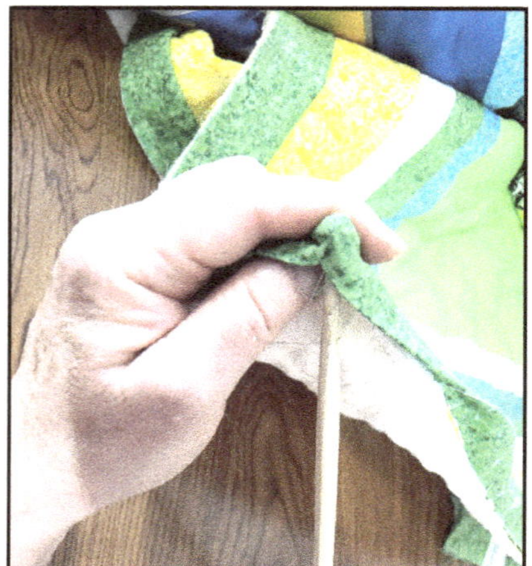

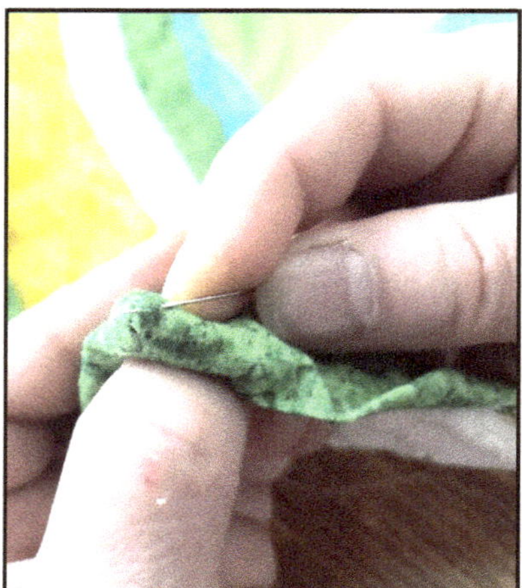

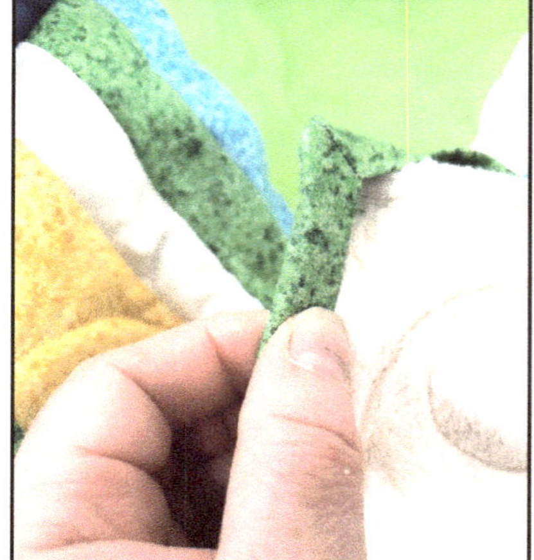

Iron the binding so that it goes out straight from the quilt.

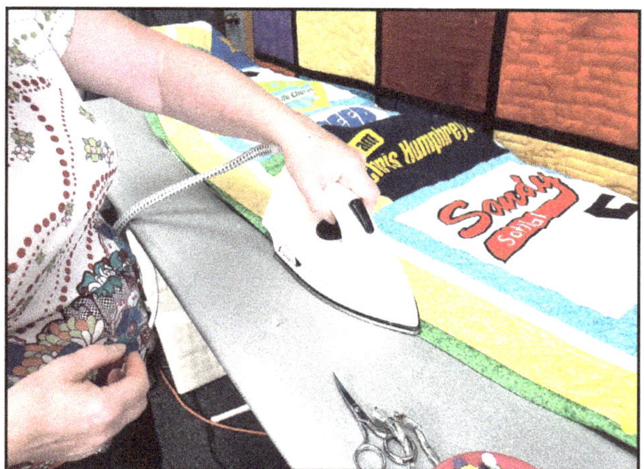
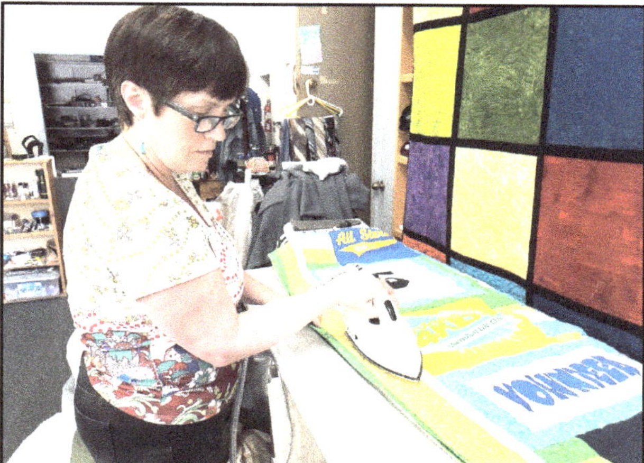

Trim the corner batting to reduce bulk . Flip the corners as you iron the binding away from the quilt.

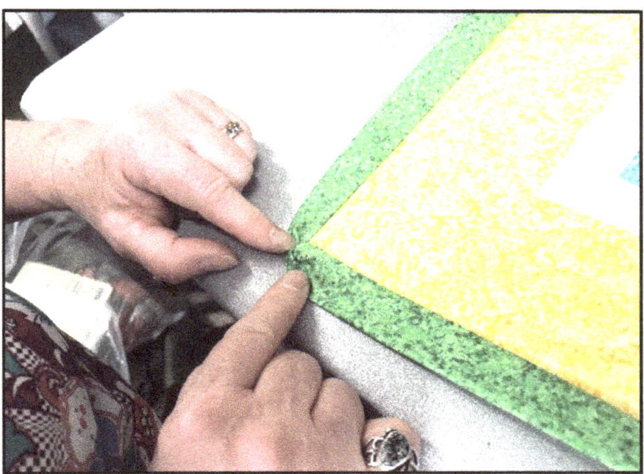
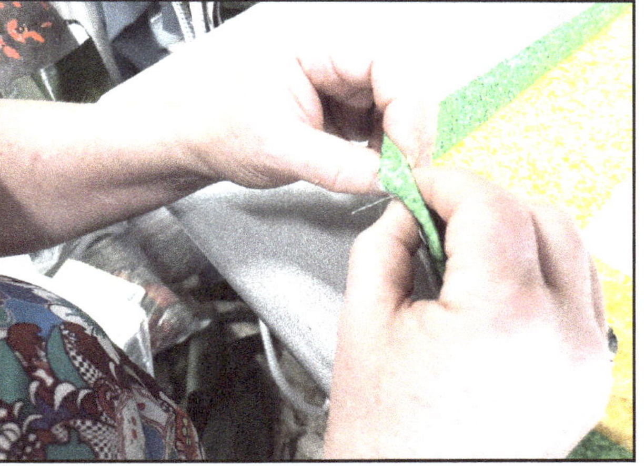

I've trimmed the corner batting and reduced the bulk (above). This makes it easier to make a nice, sharp corner.

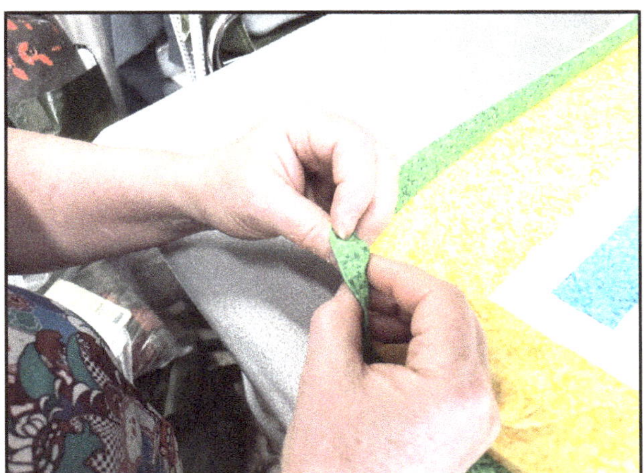
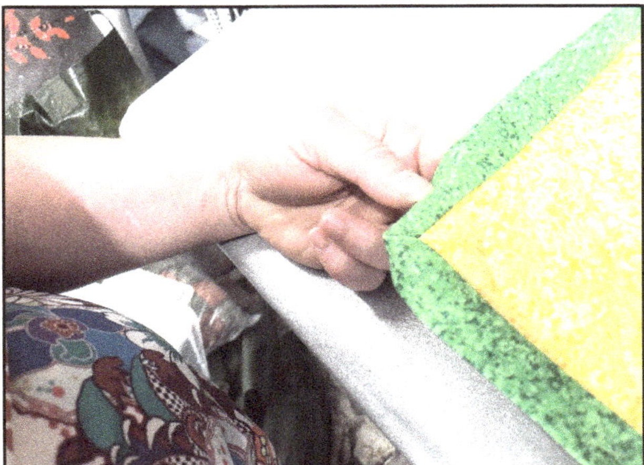

Fold the binding over and start to pin in place.

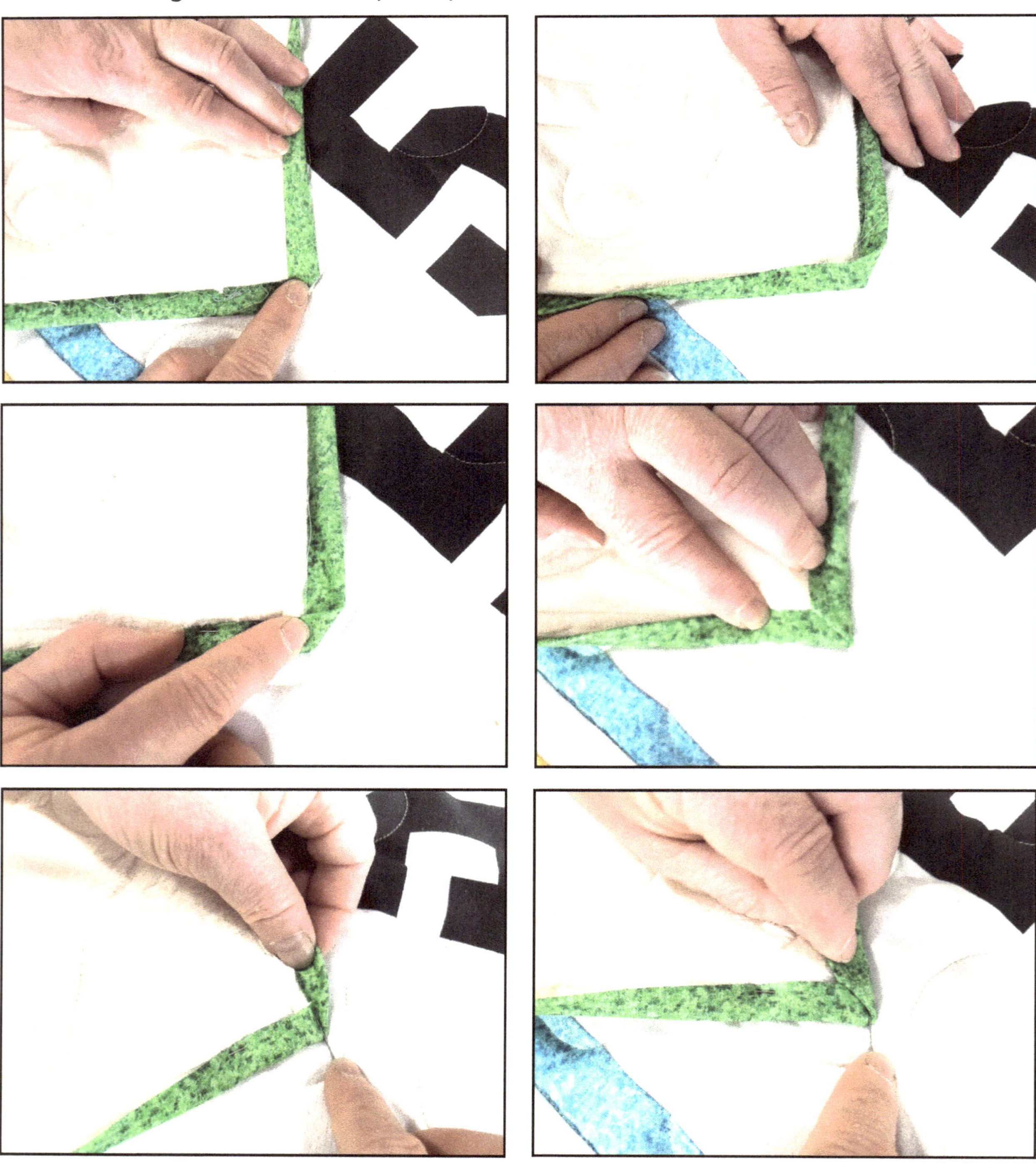

Here is what it will look like from the front of the quilt. Pin all the way around (back side view of quilt).

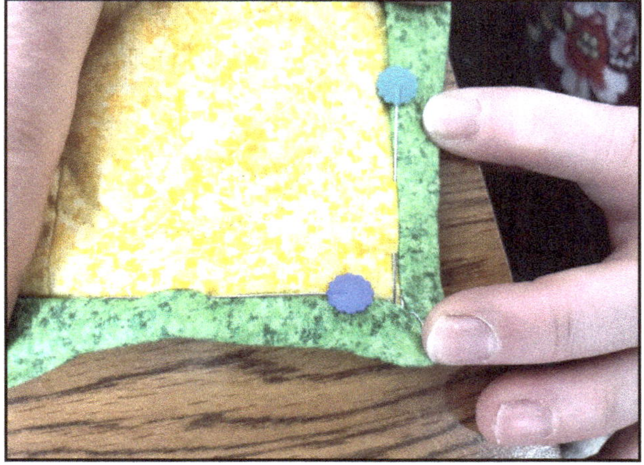
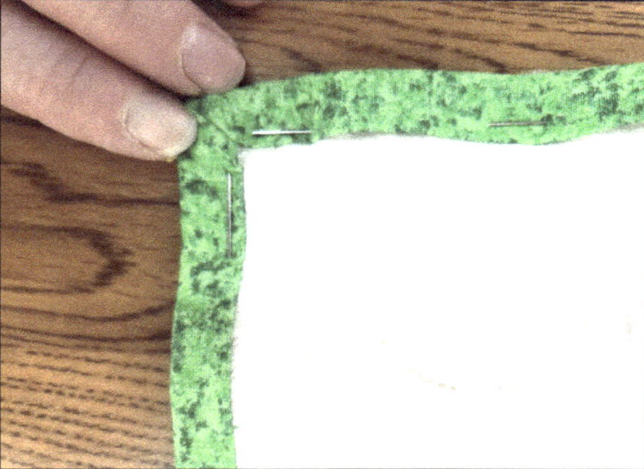

I pin a lot on this step. Since I am sewing the binding viewing from the top, I can't see the underside of the quilt. I pin the binding so that the I am catching the binding edge underside the quilt as I sew. This way I don't have to worry about missing the underside binding edge and then have to redo it all over again.

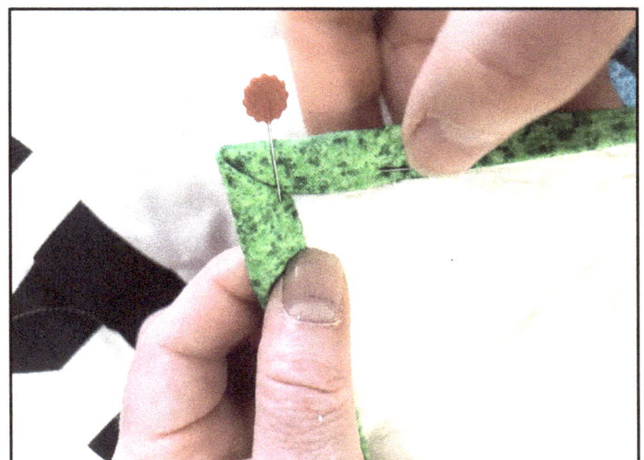
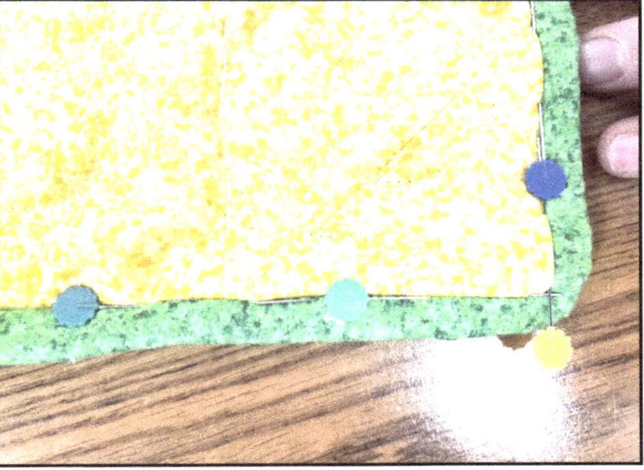

Here is how my pinning looks from the front (below left) and back of the quilt (below right).

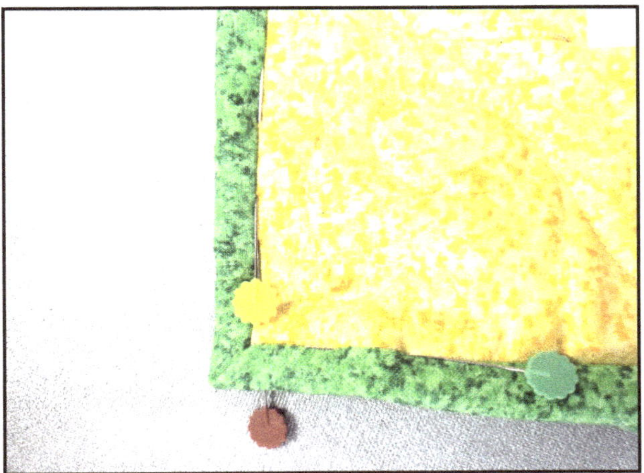
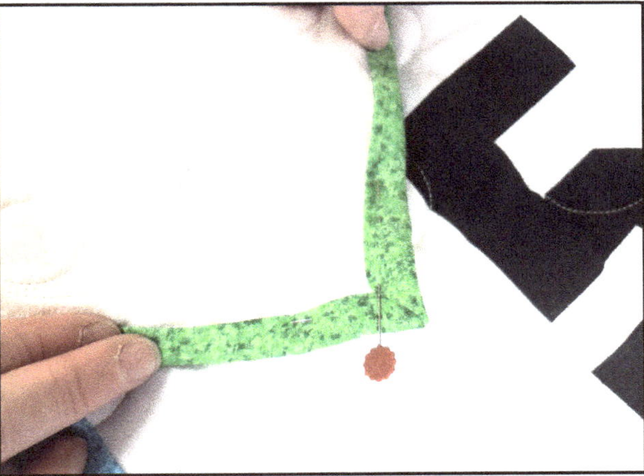

Then I sew from the front, keeping my needle in the ditch and removing pins as I go (lower left). If you are hand stitching the back you don't need to be this careful – but we aren't doing that here. Sew slowly and ensure you are catching the underside edge of the binding on the back side (lower right).

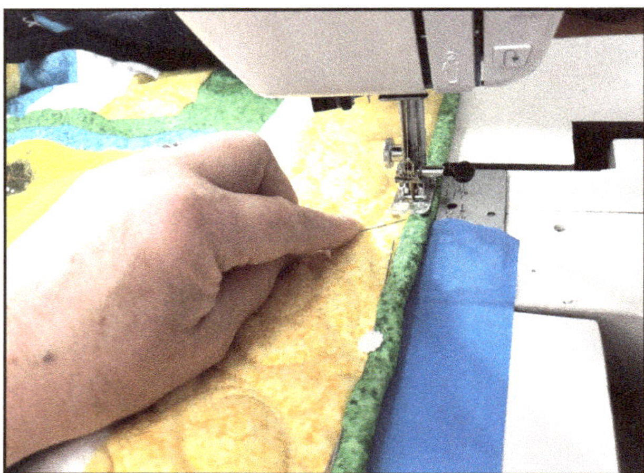
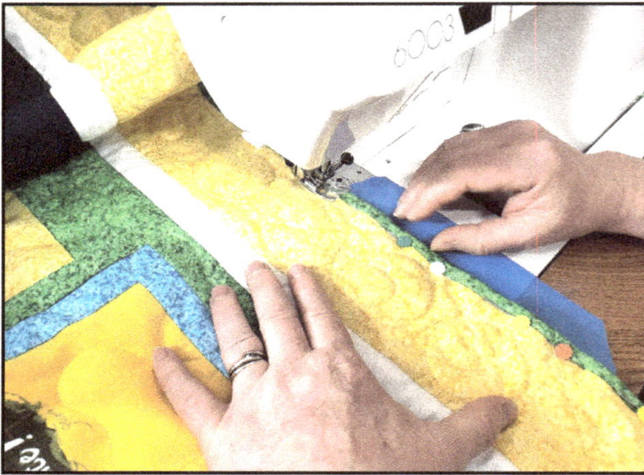

Continue. When you get to a corner, leave the needle down in the exact corner spot. Raise the presser foot and pivot the quilt. In this example I am pivoting the quilt to my right.

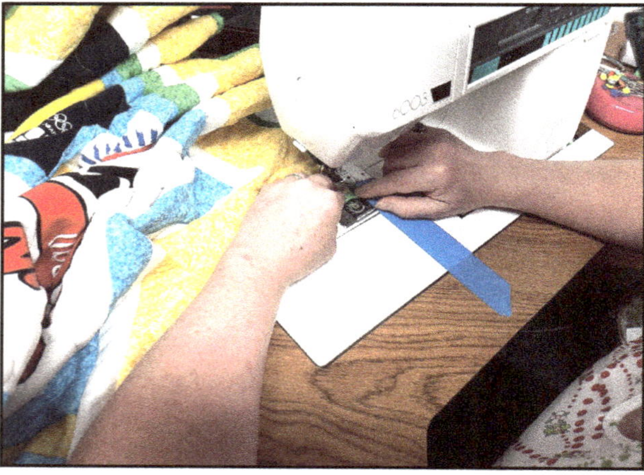
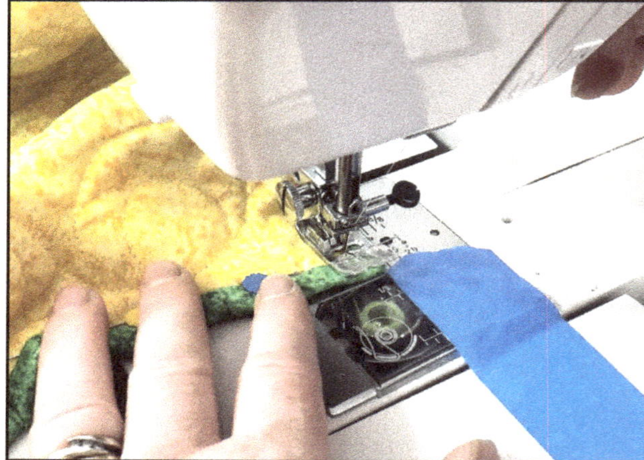
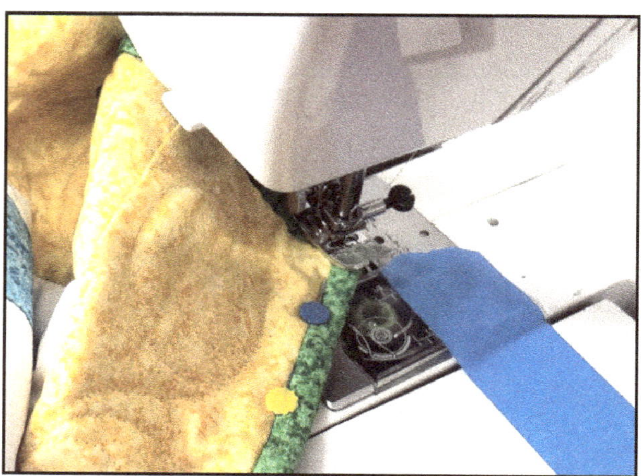
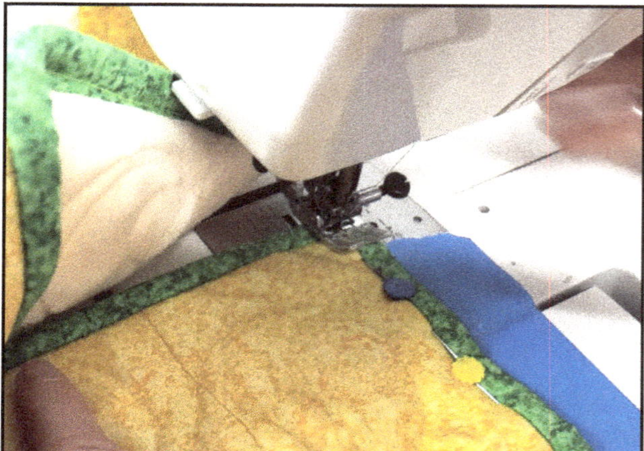

In writing this I realized that there are many ways to attach a binding – just like there are many ways to make a quilt. I have combined a few different methods on doing the corners. You can stop at the corners and cut the binding 2 ½ inches past the quilt edge. Then treat each corner as you did the first one. You can start attaching the binding mid a side and then cut to fit when you come around to where you started. You can hand stitch the binding to the back (I recommend this if this will be a quilt for show.) You can sew the binding to the back of the quilt and top stitch the finishing edge to the front.

As always there are as many ways to do things as there are people. Did you or I do it the "right way?" Well, does it work for you? Do you enjoy the process when done in this fashion? Did it give you a finished product that looks the way you want it to? I like to think of these options as one other way to do something. Not right or wrong – just another way that may work better or easier for the project I am working on at the time.

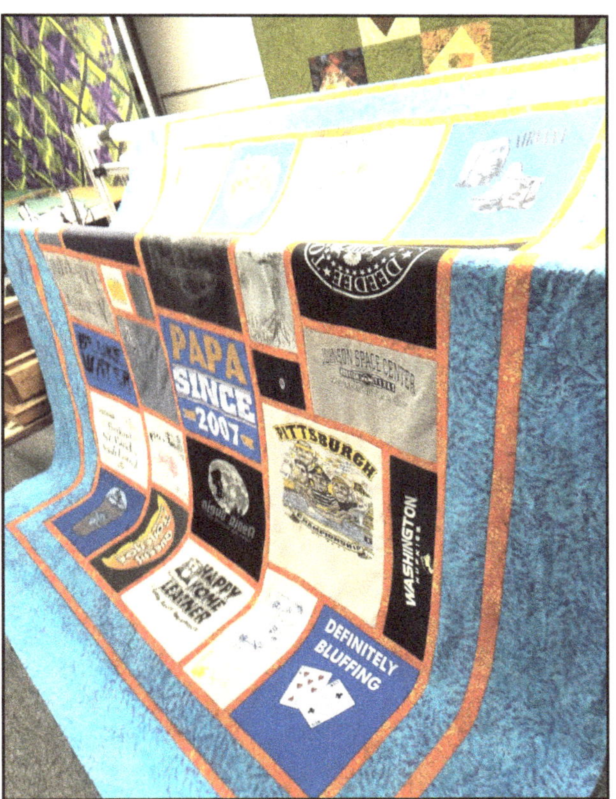

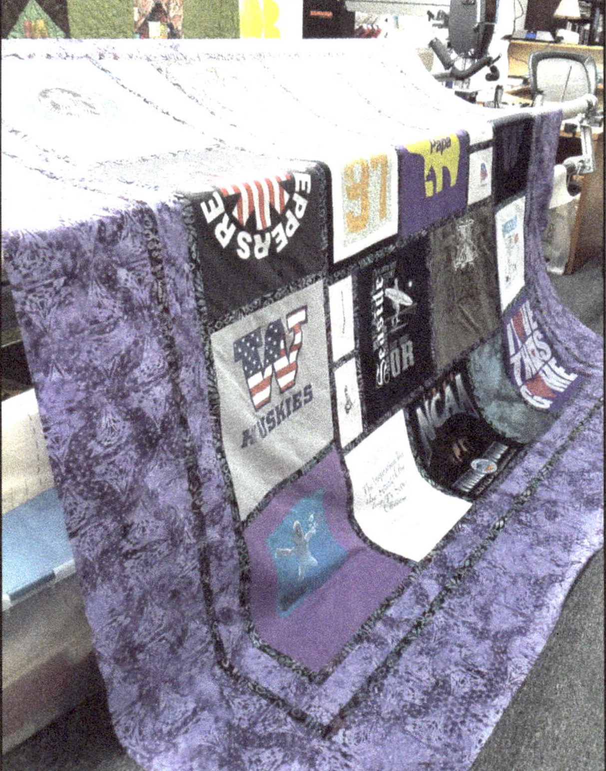

Chapter 11
Finish Work

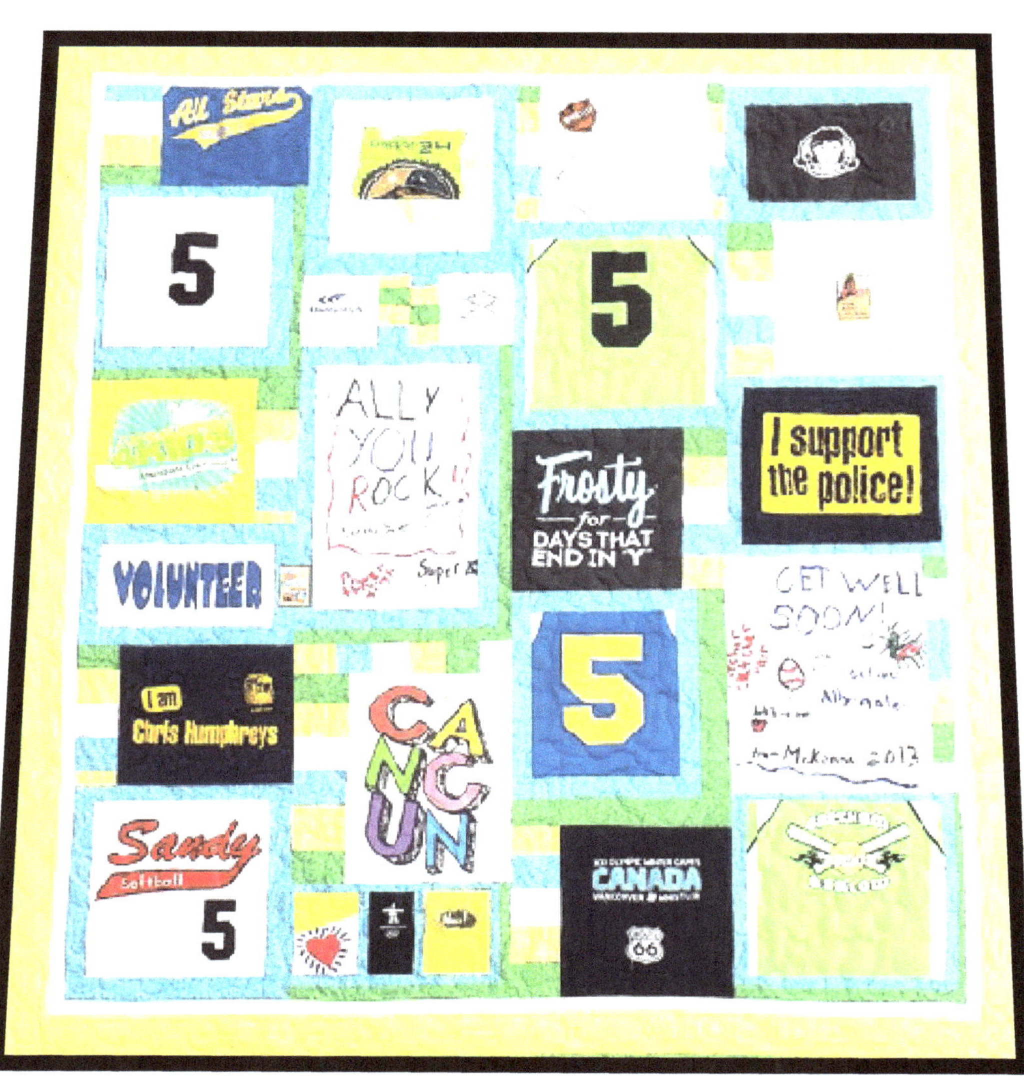

Trim threads and enjoy! Lay the quilt out and admire all your hard work.

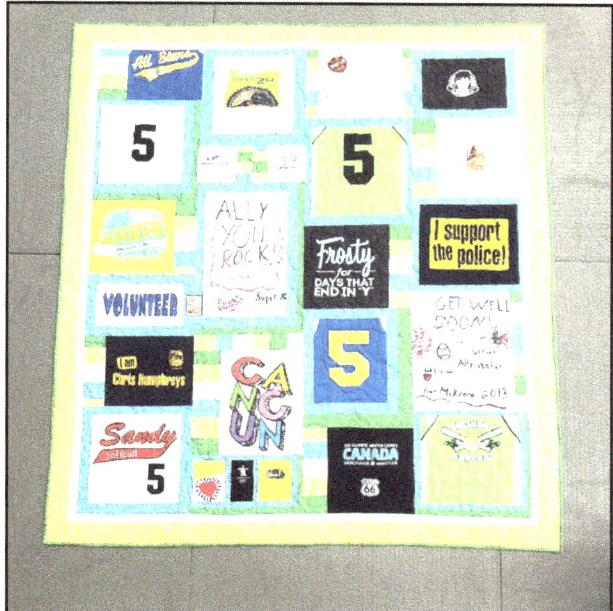 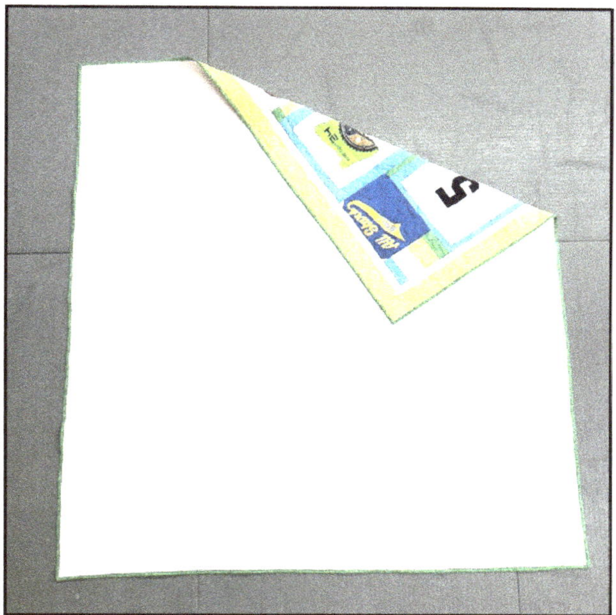

Let people tell you how beautiful it is. NEVER point out your mistakes – no one sees them!

I always tell people to wash a quilt carefully in the bathtub. Use a very mild soap. Don't wring the quilt.   Empty the water. Refill the tub. Swish mildly. Empty the water, etc. Keep rinsing till the water runs clear. Carefully lift and lay out on an old sheet on the grass. Put a sheet over the top to protect from the sun and let dry.

I'm not sure how many people follow this advice. If it is a quilt I use every day, I put it in the washing machine and the dryer. When it gets old and thread bare I'll throw it away.

But if it is special quilt that you want to have for years to come, wash it very carefully by hand and lay flat to dry.

CONCLUSION

You have now created your own memory quilt. From here you can create and design so many quilts. Your colors can be anything you want. Your blocks can be made with photos transferred to cloth, racing bibs,   pennants, monogramed clothing, embroidered articles – you will only be limited by your imagination.

If you have any questions you can contact me at marieanderson0@hotmail.com.

I am excited to see what you create, so please send me pictures of your projects!

Have fun creating your own art!

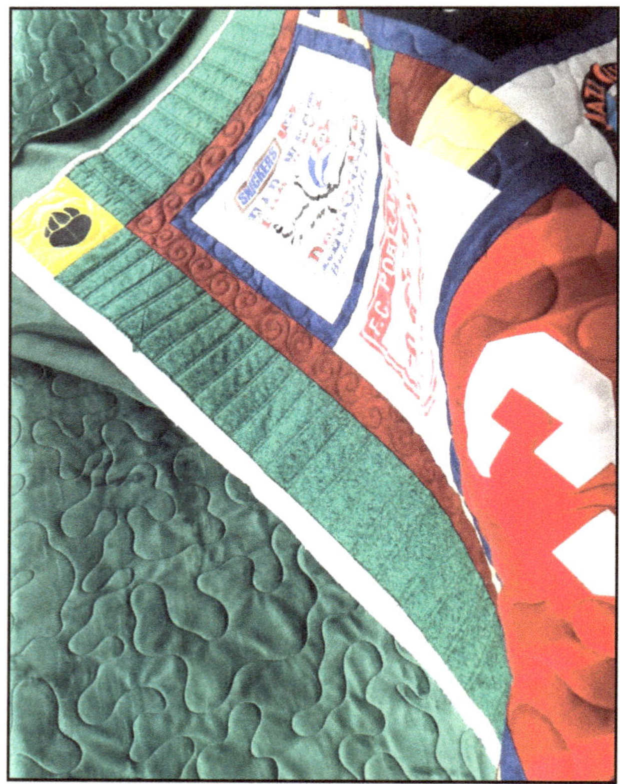

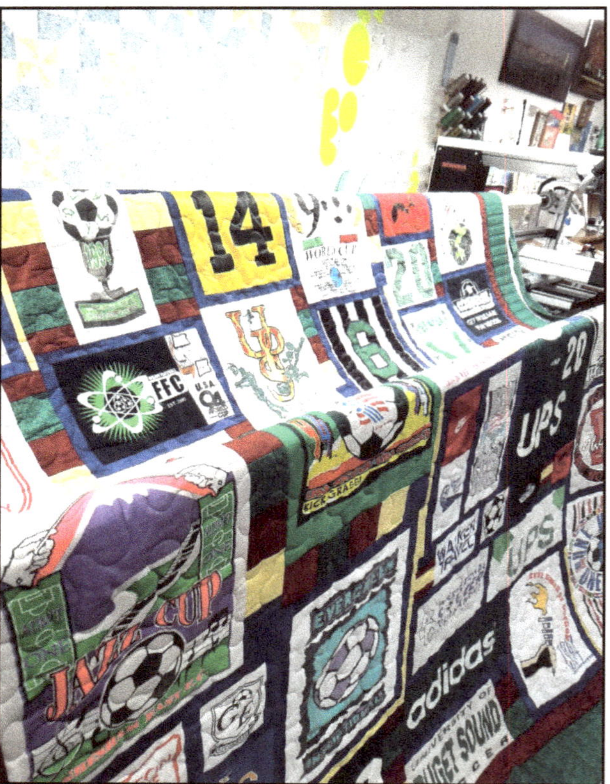

ABOUT THE AUTHOR

Marie Anderson is an artist, quilter and teacher from the Pacific Northwest Region of the United States. Growing up in the Pacific NW, she has brought her love of nature and natural color to her art. This orientation influences and inspires much of her work. Her lifelong love of sewing and creating art is evident in the items she creates today.

Anderson's first foray into sewing was creating doll clothes by hand. Taught by her mom, she learned to sew, knit, macramé, tat, hook rugs, quilt and watch

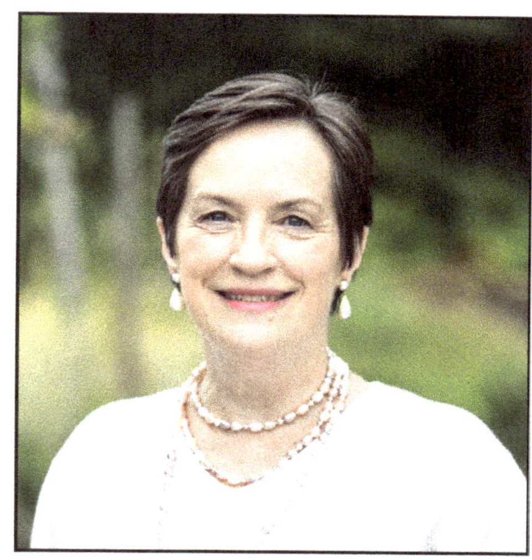

nature. Being a competing athlete as a teen has given her a desire to be the best in whatever field she is involved with. Her   natural instinct about use of color has allowed her to enter the world of quilting one step ahead of the average person.

Anderson raised 6 children over the last 30 years. She has 17 grandchildren and one other on the way. She is an accomplished seamstress, artist and quilter. Whether it is making wedding dresses, baby clothes, prom dresses or tents and bags for camping she has used her skills to create art in her life. She has designed her own patterns and followed her own path but also learned from the best teachers in the industry.

In 2010 her life took a significant turn when she and her mother started quilting and sewing together again. In 2015 her mother decided they needed a long arm to enhance their quilting hobby. Marie's father, being the practical business man insisted that they have a business to support this activity – thus Marie's Custom Quilting was born.

In the short time that Marie has been in business she has won numerous awards including the Reader's Choice Award for 2018 and 2019, International quilt show awards and Judges Choice Awards. Her latest endeavor includes quilting leather wall hangings, leather journals and leather clothes. She is a sought after artist for designing one of a kind quilts from t-shirts and or clothes. This latest activity has inspired the following book.

Marie Anderson is available to speak to your group.   To schedule a workshop or lecture, contact Marie at *marieanderson0@hotmail.com*.

Would you like to learn more about quilting on leather? In this one hour lecture, Marie will educate you on types of leather, tools to use and tips for success in your projects. Several examples of completed projects will be shown to give inspiration.

3 hour workshops are available for quilted leather journal covers. You will leave the workshop with your own journal cover or a beautiful gift for another.

Are you ready to move on to something bigger? Join the fun in a 6 hour workshop and learn to make a lined purse or tote bag.

For weekend retreats or 3 day workshops, Marie is available to teach on the subject of creating one of a kind custom quilts or t-shirt quilts.

To learn more about private consultations or lessons go to
mariescustomquilting.com

Are you anxious about starting a project? Do you want to make sure you will be happy with the end result? Would you like a professional opinion? Do you want it to look like a pro did it—but you did it all yourself?

Schedule a private consultation or lesson to get ideas and helpful tips for your project. When you arrive Marie will go over your project with you in detail, answer all your questions and give you her thoughts on enhancing the project.

Leave the consultation with a firm plan in mind of how you will approach your project and carry it through to completion.

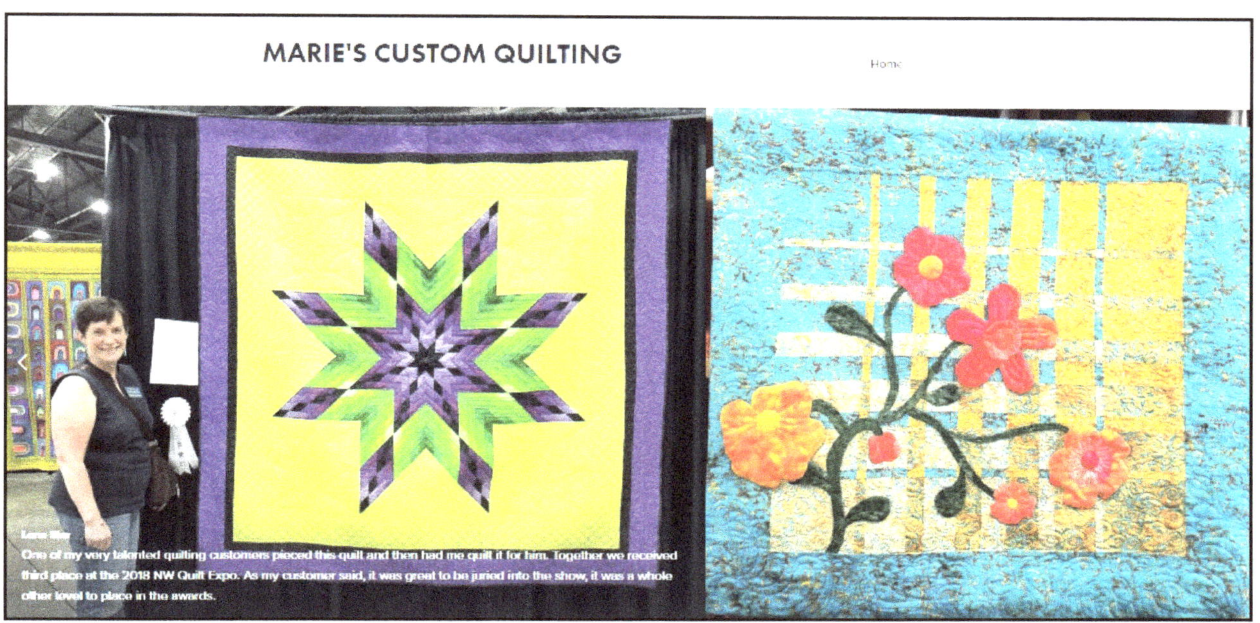

To see daily projects follow her on Facebook and Instagram at
Marie's Custom Quilting

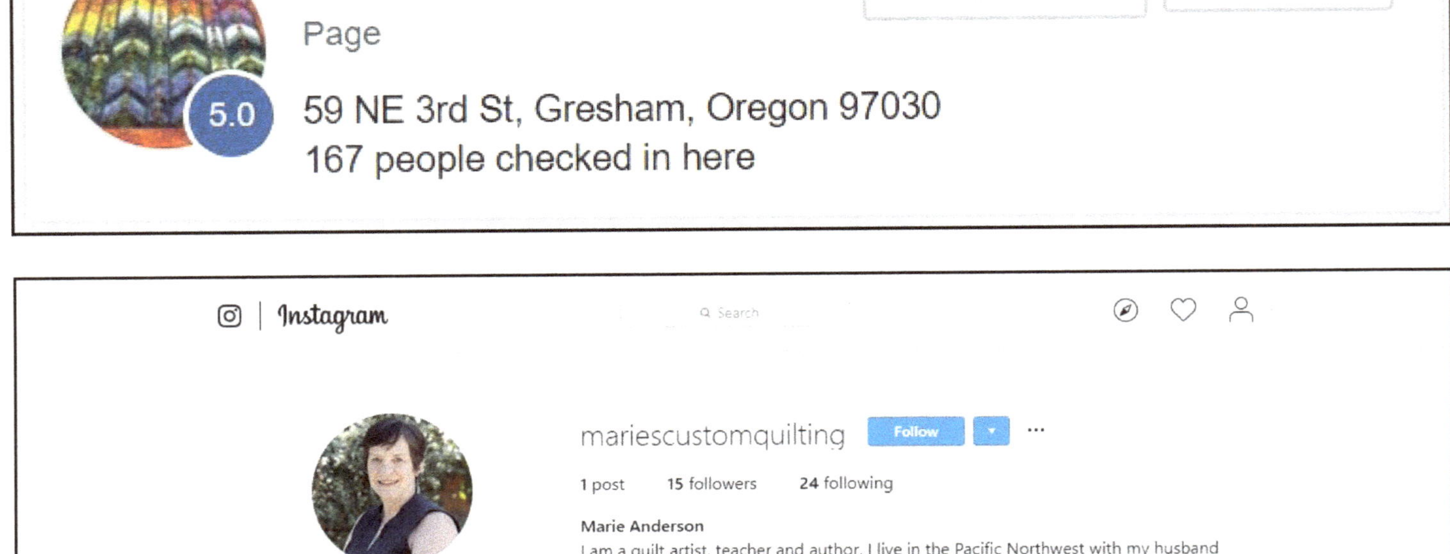